Dynamics of Virtual Work

Series Editors
Ursula Huws
Hertfordshire Business School
Hatfield, UK

Rosalind Gill
Department of Sociology
City University London
London, UK

Technological change has transformed where people work, when and how. Digitisation of information has altered labour processes out of all recognition whilst telecommunications have enabled jobs to be relocated globally. ICTs have also enabled the creation of entirely new types of 'digital' or 'virtual' labour, both paid and unpaid, shifting the borderline between 'play' and 'work' and creating new types of unpaid labour connected with the consumption and co-creation of goods and services. This affects private life as well as transforming the nature of work and people experience the impacts differently depending on their gender, their age, where they live and what work they do. Aspects of these changes have been studied separately by many different academic experts however up till now a cohesive overarching analytical framework has been lacking. Drawing on a major, high-profile COST Action (European Cooperation in Science and Technology) Dynamics of Virtual Work, this series will bring together leading international experts from a wide range of disciplines including political economy, labour sociology, economic geography, communications studies, technology, gender studies, social psychology, organisation studies, industrial relations and development studies to explore the transformation of work and labour in the Internet Age. The series will allow researchers to speak across disciplinary boundaries, national borders, theoretical and political vocabularies, and different languages to understand and make sense of contemporary transformations in work and social life more broadly. The book series will build on and extend this, offering a new, important and intellectually exciting intervention into debates about work and labour, social theory, digital culture, gender, class, globalisation and economic, social and political change.

More information about this series at
http://www.palgrave.com/gp/series/14954

Paško Bilić • Jaka Primorac
Bjarki Valtýsson
Editors

Technologies of Labour and the Politics of Contradiction

palgrave
macmillan

Editors
Paško Bilić
Department for Culture and
Communication
Institute for Development
and International Relations
Zagreb, Croatia

Jaka Primorac
Department for Culture
and Communication
Institute for Development
and International Relations
Zagreb, Croatia

Bjarki Valtýsson
Department of Arts and Cultural Studies
University of Copenhagen
Copenhagen, Denmark

Dynamics of Virtual Work
ISBN 978-3-319-76278-4   ISBN 978-3-319-76279-1   (eBook)
https://doi.org/10.1007/978-3-319-76279-1

Library of Congress Control Number: 2018935938

© The Editor(s) (if applicable) and The Author(s) 2018
This work is subject to copyright. All rights are solely and exclusively licensed by the Publisher, whether the whole or part of the material is concerned, specifically the rights of translation, reprinting, reuse of illustrations, recitation, broadcasting, reproduction on microfilms or in any other physical way, and transmission or information storage and retrieval, electronic adaptation, computer software, or by similar or dissimilar methodology now known or hereafter developed.
The use of general descriptive names, registered names, trademarks, service marks, etc. in this publication does not imply, even in the absence of a specific statement, that such names are exempt from the relevant protective laws and regulations and therefore free for general use.
The publisher, the authors, and the editors are safe to assume that the advice and information in this book are believed to be true and accurate at the date of publication. Neither the publisher nor the authors or the editors give a warranty, express or implied, with respect to the material contained herein or for any errors or omissions that may have been made. The publisher remains neutral with regard to jurisdictional claims in published maps and institutional affiliations.

Cover credit: MirageC / Getty

Printed on acid-free paper

This Palgrave Macmillan imprint is published by the registered company Springer International Publishing AG part of Springer Nature.
The registered company address is: Gewerbestrasse 11, 6330 Cham, Switzerland

Acknowledgements

This book is the result of many a vibrant discussion that took place during the training school held at the Interuniversity Centre (IUC) in May 2016, organized by the Institute for Development and International Relations and supported by the COST Action 'Dynamics of Virtual Work'. The idea for the book came out of the conversations that continued outside the scheduled sessions in the more informal settings of Dubrovnik's elegant stone-paved streets. We are therefore deeply grateful to all the participants of the training school without whose contribution and enthusiasm this collection of papers would have been impossible.

Our special thanks go to the Series editors Ursula Huws and Rosalind Gill for including this book in the 'Dynamics of Virtual Work' Series. We would also like to thank our colleagues who have helped us review different versions and/or parts of the manuscript: Daniela Agostinho, Benjamin Birkinbine, Juliet Webster, Pepita Hesselberth, Sebastian Sevignani, and Xanthe Whittaker.

We are very much indebted to our families for their support during the preparation of this book: our warmest thanks for being there for us.

And lastly, we would like to welcome into this world little Maria and Vera who were born during the writing of this book.

Zagreb, Croatia   Paško Bilić
Zagreb, Croatia   Jaka Primorac
Copenhagen, Denmark   Bjarki Valtýsson

Contents

1 Technology, Labour and Politics in the 21st Century:
  Old Struggles in New Clothing 1
  Paško Bilić, Jaka Primorac, and Bjarki Valtýsson

Part I Contradictions in Automation and Internet Platforms 17

2 Industry 4.0: Robotics and Contradictions 19
  Sabine Pfeiffer

3 From Ford to Facebook: Time and Technologies of Work 37
  Eran Fisher

4 The Production of Algorithms and the Cultural Politics
  of Web Search 57
  Paško Bilić

5 Algorithms, Dashboards and Datafication: A Critical
  Evaluation of Social Media Monitoring 77
  Ivo Furman

Part II Contradictions in Digital Practices and Creative Industries — 97

6 Efficient Worker or Reflective Practitioner? Competing Technical Rationalities of Media Software Tools — 99
Ingrid Forsler and Julia Velkova

7 In the Golden Cage of Creative Industries: Public-Private Valuing of Female Creative Labour — 121
Valerija Barada and Jaka Primorac

8 Digital Inclusion for Better Job Opportunities? The Case of Women E-Included Through Lifelong Learning Programmes — 141
Lidia Arroyo

Part III Contradictions in Human Interaction and Communication — 159

9 A Recent Story About Uber — 161
Brian Beaton

10 Protocols of Control: Collaboration in Free and Open Source Software — 175
Reinhard Anton Handler

11 Playbour and the Gamification of Work: Empowerment, Exploitation and Fun as Labour Dynamics — 193
Raul Ferrer-Conill

12 Audience Metrics as a Decision-Making Factor in Slovene Online News Organizations — 211
Aleksander Sašo Slaček Brlek

Part IV Contradictions in Democratic Participation and Regulation   233

13 Media Use and the Extended Commodification of the Lifeworld   235
Göran Bolin

14 Regulation, Technology, and Civic Agency: The Case of Facebook   253
Bjarki Valtýsson

15 Spinning the Web: The Contradictions of Researching and Regulating Digital Work and Labour   271
Pamela Meil

Index   291

Notes on Contributors

Lidia Arroyo is Researcher in the Gender and ICT Research Group at the Internet Interdisciplinary Institute (IN3) – Universitat Oberta de Catalunya (UOC). She is also a sociologist working as an Assistant Professor in the Department of Social Psychology and Organisations at Autonomous University of Barcelona. She is finishing her PhD in the Information and Knowledge Society on gender, digital skills and social inequalities. She has been a visiting research fellow at Área de Género, Sociedad y Políticas (FLACSO-Argentina) and the Fondation Travail-Univeristé (FTU-Namur) – University of Namur (Belgium).

Valerija Barada is Assistant Professor and a Head of Department of Sociology, University of Zadar, Croatia. She holds PhD in Sociology from the University of Zagreb and has also finished Centre for Women's Studies Programme in Zagreb. She teaches on interpretative approaches in sociological theory and qualitative methods. Her primary research interests include issues of gender, labour and professions, especially creative industries, but she has also worked on the topics of gender and youth social and work inequalities. Barada has authored and co-authored several articles, books and research reports on quality of life, labour conditions and gender relations in local coastal communities of Croatia. With Jaka Primorac and Edgar Buršić she has published a book on labour conditions in civil society organizations in contemporary culture and arts in Croatia, resulting from a two-year research project.

Brian Beaton is Assistant Professor in the STS Program and Director of the Center for Expressive Tech at California Polytechnic State University (Cal Poly), San Luis Obispo, USA. His research on technology recession builds on his long-standing interest in putting the technology studies field into closer conversation with recent developments surrounding digital work and culture. In addition to technology recession, Beaton is the principal architect of data criticism and humanoid capital theory, along with a principal instigator of recent debates over data science and the fourth industrial revolution (4IR).

Paško Bilić is Research Associate at the Department for Culture and Communication, Institute for Development and International Relations in Zagreb Croatia. Previously, he was International Visiting Research Fellow at the Institute for Advanced Studies, University of Westminster (London, UK) and Doctoral Research Fellow at the University of Alberta (Edmonton, Canada). His core research interest is the critical analysis of social relations mediated through digital technologies, public policies and markets.

Göran Bolin is Professor in Media & Communication Studies at Södertörn University, Stockholm, Sweden. His research spans both media production analysis and audience studies, and his latest work is focused on how media production and consumption are interrelated in the wake of datafication. He is the author of *Value and the Media. Production and Consumption in Digital Markets* (Ashgate, 2011), and *Media Generations: Experience, Identity and Mediatised Social Change* (Routledge, 2016).

Raul Ferrer Conill is a PhD Candidate in the Department of Media and Communication Studies at Karlstad University. He has published his work in Computer Supported Cooperative Work (CSCW), Journalism Studies, and Television and New Media, among others. His current research interests cover gamification, processes of datafication and digital journalism.

Eran Fisher is Senior Lecturer at the Department of Sociology, Political Science, and Communication at the Open University of Israel. He is the author of *Media and New Capitalism in the Digital Age: The Spirit of Networks* (2010, Palgrave), *Reconsidering Value and Labour in the Digital Age* (edited with Christian Fuchs, 2015, Palgrave), and *Internet and Emotions* (edited with Tova Benski, 2014, Routledge).

Ingrid Forsler is a PhD Candidate in Media and Communication Studies at Södertörn University in Stockholm, Sweden. She has a background in art and media education and her PhD project examines the relationship between media technologies and school art education.

Ivo Furman holds the position of Assistant Professor at the Department of Media and Communication Systems at Istanbul Bilgi University. He completed his PhD in Sociology at Goldsmiths College, University of London in 2015. His research interests include social media analytics, computer assisted data collection methodologies, digital sociology, the politics of (Big) Data and data journalism.

Reinhard Anton Handler studied Media and Communication, Hispanic Linguistics and Literature, and Philosophy at the University of Vienna and the Universidad Autónoma de Madrid. He received a Master's degree in Media Studies from the University of Vienna. Since 2014 he is a PhD Researcher at the Department of Geography, Media and Communication at Karlstad University (Sweden).

Pamela Meil is a sociologist of work and is currently a Senior Research Fellow, Director of international studies, and Member of the governing board at the Institute for Social Science Research (ISF München), Germany. Her research interests include: the transformation of work through digitalization; policy implications of virtual work; global value chain restructuring and consequences for the quality of worklife; and the interaction between globalization and national adaptation processes. She was the working group leader for policy in the EU COST network on the dynamics of virtual work and has published numerous articles in both English and German language books and journals, including the edited volume *Policy Implications of Virtual Work* (2017), published in this book series.

Sabine Pfeiffer is a sociologist of work and Professor of Sociology at the University of Hohenheim in Stuttgart, Germany. Her main fields of research are in work studies, innovation studies, and food studies with special focus on virtual work. Her recent publications have addressed organisational standards in production and innovation work, living labouring capacity, and the industrial Internet.

Jaka Primorac is Senior Research Associate at the Department for Culture and Communication, Institute for Development and International Relations

(IRMO), Zagreb, Croatia. She holds a PhD (2010) in Sociology from the Faculty of Humanities and Social Sciences, University of Zagreb, Croatia and has also finished Centre for Women's Studies Programme in Zagreb. Her research interests include cultural and creative industries, cultural and creative labour, women's work, media and cultural policy, digital culture and qualitative research methods. In 2016, she co-authored a book (with Valerija Barada and Edgar Buršić) on labour conditions in civil society organizations in contemporary culture and arts in Croatia.

Aleksander Sašo Slaček Brlek is Researcher at the Social Communications Research Centre of the Faculty of Social Sciences at the University of Ljubljana, Slovenia. His main research interests include critical political economy of communication, labour process analysis, theories of public opinion and the public sphere.

Bjarki Valtýsson is Associate Professor at the Department of Arts and Cultural Studies at the University of Copenhagen and has a background in literature, cultural studies, and digital communication. Research interests include cultural, media, and communication policies and regulation, particularly in terms of the politics of digital media and networked cultures. He also researches the application and reception of digital media within the area of museums, archives, libraries, and social network sites as well as how these relate to production, distribution, use, and consumption in digital cultures.

Julia Velkova is a PhD Candidate in Media and Communication Studies at Södertörn University in Stockholm, Sweden. Her research interests include computer cultures, the politics of infrastructure, economies of the Internet, and internet governance.

List of Figures

Fig. 2.1	Formula: Calculating the LC-index	29
Fig. 3.1	How can money (M) converted into a commodity (C) end up yielding a bigger quantity of money (M^i)?	38
Fig. 3.2	Marx's answer to the conundrum is that the commodity (C) actually embodies another source of value: labour (L)	39
Fig. 3.3	Regular Facebook post	46
Fig. 3.4	Post rendered into a Sponsored Story	47
Fig. 12.1	Share of active internet users of the three most visited Slovene news websites (three-month sliding averages; Source: Slovene Chamber of Advertising)	219
Fig. 12.2	Number of monthly unique users of the three most visited Slovene news websites (three-month sliding averages; Source: Slovene Chamber of Advertising)	219

List of Tables

Table 6.1	Conceptual model of software production framework in relation to knowledge in work practice	100
Table 8.1	Distribution of the sample by age group and education level	144
Table 12.1	The interviewees	218
Table 13.1	Two fields of cultural production/consumption	240
Table 13.2	Different kinds of productivity in pre-digital and web 2.0 fields of consumption. Boxes indicate the degrees to which it is possible for media and culture industries to extract value	241

1

Technology, Labour and Politics in the 21st Century: Old Struggles in New Clothing

Paško Bilić, Jaka Primorac, and Bjarki Valtýsson

The Idea Behind the Book

The idea for this book grew out of the Technologies of Digital Work international training school held at the Inter-University Centre (IUC) in Dubrovnik, Croatia between 3rd and 6th May 2016, supported by the Dynamics of Virtual Work COST IS1202 action. Early career, mid-career, and senior researchers discussed the increasing need among scholars, students, and policy makers to understand how digital technologies affect labour in contemporary societies. Do they bring social, democratic, and economic benefits? Are they inherently designed to bring positive change to society? Do they also enable surveillance? Do they create social inequalities? From a critical perspective, technologies are perceived as being used

---

P. Bilić (✉) • J. Primorac
Department for Culture and Communication, Institute for Development and International Relations, Zagreb, Croatia

B. Valtýsson
Department of Arts and Cultural Studies, University of Copenhagen, Copenhagen, Denmark

© The Author(s) 2018
P. Bilić et al. (eds.), *Technologies of Labour and the Politics of Contradiction*, Dynamics of Virtual Work, https://doi.org/10.1007/978-3-319-76279-1_1

to establish control, dominance, value extraction, and perpetuation of the capitalist system through alienated, exploited labour and various capital accumulation strategies. A gender perspective questions how technologies perpetuate patriarchal structures and contribute to digital gender divide while also providing emancipatory possibilities. From a media studies perspective, information and communication technologies enable social and cultural environments that alter communication and information production, distribution, consumption, and use. A science and technology studies (STS) perspective takes that all technologies are produced, used, and interpreted differently, while sometimes also exhibiting characteristics of social agency in various socio-material configurations. Furthermore, digital technologies present a challenge for policy makers since they develop at a faster rate than national, regional, and supranational (e.g., EU) legislative systems. The outlined perspectives share a nuanced and intricate understanding of the social, cultural, political, and economic dimensions of digital technologies. This edited volume provides a contribution to fragmented literature divided by disciplinary boundaries and professional alignments. The collection of chapters puts different views into a balanced dialogue and offers a fresh perspective for grasping the complexity of the relationship between technology, labour, and politics in the 21st century. The politics of a contradiction perspective brings to our attention how full of frictions, ambiguities, ambivalence, and difficulties implementation and use of digital technologies can be.

The global spread of information and communication technologies sparked many discussions on the ambiguous influence of technology on work and labour processes, capitalism, and modernity more generally. The classical labour process studies argued that production technologies bring new forms of managerial control under a monopoly of capitalism and create de-skilled labour (Braverman 1974). Digital technologies seem no less ambivalent and are depicted as bringing various forms of distributed capitalism through customisation, crowdsourcing, impacting the development of knowledge work and innovation, and bringing about the rise of creative jobs (Florida 2002). They also contribute to the rise of low-paid jobs, piecemeal work, and crowd-work, thus contributing to new divisions of labour that create further inequalities (Huws 2003; Dyer-Witheford 2015) and reconfiguring worker organisations (Mosco and McKercher 2009). Approaches from the digital labour perspective (e.g., Fuchs 2010; Scholz 2013; Fisher and Fuchs 2015) critically evaluated network effects of online platforms and pointed out that large numbers of users contribute to the economic sustainability of digital services by creating digital value through their online presence, cooperation, and exchange. This book argues that digital technology can be regarded not only as a conduit for monetisation of network effects or as a tool for surveillance and management control of labour processes, but also as a socially assembled and reassembled apparatus for the purpose of ambivalent, ambiguous, and contradictory implementation and use in labour-related activities. Furthermore, the book takes a twofold approach to the concept of materiality. It starts from the acknowledgment of technological materiality evident in the abundance of machines, devices, algorithms, software applications, and social media inhabiting our everyday lives and shaping our labour dynamics. It then explores how the materiality of labour is intertwined with technological materiality. In other words, it questions how labour is embedded in social inequalities and socioeconomic processes that produce and re-purpose digital technologies, and how labour is mediated, shaped, co-constructed and influenced by digital technologies. The complex interplay between technology and labour is evidenced in the upsurge of contradictions in many areas. Contradictions are taken as heuristic, epistemological devices that help us understand the frictions between technology and labour. This book maps out some of the existing contradictions and provides a theoretical and an empirical contribution to the wide ranging and continuously evolving relationship between technology, labour, and politics.

To untangle this challenging complexity, we argue that critical perspectives are much needed in contemporary discussions on the relationship between technology and labour together with visions of technology that propose alternatives strongly embedded in democratic processes, transparency, and accountability. It is therefore important to note that diverging visions of technology bring to our attention an underlying politics of contradiction in which the producers and controllers of technology have different interests and intentions when making technologies, compared to the interests of citizens, technology users, and labourers. It is a type of asymmetry and disconnection between long-standing scientific and instrumental rationality and everyday experience (Feenberg 2010) embedded in the socio-historical transformations of modernity. Labour is an integral part of the transformation as technologies need to be produced and put to use in social contexts. The realities of production and use are not always, if ever, in sync. This book looks beyond technological determinism and instead focuses on technology: first as a broader organisational, institutional, cultural, political, and economic context in which technical systems are embedded; and second as a concrete technical system with which humans and society relate. It examines how broader contexts shape digital technologies, work, and labour, and also how digital *technics* are embedded and how they alter the contexts, organisations, practices, and routines of human work, work-life balance, and labour.

Book Structure

Technologies are developed and deployed as technical tools for collaboration, communication, and information exchange, and are also (mis-)used as tools for control, dominance, and exploitation. These seemingly divergent realities point to the social embeddedness of digital technologies and also to the broader shifts in social sciences and humanities trying to tackle these socio-historical specificities with a mixture of existing and novel concepts and approaches. Unpacking these contradictions has scholarly, educational, and policy value for a critical and informed understanding of the role of digital technologies in society and more specifically in labour processes. Unlike many works in this field which tend to tackle positive or negative issues in their analysis of digital technology, this book takes a novel approach that will lay out and explore the contradictions of digital technologies. This edited volume is divided into four thematic sections where each section deals with manifest contradictions in the tensions between critical and emancipative perspectives. The list of contradictions reflected in the book structure is built solely on the work of the authors of this book. It is in no way all-encompassing, exhaustive, and completed. It does not represent the totality of the relations between technology, labour, and politics, nor does it pretend to do so. Our list is a combination of initial, analytical starting points, explored empirical realities, and professional pursuits of the authors of this book.

Part I titled 'Contradictions in Automation and Internet Platforms' deals with contradictions in automated labour, capital accumulation strategies by major Internet companies, and social media monitoring agencies. In particular, it looks at how robotics industries as well as major ICT companies and specialised local companies reorganise labour and create contradictions along new lines of struggle, forms of control, and value generation. The authors of this section suggest that non-routine activities, use-value of labour, and social engagement are relevant elements in digital capitalism. Human existence is pressured within struggles of capital, labour, time, sociality, and design contingencies of digital technologies.

In the opening chapter titled 'Industry 4.0: Robotics and Contradictions' (Chap. 2), Sabine Pfeiffer argued that regardless of current developments in robotics, human labour remains an essential aspect of the production process. Despite the discourse arguing for the replacement of routine tasks with advanced automated systems, Pfeiffer argued that such predictions are inadequate. She used qualitative data to highlight the importance of non-routine activities in highly automated environments. Based on these findings she developed the labour capacity index (LC) and applied it to a dataset of 20,000 German employees. Mechanical and automotive engineering are often regarded as highly automated sectors of the economy. Yet, the empirical data supports the thesis of the existing contradiction between use value and exchange value of human labour. This contradiction cannot be resolved through increasing digitalisation. The distinction between knowledge work as a non-routine activity and production work as a routine activity does not stand up to close scrutiny since it misses the social foundations of labour and treats them as technologically replaceable objects. She concluded succinctly: '[d]igital capitalism will not be able to resolve its immanent contradictions by means of bits and bytes, nor delegate its class conflicts to an algorithm.'

In his chapter 'From Ford to Facebook: Time and Technologies of Work' (Chap. 3), Eran Fisher analytically traced the transformation in productive technologies from the assembly line to the online platforms of major Internet companies. Social media has become the technology 'which helps construct a new model of relations between work and time' in order to 'harness our thoughts, feelings, knowledge, behaviour, and communication to the creation of economic value'. He argued that, as capitalist regimes of accumulation change, the construction of time is transformed and the techno-social constellation is reconfigured to regulate time. Time, therefore, represents the central point of contradiction and struggle between capital and labour. Based on such an analytical framework, Fisher presented a class-action lawsuit filed by Facebook users against the company and argued that the online platform becomes a site of struggles over productive time, free-time/work-time ratios, and arrangements that distinguish work time from free time.

In the following chapter, Paško Bilić focused on another online platform that has come to dominate the global experience of the Internet. In the chapter titled 'The Production of Algorithms and the Cultural Politics of Web Search' (Chap. 4), he traced contingencies built into Google's search algorithms. He grounded his analysis in the works of Herbert Marcuse and argued that the contradictions in Google's technical design and cultural politics of web searching are the result of an uneven and partly hidden global division of search engine labour. Google's evolving algorithms are not just technical artefacts but also business strategies for market control and dominance. Algorithms are not conducive to democracy as they are constructed to operate under a limited vision of society and a skewed horizon of human experience. Algorithms cannot be separated from political, economic, and cultural contextualisation. They are 'commodified objects whose embeddedness in market relations is reified by techno-utopian visions of digital technology and hidden human labour'. Such technical artefacts adversely affect public visibility and advertising revenue flows in the digital economy.

In the final chapter of the section entitled 'Algorithms, Dashboards, and Datafication: A Critical Evaluation of Social Media Monitoring' (Chap. 5), Ivo Furman argued that social engagement has become a vital aspect of the affective economy. Such engagement increases brand value and introduces a need for continuous monitoring and surveillance of online activities. Social media monitoring (SMM) agencies enable organisations to have direct and real-time access to customers' opinions, complaints, and questions. The pilot study focuses on a specific case of an SMM tool in Turkey, paying particular attention to technologies that capture, analyse, and visualise data. Furman argued that the data collected from the social web is a simulated, simplified version of reality. This reality passes through numerous filters. In the process, certain aspects of reality are lost and others are retained. Aside from the technical characteristics of the analysed tools in his case study, what is essential about such technologies is that they are 'used to manage the risks associated with online communication strategies'. Yet, the technologies themselves, as the author continued, are not enough to resolve the risks they identify.

Part II titled 'Contradictions in Digital Practices and Creative Industries' explores the contravening consequences of digital practices for (female) creative labour that also contribute to the emergence of new gender inequalities. Technical affordances of software applications are analysed through contradictions in digital practices within specific creative industries. Contradictions vary from enabling human creativity to controlling and monitoring work environments. Digital skills and gender are the main focus of the analysis in the context of employment opportunities for women, while also opening the floor for discussion on the social valuing of female work.

In the chapter entitled 'Efficient Worker or Reflective Practitioner? Competing Technical Rationalities of Media Software Tools' (Chap. 6), Ingrid Forsler and Julia Velkova argued that specialised software is not just an instrument of labour. They contended that social hegemonies are built into different rationalities of the technologies of labour. The goals of technology creators become embedded within their technical designs. The authors presented an analysis of three industrial and user-driven manufacturers of software tools for computer graphics. They built a conceptual theoretical model explaining different epistemological assumptions and competing visions of media practitioners and their digital tools: 'each distinct framework of software production assumes a different way of knowing and understanding knowledge in relation to practice'. Such 'competing visions' are not inevitable but always contestable, malleable, and changeable at the level of practice.

Valerija Barada and Jaka Primorac in their chapter entitled 'In the Golden Cage of Creative Industries: Public-Private Valuing of Female

Creative Labour' (Chap. 7), argued against the techno-optimistic notion of the emancipatory potential of female creative labour. Although economically independent with lucrative jobs that they consider a personal choice, female creatives are facing the implosion of the public into the private sphere as their labour practices become embedded into their private homes and daily activities while the social value of their work is decreasing. In their paper that draws upon empirical data on women in cultural and creative sectors in Croatia, Barada and Primorac argued that even if socio-economic changes are redefining labour as such, women's work, and especially female creative labour, is changing at a different pace since it is additionally engulfed in patriarchal social relations. Thus, the redefining of women's work is underway and technology plays a contradictory role in that process. The authors show how female creatives' labour is becoming a golden cage, since it encourages non-paid, underpaid, and self-exploitative practices that put women in more precarious positions than men.

In the final chapter of the section 'Digital Inclusion for Better Job Opportunities? The Case of Women E-Included through Lifelong Learning Programmes' (Chap. 8) Lidia Arroyo explored the limitations of digital inclusion programs for women. The analysis is based on a qualitative study of disadvantaged women who attended a basic digital skills course through a lifelong learning program in Spain. The results showed that digital skills are not enough to alleviate entrenched social inequalities. Such contradictions are the result of misplaced policies arguing for a positive impact of digital technologies on creating new labour opportunities and market access for underprivileged women. She wrote:

> digital programmes for better job opportunities must not only promote the acquisition of digital skills but also other basic skills such as knowledge of a foreign language. Moreover, these policies have to be coordinated with other social policies that avoid age, race and gender discrimination.

Part III brings chapters that interrogate 'Contradictions in Human Interaction and Communication'. The section opens with the discussion on the notions of embodied and disembodied work inside Uber rides. Contradictions in human interaction are also tackled within open-source software production. Such production processes orient human interaction towards a mixture of coordination, control, and innovation. The trend of work gamification is studied as bringing contradictions between empowerment and exploitation. Furthermore, the technologically enabled trend of audience monitoring in online news websites is analysed as an important element of change in professional practices within communication industries.

In a chapter titled 'A Recent Story about Uber' (Chap. 9), Brian Beaton examined how apps manifest within contemporary literature. He scrutinises a recent story about Uber by the American author and former Iraq war veteran, Colby Buzzell. Beaton argued that this story clearly outlines some of the contradictions that surround apps in their specific contexts of use. He provided a vivid analytical argument for a larger process of the struggle between capital and labour and alienation in technologically mediated environments of the sharing economy. Uber drivers are often stuck between conflicting screens of the driver and the passenger. The driver 'has to maintain continuous engagement with a navigation app. The overall effect (…) is an immersive, cocooned experience marked by near-total disconnection between the driver and passenger(s)'. The driver's war medal is displayed on the dashboard, yet it fails to capture the interest of his customers who are too immersed in their own mobile phone screens. In this alienating environment, Beaton also saw an element of what he called 'technological recession'. Some technologies have 'lost their cultural value, user communities, maintainability, or everyday legibility'. His chapter offers a reminder of the fragile nature of the social existence of technology.

In his chapter titled 'Protocols of Control: Collaboration in Free and Open Source Software' (Chap. 10), Reinhard Anton Handler analysed strategies for producing software. While often promoted as de-centralised, flexible, and flat, he argued that f/oss production operates on the basis of specific control mechanisms. Both the commons and the commodities model share a computational logic that relies on control. Decisions are not always made in a democratic manner, and hierarchies often inform the collaborative process. Contrary to popular discourse, the field of f/oss production is teaming with power imbalances along social, philosophical, political, economic, technological, and practical lines. Tracking work activities by computers is a fundamental component for collaborative production. Therefore, software is not a neutral tool. It 'not only transforms industries along computational processes, but also activates the imagination of society with a computational logic of decentralized networks', Handler contended.

In the chapter titled 'Playbour and the Gamification of Work: Empowerment, Exploitation, and Fun as Labour Dynamics' (Chap. 11), Raul Ferrer-Conill critically analysed the trend of incorporating playful thinking, worker empowerment, and self-realisation within labour processes. Such trends display a contradictory tension between fun and enjoyment on the one hand, and exploitation, surveillance, and control on the other hand. Work and play are mediated by labour dynamics embedded in a technological assemblage that empowers and exploits employees. The gamification of work creates a contradiction between 'the promise of empowerment and free will of play, and the tactics of control and for-profit determinism of capitalist ventures'. Ferrer-Conill argued that the only available choice is to play or revolt.

Aleksander Sašo Slaček Brlek, in his chapter entitled 'Audience Metrics as a Decision-making Factor in Slovene Online News Organisations' (Chap. 12), studied the dramatic increase in information gathering and analysis practices. While struggling to attract advertising investments in competition with major Internet platforms such as Facebook and Google, news organisations are under increasing pressure to utilise audience metrics and monetise their fragmented audiences. Based on a series of interviews with journalists, editors, and advertising sales agents in Slovenia, Slaček Brlek found that the number of clicks has become the dominant metric in digital newsrooms. Simultaneously, journalists do not see this process as being an obstacle to their professional autonomy and integrity. He argued that digital technologies are 'bringing back rather primitive methods of increasing surplus value through lower wages, precarious working arrangements and longer working hours'.

Part IV titled 'Contradictions in Democratic Participation and Regulation' uncovers challenges and contradictions in studying and regulating digital work and labour. It looks at contradictions in social media use, democratic participation, commercial ownership, and commodification of communication via major social media companies. The section concludes with a chapter outlining some of the key dimensions and lessons for studying and regulating multiple dimensions of digital work and labour.

Göran Bolin, in the chapter 'Media Use and the Extended Commodification of the Lifeworld' (Chap. 13), studied how media users produce social, aesthetic, and cultural value that becomes expropriated by the media industries and transformed into economic value. Two types of commodities circulate over digital networks: the general traffic commodity, or data bits flowing through the network; and the specific traffic commodity that is the algorithmically processed version of these bits. Based on empirical research executed in Sweden and Germany, Bolin concluded that social media users are largely unaware of the objectified commodity of their online labouring activities. Media users largely misrecognise the fact that their activities take the form of a commodity circulating within the media and communication industries.

In the chapter titled 'Regulation, Technology and Civic Agency: The Case of Facebook' (Chap. 14), Bjarki Valtýsson problematized the notions of creativity and control of Internet communication. He analyses Facebook's contractual agreements in relation to current EU regulation. These structural elements are contrasted with empirical data of citizens' perceptions of Facebook as a space for realising civic agency. Facebook users are unsure about the regulatory aspects of their content production: '[i]t is thus not that citizens are uninformed and unclear in their perceptions of their commercial social media but instead that there is a lack of clarity within the regulatory frameworks that are meant to ensure citizens' rights'. He concluded that the platform cannot be dismissed as an agent seeking control, nor as an agent offering space for creative and democratic expression. Instead, the social field opened by the platform can be situated as somewhere in between these two poles.

In the concluding chapter 'Spinning the Web: The Contradictions of Researching and Regulating Digital Work and Labour' (Chap. 15), Pamela Meil provided an analytical perspective on the multifaceted reality of digital technologies and labour. Three contradictory relationships characterising virtual work are outlined: the compression of time and place versus the global reach of virtual spaces; autonomy versus control; and collaboration versus competition. Meil looked at these contradictions from the perspective of the institutional embeddedness of labour markets as well as conceptual positions for understanding value capture in digital environments. She concluded that dis-embedded institutions and amorphous labour markets stifle the development of effective policy and regulation. Traditional organisations and institutions are being bypassed, which facilitates a deregulation of work, jeopardises intellectual property rights, and exploits workers by profiting from unpaid labour. She concluded: 'work contracts and the employment relationship also impact on social systems and the legal and institutional frameworks for governing work and employment at the societal level'.

Analytical Takeaways

Many of the chapters, particularly the ones focusing on global Internet platforms, carry with them the biases and experiences of the authors studying and most likely using the platforms at the same time. While keeping in mind the need for academic rigour and standards, the editors of the book do not aim to take the position of objective, outside observers. Precisely from such experiences, we can start building arguments about corporate power to influence daily lives and to commodify and valorise human existence through digital technologies. Therefore, the book has an underlying political dimension in which contradictions are taken as an indicator of social imbalances and tensions, potentially leading to social change through democratic policy, regulation, or other courses of action. The wider framework of these contradictions is that of capital producing systemic crises (Harvey 2014). In the sphere of labour and technology, capital accumulation restructuring is happening along the lines of automation, digitalisation, datafication, and the accompanying discourses of flexibility, efficiency, progress, and innovation. To understand the wider as well as the more specific frameworks, it is necessary to look at how contradictions actually play out in concrete empirical realities that are often hidden at first sight. We can identify three topics cutting across different chapters of the book. Other analytical points could potentially be traced within the rich material of the book. However, we believe that these three central axes deserve special attention.

First, many authors share an implicit, or explicit, understanding of *labour and economic valorisation occurring outside of the traditional concept of work* as a paid activity confined within a single, or distributed, organisational structure. Working 9-to-5 has ceased to be the central trope of capitalism for some time now. While certain sectors of the economy are more standardised around such a time-management premise, the predominant, persistent discourse is the one about flexibility amplified by digital technologies. This change occurs along the blurred lines between the private and the public, free-time and work-time, exploitation and emancipation, alienation and fulfilment, and work and play. Nowhere is the aspect of non-standardised and non-remunerated labour more emphasised than in the activities on different types of Internet platforms. Financially successful business models are mostly built around the social exchange of free services for personal data and surveillance. The communicative, reflexive, interpretive, playful, and creative aspects of a fulfilling human existence are no longer reserved for leisure time. This dramatically extends to commodified online communication and becomes a key resource for the creative industries, knowledge economy, and the sharing economy. It is not just time but also human qualities in non-routine activities that matter. As a number of papers in this volume show, human existence has equal value in the assembly line, despite the dominant discourses claiming otherwise.

Second, *technology does not only imply a material, fixed existence under capital. It is malleable and mouldable* based on the process of creating and using technology in different ways. Technology itself can potentially be changed to reflect social equality and democratic policy. The obsolescence of human labour amid new developments in hardware, software, apps, algorithms, and other technologies is a recurring theme that captures public attention. Yet, instead of being replaced, labour becomes increasingly entangled with technology in new and complex ways. Malleability of digital technology is one of the constitutive elements in our struggle to precisely define what academics actually mean by digital work and labour. Science and technology studies have known for a long time that technologies are interpretatively flexible (Pinch and Bijker 1984). However, what is missing from many works in that field, according to Feenberg (2010), is a normative concern over democratic rationalisation of technologies within broader social contexts. Many authors in this volume focus on technology, or *technics* (Marcuse 1941), as one of their central analytical categories, while keeping in mind the political and economic conditions under which technologies operate and exert influence.

Third, outlined contradictions display *political tensions without organised awareness or dissent*. Whether we talk about labour, or how technology is utilised and shaped by labour, policy and democratic regulation are lagging behind this dynamic change. The general trend with digital technologies supporting globally dispersed labour markets seems to be one of de-regulation or a lack of democratically meaningful policy action. Many of the contradictions surrounding Internet platforms are difficult to resolve within the confines of national or transnational legislative measures. For example, should Internet users demand remuneration based on the economic valorisation and exploitation of their online activities? Should Internet users protest against technical affordances of digital platforms they use? Other regulatory areas are equally ambivalent. How should workers in many affected industries respond to the possibility of technological unemployment? How should creative workers fight for standard working hours when faced with project-based, precarious employment? This book is far too short to respond to all the issues that technologies of labour bring into the 21st century. The difficulty for political subjects carrying the load of changing such conditions is the global reach of digital labour markets and the inability to find a political framework to support the demand for change. Many legal battles are fought in more traditional policy arenas of intellectual property, privacy, freedom of expression, audio-visual media services, and so on. Yet, these areas do not capture the essential contradictions of workers' rights in technologically mediated environments.

Moving Forward

Chapters in this book suggest that technologically-mediated labour dynamics are a part of activities appearing inside and outside of traditional workplaces and workspaces. Regardless, human existence remains pressured in the old struggle between capital and labour. The shifting coordinates of this struggle are the result of the global compression of time and space, the lack of institutional embeddedness of new labour markets, and design characteristics of digital technologies. Every book anthology focusing on such a moving target runs the risk of being outdated as soon as the new gadget, software, or app enters the market, or when social media platforms make changes in their contractual agreements. Yet, our goal was not to chase the latest technological developments in an attempt to situate them within a field of social and academic relevance. Instead, the book tries to build an emergent theoretical argument for new manifestations of technologically-mediated labour. These new labour processes are appearing under weak political, democratic, and regulatory activity. However, as the authors in the book show, the process is by no means smooth and frictionless. In the quest to outline the richness of these contradictions, a variety of human subjects and case studies are presented, cutting across time and space, gender, income, social status, and class of many research subjects. Analysed technologies will undoubtedly evolve, and many others recede into distant memory, but the social struggles and contradictions between capital and labour, exploitation and emancipation, alienation and fulfilment, and creativity and control will remain. Understanding unequal power relations helps one to see beyond promotional and utopian discourses of digital technologies, often only thinly veiled behind corporate interests. Digital technologies come in different shapes and sizes and also include f/oss and other tools assembled and re-organised for different purposes. These cases remind us that human relations are always the focal point of technology and that, regardless of flexible appearances, such projects also reflect the social and material foundations upon which they are built and utilised. Whether systemic or embedded in everyday life and social interaction, technology cannot escape its social foundations, despite many misplaced policies promoting the immediate positive impact of technology on society, economy, and politics. Keeping this in mind is a valuable lesson for scholars, students, and policy makers. Hopefully, the readers of this book will also come to the conclusion that technology always entails a political dimension. An understanding of the contradictory politics of the technologies of labour remains for you, the reader, to be discovered in the following pages.

References

Braverman, H. (1974). *Labour and monopoly capital: Degradation of work in the twentieth century.* New York: Monthly Review Press.

Dyer-Witheford, N. (2015). *Cyber-proletariat: Global labour in the digital vortex.* London/Toronto: Pluto Press.

Feenberg, A. (2010). *Between reason and experience: Essays in technology and modernity.* Boston: MIT Press.

Fisher, E., & Fuchs, C. (2015). *Reconsidering value and labour in the digital age.* Basingstoke: Palgrave Macmillan.

Florida, R. (2002). *The rise of the creative class and how it's transforming work, leisure, and everyday life.* New York: Basic Books.

Fuchs, C. (2010). Labour in informational capitalism and on the Internet. *Information Society, 26*, 179–196.

Harvey, D. (2014). *Seventeen contradictions and the end of capitalism.* London: Profile Books.

Huws, U. (2003). *The making of a cybertariat: Virtual work in a real world.* New York: Monthly Review Press.

Marcuse, H. (1941/2004). Some social implications of modern technology. In D. Kellner (Ed.), *Herbert Marcuse: Technology, war, fascism* (pp. 39–65). New York/London: Routledge.

Mosco, V., & McKercher, K. (2009). *The labouring of communication: Will knowledge workers of the world unite?* Lanham/Boulder/New York/Toronto/Plymouth: Lexington Books.

Pinch, T., & Bijker, W. (1984). The social construction of facts and artefacts: Or how the sociology of science and the sociology of technology might benefit each other. *Social Studies of Science, 14*(3), 399–441.

Scholz, T. (Ed.). (2013). *Digital labour: The Internet as playground and factory.* New York/London: Routledge.

Part I

Contradictions in Automation and Internet Platforms

2

Industry 4.0: Robotics and Contradictions

Sabine Pfeiffer

Digital Capitalism, Robotics and Human Labour: An Introduction

In light of predicted dramatic technological changes ahead, debates on the potential automation of human labour are returning with an almost forgotten vehemence. The last years have seen a widespread debate of Industry 4.0 (Pfeiffer 2017) that is premised on two assumptions. First, it is often assumed that Industry 4.0 arose in reaction to a new quality of technological development. In future, at least according to the story told, businesses will network their machines, warehouse systems, and operating equipment as worldwide cyber-physical systems (CPS). This vision of

---

Work for this chapter originated within the research projects 'RAKOON—Innovation by active collaboration in open organisations' and 'diGAP—Decent Agile Project Work in the digitised World'; funded by the German Federal Ministry for Education and Research (BMBF) and the European Social Fund (ESF).

S. Pfeiffer (✉)
Nuremberg Campus of Technology (NCT), Friedrich-Alexander-Universität Erlangen-Nürnberg, Nürnberg, Germany

an industrial Internet of Things (IoT) concerns the digital networking of the physical elements in the production process, support services, and logistics. Customized production that is responsive to individual needs and on-demand-only is one of the ideas put forward. Data volume will increase exponentially during the course of CPS. It is not only the elements moving through the production process which continuously generate status data but also all the sensors and activators of all the machines and plants involved. Further technical developments are also central to the Industry 4.0 scenarios under discussion, such as adaptive robots, 3D-printing, or wearables. All these technical capabilities could be integrated into the factory. From its beginning, this debate has been claiming that Industry 4.0 in its core is a 'human-centric approach to manufacturing' (Kagermann et al. 2013, p. 57). In contradiction to that claim, other studies predict future job losses on an unprecedented scale. Frey und Osborne (2017), for example, predict that 47% of jobs in the US labour market are at risk of computerisation, and those who work with machines and in the production sector will bear the brunt of these developments. Frey and Osborne estimate that 98% of such jobs may be susceptible to automation.

Although this process has been underway for some decades now, particularly in Germany, it has only recently attracted renewed attention in academic research and public debate. Here it is important not to underestimate the extent to which new forms of robotics are now being discussed that have little in common with previous industrial robots. Increased attention has been given to intelligent robots (Frick 2015), as well as robots connected to the cloud (Kehoe et al. 2015). Furthermore, software algorithms are also increasingly termed robots, for example the so called journalistic robot (Cohen 2015), and even automated cash machines now are classified as robots (Bessen 2015).

This chapter will be exclusively concerned with hardware-based robots and their effect on human labour in the areas of production and assembly. Sales of robots here have increased in year on year, and are predicted to continue to do so in future (IFR 2016). Nevertheless, in the age of digital capitalism, the significance of classical industrial robots for human labour in the production sector cannot be considered in isolation from other technological developments and economic strategies (Aneesh 2016;

Dolata 2017; Fuchs 2013). Such robots are interconnected, intelligent, adaptive, and are beginning to emerge from their protective cages. They are also becoming cheaper and lighter, and are increasingly coming to supplant human beings on the production line—the very place where Industry 4.0 is supposed to offer human workers a new, central, and more highly valued role, at least according to its own mantras (Pfeiffer 2017).

In labour market research, forecasts for the future are equally varied. On the one hand, we find studies by those such as Frey and Osborne (2017), which make predictions about the future on the basis of certain assumptions concerning automation. Likewise, a recent study by the National Bureau of Economic Research drew on past data to present strong evidence for the continued automation of human labour through robotics (Acemoglu and Restrepo 2017). Despite methodological differences, then, these studies predict similar future trends, at least at the quantitative level. In the eyes of many labour market statisticians, production and machine-based work is monotonous, repetitive, and physically challenging; the loss of such jobs is therefore not on the whole seen as problematic in itself, but rather as a positive development. While on the one hand, then, commentators unanimously hold that machine-based work is under threat from robotics, other voices have also affirmed that it will be possible to shape these developments—potentially through social innovations (Kaivo-oja and Roth 2015). Yet others have argued that the polarisation of the labour market is not limitless and have indicated the importance of developing a strata of qualified, mid-level employees within the overall employment structure (Autor 2015). Finally, others sought to demonstrate the positive effects of robotics on the labour market (Gorle and Clive 2013).

In section "Developing Digital Productive Forces: New Contradictions?", the empirically based argumentation of this chapter is initially discussed against the backdrop of a critical and theoretical framework, asking for new contradictions within the developing digital productive forces.

In this perspective, the section "The Exchange Value of Living Labour Capacity: The Limits of the Notion of Routine" critically discusses recent labour market research on the potential for automation through new technology. Particularly where robotics is concerned, such research tends to see human labour as highly susceptible because labour in production and assembly is assumed to be highly routinized.

Section "Beyond Routine: The Significance of Living Labour Capacity" sets out to challenge this view based on a plethora of qualitative research providing an alternative insight into work in production and assembly. From this viewpoint, immanent limits of automation can be found as well as a mostly overseen relevance of non-routine work especially in highly automated and digitalised work environments.

It is nonetheless difficult to argue against the ever more objective-seeming quantitative data on the basis of qualitatively dense empirical studies. In order to address this difficulty, section "Making the Invisible Measurable: The LC Index" develops an index that highlights non-routine activity. This novel approach uses the presented qualitative results to measure the otherwise 'unmeasurable'. Utilising indicators from the BIBB/BAuA Employment Survey (Rohrbach-Schmidt and Hall 2013), the *labour capacity index* (LC index) unveils the extent to which individuals are confronted with complexity, unpredictability, and change in the workplace today, thus illuminating the use value of human labour.

Section "Labouring Capacity in the Industrial Sector" presents a number of index scores in the fields of mechanical and automotive engineering. These results show that where the most significant effects of robotics have been predicted on the automation of living labour that the immanent limits of this automation may already have been reached. Finally, section "Exposing Contradictions by Attending to Living Labour Capacity Rather than Automation Forecasts" discusses these findings concerning robotics and labour in the context of digital capitalism and from the perspective of contradictions presented by Harvey (2014).

Developing Digital Productive Forces: New Contradictions?

In these debates and studies, two questions nonetheless remain open: first, what is the exact nature of the work that is supposed to be taken on by robots? Second, what is the value of human labour and is the question of what tasks will be taken on by robots and at what cost a purely technical one? *These questions ultimately revolve around a fundamental contradiction within capitalistic modes of production, namely that although human beings are the only genuine source of all value creation, automation and technological innovations are almost always used to supplant this very source of value creation.*

Contradictions are complex phenomena. In his recent critique, McGovern (2014) consistently affirms that the concept is often approached too arbitrarily and in the absence of a clear theoretical basis or empirical operationalisation. Not every instance of tension, conflict, or phenomenal opposition indicates a genuine contradiction. It is therefore important to take a more analytical approach to the concept, in the manner of David Harvey, who dissects the fundamental contradictions of capitalism in an analytically rigorous manner. Among the contradictions he identifies, two are particularly relevant in the present context: first, the 'moving contradiction' constituted by the interlinking of technology, work, and 'human disposability' (2014, pp. 91–112), and secondly, the 'foundational contradiction' between 'use value and exchange value' (2014, pp. 15–25).

This chapter aims to make an empirically supported contribution to the discussion of these two contradictions, without thereby wishing to suggest that Industry 4.0—as an interest-based narrative as well as a material contribution to the development of productive forces (Pfeiffer 2017)—can be explained on the basis of these two contradictions alone or understood via their effects.

In elaborating his first contradiction, Harvey, like Marx, indicates that as capitalism uses new technologies to control and to replace human labour, also the true source of value creation is minimised. Other means of ensuring profitability thereby become more important—even at the cost of destabilising the economy and society more broadly. This is Harvey's central contention concerning the replacement of living labour.

Here the contradiction Harvey draws between use value and exchange value, also derived from Marx, is likewise helpful. 'Nothing could be simpler' (2014, p. 15), Harvey writes at the outset of his chapter on the topic, before proceeding to explain these Marxist concepts in terms of commodities—though not the commodity of labour power. The latter too has its use value, though even in Marxist debates this is rarely systematically attended to. Kluge and Negt, however, have illuminated this use value as a central element in the political economy of labour power (2014), and it is on the basis of this elucidation that we can operationalise the concept with a view to the empirical assessment of the use value of labour—particularly within the context of digital capitalism (Pfeiffer 2014).

The Exchange Value of Living Labour Capacity: The Limits of the Notion of Routine

In the scientific as well as public discourse on Industry 4.0 Frey and Osborne's study (2017) has played a particularly prominent role. The authors derive their conclusions on digital technology's streamlining potential and the associated effects on the labour market on the basis of US labour market data and the views of technical experts. Frey and Osborne assume that there are barely any remaining limits to computerisation, but still some engineering bottlenecks, i.e. tasks that at least make automation more difficult or delay its implementation. These include perception and manipulation tasks, creative intelligence tasks, and social intelligence tasks (Frey and Osborne 2017, p. 264). This approach, which juxtaposes task-specific mass data with views on the feasibility of technological automation, has two general limitations. Firstly, in the corporate world, what determines whether a given technology is implemented is not simply its technical feasibility, but rather economic considerations. Secondly, decisions concerning the use of technologies are often determined more by the objective relations and power structures within the value creation chain than by individual business strategies.

Alongside these general objections, however, what particularly interests us here is the question of routine. Frey and Osborne (2017) subscribe to certain distinctions that almost always form the basis of assessments of the effects of technological change. Drawing on employee data from the USA, Autor et al. (2003) ask why the greater use of computers leads to an overall rise in more highly skilled work, setting out from a classificatory distinction between non-routine (analytic or interactive) tasks and routine (cognitive or manual) tasks. Frey and Osborne (2017, p. 255), meanwhile, illustrate changes in the technical feasibility of computerisation using the example of driverless cars, just because Autor et al. had used the latter to indicate the limits of automation.

What interests us most of all here, however, is the distinction between routine and non-routine tasks—a distinction that plays a central role in these studies' assessments of the technical feasibility of automation. Ultimately, all such task-based approaches set out from the hypothesis of routine-based technical change (RBTC) (Fernández-Macías and Hurley 2014, p. 37) and almost always equate routine with repetitive, monotonous work. Their classification of tasks as either routine or non-routine—which represents a crucial step in almost all of the studies discussed here—is rather obscure and risks becoming circular (Fernández-Macías and Hurley 2014, p. 48). It therefore distorts our understanding of the significance of living labour capacity and clouds our perception of the associated contradictions and their transformation over time. In these studies, machine-based labour is seen as particularly susceptible to automation, in two respects: first, such work is held to consist largely of routine tasks; second, production and assembly are seen as the most important areas of application for new developments in robotics. The author's own workplace investigations (Pfeiffer 2016) have nonetheless shown that things are not so simple. A typical automobile assembly line in a German car manufacturing plant is already over 95% automated, and there is on average one employee for every robot. But the work done by such employees is far from routine. They supervise eight robots, and in a normal work day intervene in this highly complex process between 20 and 30 times. In order to do so, they not only require a great deal of specialist knowledge (about controlling robots, for instance, or welding technologies) but also context-specific knowledge (concerning quality control, for example, and upstream and downstream processes), as well as experiential knowledge (about the causes of previous disturbances, wear and tear, the way materials react to temperature changes, and so on). Their frequent interventions are sometimes responses to irregularities or disturbances, but mainly serve to ensure that these do not arise in the first place. What we encounter here, then, is a striking contradiction: while in highly complex and heavily digitised production environments the significance of living labour is quantitatively decreasing, its role in maintaining these complex production processes is becoming ever more important. This fact nonetheless remains invisible to most statistical approaches to the issue.

Beyond Routine: The Significance of Living Labour Capacity

Contrary to what is implied by Frey and Osborne (2017), experience here would then seem to be an expression of non-routine activity and its importance in complex and heavily automated and digitised working environments (Hirsch-Kreinsen 2016). This was already shown by studies conducted in the 1980s on the transition from traditional machines to CNC tools (Böhle and Milkau 1988) and on the management of complex operations in the process industry (Böhle 1994). These studies indicated the importance of 'subjectifying work action', whose central dimensions include holistic perception, an explorative and dialogical approach, intuition and instinct, and an empathetic bearing. While specialist theoretical knowledge and routine-based practices are important in standardised processes and repetitive, unchanging tasks, subjectifying action helps employees to deal with the (as yet) unknown. The notion of subjectifying work action thus recalls those aspects of knowledge and action that figures such as Polanyi (1983) and Dreyfus (1992) identified as hidden and informal and—as genuine human capacities—superior even to intelligent forms of technology. A range of empirical studies have lent further weight to the notion of subjectifying work action and highlighted its significance in various work-related tasks, particularly in non-routine situations. In the above studies, this has been empirically demonstrated in relation to the way employees deal with uncertainty in project-based work (Böhle et al. 2016) as well as the contradictory demands placed on R&D engineers (Pfeiffer et al. 2010) and on customers using self-service systems in the service and Internet economies (Böhle 2013).

In the labour market studies in question here (Frey and Osborne 2017), these three sectors are also classed as non-routine-based. By consensus, they are held to consist of knowledge work, innovation work, or creative work. Here it is interesting to compare these studies on knowledge and service work with the studies on production work cited at the outset (Böhle and Milkau 1988; Böhle 1994). Although knowledge and service work differs greatly from production work in many respects, there are similarities between the subjectifying work action involved in both areas and the situations in which such non-routine action is called for. *From the perspective of qualitative labour research, then, the customary distinction between knowledge work as a non-routine activity and production work as a routine activity does not stand up to close scrutiny.*

More recent studies have also demonstrated that the increasing globalisation and standardisation of production systems, along with their associated technological transformations, have made production work more complex and thereby increased the significance of non-routine activities. The importance of a 'high-tech instinct' was indicated by Bauer et al. (2006) in their study on process chemistry—an area marked by particularly high levels of automation and the early introduction of process management IT systems. Other studies have shown that in automobile assembly and serial production processes, employees increasingly have to deal with more rather than less complexity (Levitt et al. 2012), even when carrying out so-called 'simple' work. Such developments have been observed in the very areas in which robotics have long played an important role (Pfeiffer 2016). Qualitative studies at the shop floor level and in the production sector have arrived at very different conclusions than quantitative labour market research, which tends to make rather far-reaching predictions about automation-induced job losses on the basis of its findings. What qualitative studies bring to light, then—namely the ongoing centrality of living labour, even for value creation—vanishes when we adopt a quantitative perspective. What is crucial here is that the significance of living labour cannot simply be described as a residual element that has somehow retained its relevance. The *increasing qualitative significance of living labour in the face of its quantitative reduction is rather an immanent consequence of the contradictions in the dominant modes of production and the current leap in productive forces resulting from digitisation.*

This originally theoretical thesis can be translated into an empirically fruitful concept: the notion of *living labouring capacity* stands for the use value of the commodity that is labour power (for a more detailed theoretical development see Pfeiffer (2014), which draws on Kluge and Negt (2014)).

On the theoretical elaboration of this analytic concept, living labouring capacity is developed, with the aid of subjectifying work action, through the active appropriation of the object and means of work (whether material or immaterial) within a historically concrete form of labour organisation.

In the above discussion, we have then briefly presented the recent qualitative research on the empirical significance of non-routine activities in production environments. Yet we can also link this back to the contradiction between use value and exchange value at the level of labour. Even so, this will not suffice to provide a counter-argument to the claims of quantitative labour-market studies. As noted, such studies forego any serious clarification of the concepts of routine and non-routine activity, although these play a crucial role in their derivations of their conclusions. A rigorously critical approach that appeals to the notion of contradiction should also attempt to empirically support its analytic arguments. This will be undertaken in the following section.

Making the Invisible Measurable: The LC Index

Given the qualitative studies on the significance of non-routine tasks in production work presented in section "The Exchange Value of Living Labour Capacity: The Limits of the Notion of Routine" are of empirical relevance, and presumed—from a contradiction-oriented theoretical perspective—the significance of living labour will endure to be important for value creation in the context of digital capitalism, is there a way to quantify the share of non-routine and therefore human labour that is not that easy to replace? In the present section, we shall do this on the basis of the 2012 BIBB/BAuA Employment Survey (Rohrbach-Schmidt and Hall 2013). This is an occupation-based representative survey that has been repeated at regular intervals since 1979. The survey asks around 20,000 employees in Germany about changes in their work and their occupational roles. Though the survey items only allow us to sketch an approximate picture of the above-mentioned special and genuinely human capacities, certain items would seem to be congruent with the findings of the wealth of qualitative research on the topic. Our targeted search looked specifically for the non-routine aspects of occupations.

During this first stage, the aim was *not* to predict the probability of automation in light of new technologies, but rather to highlight the limits of such forecasts. The following elaboration of an appropriate index attempts to make the use value of labour 'measurable'. Our starting point here is the contemporary qualitative research outlined in section "Beyond Routine: The Significance of Living Labour Capacity" . The LC index should incorporate both situational and structural challenges for employees resulting from complexity, change, and unpredictability in the workplace (cf. Pfeiffer and Suphan 2015). The index is comprised of three components and a multiplier, and is generated as follows (Fig. 2.1):

The *sitCOM index component* stands for '*situation-specific handling of complexity*'. Here, three items[1] measure the frequency with which employees engage in situative problem-solving and decision-making activities, both alone and in collaboration with others. Seven further items[2] make up the *sitUP index component, and measure 'situation-specific unpredictability*', including improvised action under pressure. The *strCOM index component*, likewise comprised of seven items,[3] measures '*increasing structural complexity*' and thus the changes in the tools, objects, and organisation of work over the last two years, insofar as these were accompanied by increased stress levels. Finally, the rEX multiplier stands for the 'relevance of *acquiring experience*'. The LC index can be calculated for a

$$LC = \left(\frac{\overline{sitCOM} + \overline{sitUP} + \overline{strCOM}}{3} \right) \cdot rEX = [0;1]$$

Whereby:

$$\overline{sitCOM} = \frac{1}{3} \sum_{i=1}^{3} x_i = [0;1]$$

$$\overline{sitUP} = \frac{1}{7} \sum_{i=1}^{7} y_i = [0;1]$$

$$\overline{strCOM} = \frac{1}{7} \sum_{i=1}^{7} z_i = [0;1]$$

Fig. 2.1 Formula: Calculating the LC-index

total of 17,479 cases. The measurable index scores (LC > 0) are normally distributed. The LC index mean score was 0.56. Overall, an LC index score of over 0.5 was registered for the occupations of 74% of all workers surveyed. The majority of employees in Germany had therefore developed informal skills to help them deal with unpredictability, change, and complexity. This dynamic ability to learn from experience and to bring this learning to bear when complex workplace situations require it is found among a majority of employees. This high score shows that the contrast usually drawn between routine and non-routine tasks is inadequate. Thus far, however, we have considered all occupations together; in the following, we shall consider the significance of living labour capacity in production and assembly work.

Labouring Capacity in the Industrial Sector

The production and assembly in automotive and mechanical engineering are key to the implementation of Industry 4.0 and new applications in robotics. Of all respondents we now consider mechanical engineering (N=533) and automotive engineering (N=663), along with certain machine-based occupations—i.e. those that are regarded as routine and particularly susceptible to automation. The LC index shows that these core industrial branches exhibit well above average mean LC scores, at 0.65 each (mechanical engineering=477, SD=0.229; automotive engineering=593, SD=0.265). In contrast to Frey and Osborne (2017), this suggests that it is precisely in such heavily industrialised and highly automated industrial branches that employees are called upon to exhibit an above-average level of non-routine activity.

We shall now turn to the LC index scores for five occupations particularly relevant to Industry 4.0 within both industries: The LC scores for occupations in 'metal production/metalwork' (øLC=0.61, SD=0.269; N_{LC}=115) and 'automotive mechanics' (øLC=0.65, SD=0.258; N_{LC}=319), as well as those recorded in the areas of 'mechatronics' (øLC=0.73, SD=0.167; N_{LC}=61) and 'technological development, construction, and production management' (øLC=0.70, SD=0.196; N_{LC}=124) were not only well above average, but also just as high as the scores recorded for the occupations in 'information and communications technology' (øLC=0.71, SD=0.182; N_{LC}=34). This clearly shows that machine and production-based workers are often confronted with unpredictability, change, and complexity. The idea of dull routine work therefore does not apply here, and the quantitative figures support the above qualitative research. The frequent devaluation of machine-based production work as easily automated routine work is thus empirically untenable in the context of contemporary digitisation. *On the contrary: in the very branches of industry that already exhibit a high level of automation and robot usage, living labour capacity has an above average significance.*

Exposing Contradictions by Attending to Living Labour Capacity Rather than Automation Forecasts

Capitalism always has and always will use technology to increase the abilities of workplace control and to reduce the costs for human labour. Automation especially by robots thus first of all aims to replace workers, and those in production or assembly again are seen as the first to go according to recent studies (Frey and Osborne 2017). Their conclusions on the replaceability of human labour by robotics on the basis of a notion of routine work have been neither empirically nor theoretically validated. In contrast, we gave an overview of qualitative research in the area, which showed that it is precisely in highly automated environments that non-routine action plays a central role. We then quantified that by inventing an index that makes evident what so often is overseen and neglected: phenomena of living human labour. Initial results generated on the basis of a representative study of approximately 20,000 German interviewees made apparent that 74% of all employees in Germany often need to carry out non-routine work. This can be taken as evidence of the importance of living labour capacity, though it does not by itself show whether similar scores might also be observable in the highly automated fields of production and assembly work. We therefore calculated the relevant LC index scores for the branches of mechanical and automotive engineering and for machine-based occupations. Though the particular significance of living labour capacity may quantitatively decrease as a result of increasing digitisation and robotics usage, the qualitative significance of the use value of labour remains constant or even increases. Following David Harvey, two of whose seventeen contradictions form the theoretical framework of this essentially empirical chapter, we draw the following dialectical conclusion: instead of disappearing entirely, the significance of living labour capacity will rather increase—though fewer people will directly benefit from this. Digital capitalism will not be able to resolve its immanent contradictions by means of bits and bytes, nor delegate its class conflicts to an algorithm. The tendency of the falling profit rate will remain an economic problem characteristic for capitalism, be it digital or not. And the very economy that gives rise to it will be unable to deliver an antidote for it. Living labour capacity remains the guarantor of value creation.

That it is precisely production work that is characterised as routine and thus as replaceable is perhaps no coincidence. It is interesting to note here, finally, that what is thereby devalued and rendered discursively invisible are the very forms of labour that were the cultural models of the Fordist era, namely, skilled, traditionally male production work. Only recently, Hatton (2017) developed an analytical theory of invisibility on the basis of numerous studies. Such empirical studies have nonetheless traditionally focussed on female reproductive work or taboo forms of body work, i.e. forms of work that lie outside the sphere of gainful employment/the cultural mainstream, but which in both cases are predominantly undertaken by women. Hatton identifies three 'mechanisms of invisibility': sociocultural, sociolegal, and sociospatial. On the one hand, the broad public debate around Industry 4.0—as has been shown on the basis of a discourse analysis (Pfeiffer 2017)—has emphasised the new significance of industrial labour and affirmed that human beings will remain at the heart of the production process. At the same time, however, with its continual appeal to studies such as those by Frey and Osborne (2017), this discourse—strategically instigated by management consultancies and the World Economic Forum (WEF)—can also be seen as contributing to the devaluation of what at least in the core industrial production countries once amounted to relatively well safeguarded and trade union-protected, skilled, traditionally male work. Arguing against this devaluation is not only politically necessary; indeed, the main aim of the present chapter was to show that such arguments are also scientifically well-founded: 74% of all employees in Germany need to utilise their labouring capacity to deal with complexity and unpredictability, and in the two production branches we investigated, this figure was even higher, at 83%.

Certain recent studies have then interpreted the reduction in the numbers of mid-level employees and the increasing polarisation of the workplace as a consequence of digitisation, and have forecast these trends to continue (Collins 2013; Pew 2016). Others, however—likewise drawing on labour market data—have pointed to the new significance of this middle level (Autor 2015) or even to the emergence of a 'new middle' (Holzer 2015). The aim of this study is not to endorse either one or the other of these positions. In future, management strategies will continue to seek to replace living labour by means of technology (among other things). We can nonetheless observe that previous assessments of the technologically conditioned potential for job streamlining have been based upon conceptions of routine and non-routine tasks that were neither empirically nor conceptually well founded. These assessments therefore have to be considered inadequate, particularly where work with machines is concerned. The more digitisation succeeds in creating autonomous and adaptable systems, the more those dimensions of living labour that have thus far endured on account of their capacity to respond to complexity will also be subject to streamlining processes. At the present time, then, it is not possible to make a credible prediction as to whether living labour capacity may gain in significance within even more complex and vulnerable overall systems, or whether as a result of developments in the field of deep learning and artificial intelligence it may be subject to dramatic displacements and an associated escalation of the above-mentioned contradictions. The present chapter expressly does not seek to offer its own predictions, but rather describes and applies a set of analytic tools that will allow at least one of Harvey's 'moving contradictions' to be empirically investigated in future. The more disruptively digital capitalism develops—and the more dynamically 'moving contradictions' manifest themselves and the more explosively 'foundational contradictions' erupt and escalate—the more important it will be to examine such upheavals in an empirically rigorous manner.

Notes

1. How often does it happen in your occupational activity…: …that you have to react to and solve problems?; …that you have to take difficult decisions autonomously?; …that you have to communicate with other people in your occupational activity?
2. How often does it happen in your occupational activity…: …that you have to work under strong pressure of time or performance?; …that your work is disturbed or interrupted, e.g. by colleagues, inferior materials, machine malfunctions or phone calls?; …that you are expected to do things you have not learned or you are not proficient in?; …that you have to keep an eye on different work processes or sequences at the same time?; …that even a small mistake or a slight inattentiveness can lead to larger financial losses?; …that you have to work very quickly?; …that you don't receive all the information necessary for performing your work correctly?
3. In the last two years, have…: …new manufacturing or process technologies been introduced?; new computer programs been introduced?; …new machines or equipment been introduced?; …new or significantly changed products or materials been employed?; …new or significantly changed services been provided?; …there been significant restructurings or reorganisation pertaining to your immediate work environment? How did work pressure and stress change in the last two years?

References

Acemoglu, D., & Restrepo, P. (2017). *Robots and jobs: Evidence from US labor markets*. Cambridge: National Bureau of Economic Research.

Aneesh, T. (2016). *Technologically coded authority: The post-industrial decline in bureaucratic hierarchies*. Stanford: Stanford University.

Autor, D. H. (2015). Why are there still so many jobs? The history and future of workplace automation. *Journal of Economic Perspectives, 29*(3), 3–30.

Autor, D. H., Levy, F., & Murnane, R. J. (2003). The skill content of recent technological change: An empirical exploration. *The Quarterly Journal of Economics, 118*(4), 1279–1333.

Bauer, H. G., Böhle, F., Munz, C., Pfeiffer, S., & Woicke, P. (2006). *Hightech-Gespür: Erfahrungsgeleitetes Arbeiten und Lernen in hoch technisierten Arbeitsbereichen*. Bielefeld: Bertelsmann.

Bessen, J. (2015). Toil and technology. *Finance & Development, 52*(1), 16–19.

Böhle, F. (1994). Relevance of experience-based work in modern processes. *AI & Society. Journal of Human Centered Systems and Machine Intelligence, 8*(3), 207–215.

Böhle, F. (2013). "Subjectifying action" as a specific mode of working with customers. In W. Dunkel & F. Kleemann (Eds.), *Customers at work—New perspectives on interactive service work* (pp. 149–174). Basingstoke: Palgrave Macmillan.

Böhle, F., & Milkau, B. (1988). Computerised manufacturing and empirical knowledge. *AI & SOCIETY, 2*, 235–243.

Böhle, F., Heidling, E., & Schoper, Y. (2016). A new orientation to deal with uncertainty in projects. *International Journal of Project Management, 34*, 1384–1392.

Cohen, N. S. (2015). From pink slips to pink slime: Transforming media labor in a digital age. *The Communication Review, 18*(2), 98–122.

Collins, R. (2013). The end of middle class work: No more escapes. In I. Wallerstein, R. Collins, G. Derlugian, & C. Calhoun (Eds.), *Does capitalism have a future?* (pp. 37–70). Oxford/New York: Oxford University Press.

Dolata, U. (2017). Apple, Amazon, Google, Facebook, Microsoft. In *Market concentration—Competition—innovation strategies*. Stuttgart: Universität Stuttgart.

Dreyfus, H. L. (1992). *What computers still can't do*. Cambridge: MIT Press.

Fernández-Macías, E., & Hurley, J. (2014). *Drivers of recent job polarisation and upgrading in Europe: Eurofound Jobs Monitor 2014*. Luxembourg: Eurofound.

Frey, C. B., & Osborne, M. A. (2017). The future of employment: How susceptible are jobs to computerisation? *Technological Forecasting and Social Change, 114*, 254–280.

Frick, W. (2015). When your boss wears metal pants. Insights from the frontier of human-robot research. *Harvard Business Review, 96*, 84–89.

Fuchs, C. (2013). Capitalism or information society? The fundamental question of the present structure of society. *European Journal of Social Theory, 16*(4), 413–434.

Gorle, P., & Clive, A. (2013). *Positive impact of industrial robots on employment*. London: Metra Martech, International Federation for Robotics.

Hirsch-Kreinsen, H. (2016). Digitization of industrial work: Development paths and prospects. *Journal for Labour Market Research, 49*(1), 1–14.

Harvey, D. (2014). *Seventeen contradictions and the end of capitalism*. London: Profile. http://libro.eb20.net/Reader/rdr.aspx?b=1641562

Hatton, E. (2017). Mechanisms of invisibility: Rethinking the concept of invisible work. *Work, Employment & Society, 31*(2), 336–351.

Holzer, H. (2015). *Job market polarization and U.S. worker skills: A tale of two middles*. Washington, DC: The Brookings Institution, Economic Studies at Brookings.

IFR. (2016). *World robotics. Industrial robots 2015*. Frankfurt/M./New York: International Federation for Robotics.

Kagermann, H., Wahlster, W., & Helbig, J. (2013). *Recommendations for implementing the strategic initiative INDUSTRIE 4.0* (Final report of the Industrie 4.0 Working Group). Frankfurt/M.: Plattform 4.0.

Kaivo-oja, J., & Roth, S. (2015). *The technological future of work and robotics*. Genève: Inderscience.

Kehoe, B., Patil, S., Abeel, P., & Goldberg, K. (2015). A survey of research on cloud robotics and automation. *IEEE Transactions on Automation Science and Engineering, 12*, 398–409.

Kluge, A., & Negt, O. (2014). Elements of a political economy of labor power. *October, 149*(Summer), 9–34.

Levitt, S. D., List, J. A., & Syverson, C. (2012). *Toward an understanding of learning by doing: Evidence from an automobile assembly plant*. Cambridge: National Bureau of Economic Research.

McGovern. (2014). Contradictions at work: A critical review. *Sociology, 48*(1), 20–37.

Pew. (2016). *America's shrinking middle class: A close look at changes within metropolitan areas*. Washington DC: Pew Research Center.

Pfeiffer, S. (2014). Digital labour and the use-value of human work. On the importance of labouring capacity for understanding digital capitalism. *tripleC. Journal for a Global Sustainable Information Society, 12*(2), 599–619.

Pfeiffer, S. (2016). Robots, Industry 4.0 and humans, or why assembly work is more than routine work. *Societies*, 6. Special Issue Robots and the Work Environment, 2, 16. http://www.mdpi.com/2075-4698/6/2/16

Pfeiffer, S. (2017). The vision of 'Industrie 4.0' in the making—A case of future told, tamed, and traded. *NanoEthics, 11*(1), 107–121. http://rdcu.be/oN8l

Pfeiffer, S., & Suphan, A. (2015). *The labouring capacity index: Living labouring capacity and experience as resources on the road to Industry 4.0*. Stuttgart: University of Hohenheim, Chair of Sociology.

Pfeiffer, S., Schütt, P., & Wühr, D. (2010). Innovation, market, networks—Interdependencies, synergies and contradictions in technical innovation processes. In T. Chavdarova, P. Slavova, & S. Stoeva (Eds.), *Markets as networks* (pp. 165–180). Sofia: St. Kliment University.

Polanyi, M. (1983). *The tacit dimension*. Gloucester: Peter Smith.

Rohrbach-Schmidt, D., & Hall, A. (2013). *BIBB/BAuA employment survey 2012*. Bonn: BIBB. https://doi.org/10.7803/501.12.1.1.30

3

From Ford to Facebook: Time and Technologies of Work

Eran Fisher

Time Is Money

Here is something both Marxists and Capitalists can agree on: that time equals money. Since the invention of the clock and the emergence of universal time (Mumford 2010), and more forcefully since the beginning of modernity, time has become one of the central measures of economic value and labour productivity (Postone 1996). It has therefore also become *the* bone of contention between capitalists and workers. We might describe the history of labour struggles in capitalism as struggles over time: work time, wages for a given unit of time, duration of break time, paid vacation time, and the quality of free, or leisure time. In this struggle technology played a crucial role. Capitalists sought to design production technologies in ways that anchor their control over the time of their workers (Braverman 1974). Workers, on the other hand, fought these attempts, and even exercised practices of resistance while utilizing

E. Fisher (✉)
The Open University Israel, Ra'anana, Israel

© The Author(s) 2018
P. Bilić et al. (eds.), *Technologies of Labour and the Politics of Contradiction*, Dynamics of Virtual Work, https://doi.org/10.1007/978-3-319-76279-1_3

the very same technologies (Noble 1984). Time is therefore mired with contraction in the context of capitalist production.

But the nature of this contradiction transforms as the nature of capitalism, or its regime of accumulation, changes (Aglietta 2001; Boyer 2002). With the rise of network capitalism—with its characteristic blurring of the distinction between work and play, production and leisure, economy and "life itself"—the contradiction increasingly takes on a new face: now it is leisure time and the private sphere which are increasingly under threat to be colonized by productivist categories, encouraging individuals to produce content, communication, and data, which can be rendered into commodities.

To fully appreciate the novelty of that contradiction, we need to recall the regime of time under industrial capitalism. As early as the mid-19th century Karl Marx identified time as a central axis for analyzing how capitalism operates. His key concept of exploitation—coined in order to explain capitalism as power relations between human beings, rather than merely a technical economic system—is closely tied with time. By employing the notion of exploitation Marx clarifies the process of capital accumulation. How, Marx asks, does capital grow? How does investing a given quantity of capital in the production of commodities to be sold in the market end up yielding a larger quantity (Fig. 3.1)?

Given the Newtonian notion of conservation of energy, which proposed that the quantity of energy does not change over time, i.e., that energy cannot be created out of energy Marx asks, where this surplus 'energy', or capital, comes from? How does the transformation of money into commodities and back again into money results in an increase quantity?

Marx's answer was that the commodities produced in fact embody an additional quantity of 'energy' on top of the original quantity of money: human energy, of muscle power, cognitive abilities, and embodies skills; i.e., labour (Fig. 3.2).

$$M \rightarrow C \rightarrow M^i$$

Fig. 3.1 How can money (M) converted into a commodity (C) end up yielding a bigger quantity of money (M^i)?

$$M \rightarrow C (+L) \rightarrow M^i$$

Fig. 3.2 Marx's answer to the conundrum is that the commodity (C) actually embodies another source of value: labour (L)

Hence, Marx's argued that the increase in value of M^i over M occurs due to the input of another source of value; labour. But this important discovery creates an even bigger conundrum: how does the creation of value through labour result in the increase of capital? After all, capitalists need to pay for the labour that they hire, just as they need to pay for raw materials they buy, or the factory they build. Assuming a perfectly functioning market any commodity will be exchanged for its real value. Where from can any extra capital arise? One of Marx's great discoveries and one of the keys for a critical understanding of capitalism was that capital accumulation was based on a unique form of exchange which does not exist anyplace else in the market with any other commodity: the unequal exchange between the value that workers create through labour—and embody into the commodity—and the value they receive as wages.

The 'trick' behind this market oddity of unequal exchange, which allows capitalist to leave the exchange having more money then what they have entered with, is anchored, according to Marx, in time. Marx suggests we think about this odd exchange thus: when we go to an eight-hour workday, we actually work the first seven hours in order to create the value needed for the reproduction of our own life, whereas in the additional hour we create value for the capitalist. The wages we are paid represent the value we have created in the first seven hours of work. The value we have created in the last hour—which Marx calls surplus-value, as it is superfluous to what the worker actually needs for the reproduction of his life—is not remunerated in wages, but rather added to the infinite circulation of capital accumulation—the beating heart of capitalism. Indeed, we might think of the distinction between money and capital by placing them on the axis of time: while money is directed into consumption, capital is money which is directed into production, and therefore harbors a potential for its augmentation over time, after going through a cycle of $M \rightarrow C \rightarrow M^i$.

Managing Labour Time

In light of such description of reality it is no surprise that time has stood at the center of class struggle (Fuchs 2014). On the one hand, capitalists sought to exert as much value as possible from the time that workers are subject to their control, striving for longer working hours and increased efficiency of the work process. On the other hand, workers struggled to reduce as much as possible the time of exploitation, by shortening the workday, elongating vacation time, and securing paid work breaks. The fact that time was the key variable in allowing only a partial remuneration for labour, required capitalists to develop new techniques of control over workers in order to ensure that their time management is improved and allows better extraction of value.

Some of these techniques were direct practices of surveillance and control, such as the introduction of time clock, which monitored workers' presence at work. These techniques risked evoking resistance because they were quite overt and blunt attempts at control, and because they were external to the work process. More covert—and hence requiring more careful critical analysis to be deciphered—were techniques of control that were seamlessly weaved into the work process by technological means. These seem to be emerging from the internal logic of the work process itself. The epitome of such techniques has been the assembly line, which was first implemented on a large scale in Ford's auto factories. Marxist scholars of technology such as Harry Braverman (1974) and David Noble (1984) have suggested how the assembly line allowed not merely improved efficiency and quality control, but also deeper command and control of factory management over the time of workers. The assembly line enabled capital to dictate the rhythm of production externally—it could now be accelerated by merely controlling the machinery and forcing labour to adjust to the new rhythm; it prevented workers to freely move on the shop floor and anchored them to a given point in space; it also contributed to a physical separation of workers from one another and prevented them from communicating during work—a practice which not only 'wasted' time, but also contributed to something much more troubling from the point of view of capital: developing class consciousness, solidarity, and political organizing.

Enters Immaterial Labour

This constellation of work, time, and technology has reached its zenith in the first half of the 20th century. However, in the second half of the century capitalism has encountered another of its recurring crises, which put this constellation into question. The very success of the capitalist machine brought a reduction in the rate of profit and a systemic failure to create capital from labour (Mandel 1999; Harvey 2007). Just as in previous cyclical crises, now too, the route out of the crisis required capitalism to search for new sites that can be mobilized to the process of capital accumulation, and to restructure the work/time/technology constellation (Fuchs 2014).

One of these new sites for value extraction was what Autonomist Marxists refer to as general intellect (Marx 1993), life itself (Virno 2004; Morini and Fumagalli 2010), or immaterial labour (Lazzarato 1996), which refers to cognitive, emotional, communicative, relational, erotic, aesthetic, and sensual human facets, which are mobilized to the project of capital accumulation via the production of commodities. It is therefore 'labour', but one which largely takes place outside of the factory and the office, as part of everyday life, culture, the lifeworld, and subjectivity. It entails facets of human existence which are performed during leisure time, playing, or resting, with family, friends, or community. These were seen as resources in the creation of affective and symbolic commodities in an economy which increasingly drew on culture for the creation of economic value.

But in the newfound promise to mobilize new sources for the accumulation process lies also a weighty challenge. How can life itself be integrated into the production process? After all, life happens in the street, at home, while we play, cook, do yoga, or talk with friends` it happens in the semi-public and private spheres of life, sometimes in the most intimate of them. The activities we now put under the heading 'immaterial labour' had of course always been part of human life, but the ability to mobilize 'life' to the process of capital accumulation was very limited.

But something has changed. And it was not just the scale of mobilizing life. Indeed, to be able to reach such a scale and depth of penetration into life itself a new constellation of work/time/technology had to be put in place. One means to overcome the challenge of drawing life itself closer to the accumulation process was blurring and even eliminating the boundary between labour time and leisure time. This boundary has been a staple of the Fordist model of capitalism: value from labour could only be extracted in the factory. If anything, because time outside work time could not be mobilized towards the creation of value, it was laboriously constructed as time for consumption (Bauman 2004). While work time was constructed as rational and instrumental, leisure time was seen as its opposite: unpurposeful and erotic.

In this case too, a central means that capitalism employed in order to penetrate leisure time, and with it penetrate the lifeworld of play and creativity, and private lives and relationships that take place outside the office and the factory, was technological. This time it was digital technology, first and foremost the computer, the internet, and the smartphone. The immediate transformation of these technological means was their ability to make working hours more 'flexible', as this is called in business lingo, or, to use critical terms, the ability to usurp leisure time to the process of capital accumulation (Fisher 2010). We have thus found ourselves always readily accessible to employers via our mobile devices, or answering work-related emails in the evenings, or during vacation.

But this new constellation of work/time/technology meant something even more untraditional: At the same time that capitalism tried to penetrate leisure time, it also transformed the workplace dramatically so as to let leisure time penetrate work. Factories that are based predominantly on immaterial labour have replaced the assembly line, which enabled command and control over time in the case of material labour, with shared workspaces that combine elements from the lifeworld, such as cafés and game parlors, thus facilitating and encouraging the arousal of human qualities such as passion, creativity, joy, friendship, and communication—to be experienced not with loved ones, but this time with work colleagues (Fisher 2008).

One of the most eloquent manifestations of this new conceptualization of space and time can be found in Google. In order to make its products, Google needs its workers to speak with one another, exchange knowledge and information, cooperate in solving problems, and be creative. The playful and agreeable atmosphere in its offices—such an anathema to the cool, metallic, dehumanizing and alienating space of the Fordist factory—is not external to the work process, an add-on to an otherwise autonomous mode of working, introduced solely to make workers more content. It is not, in other words, a, office day trip, supposed to take workers out of the work context and put them—very temporarily—in a fun, amicable environment. Instead, it is part and parcel of the technical organization of production in factories that are founded on knowledge, information, communication, and creativity. Put simply, a billiard table at the center of a colorful workspace signals that this is a place for play, fun, and communication; that these are not anathema to work but precisely its new foundations.

But perhaps the more radical revolution of the new constellation of work/time/technology took place not in the factory and the work place, but rather outside of it. That's because, as aforementioned, the bulk of immaterial labour occurs outside the immediate control of capitalists—in the private sphere, during leisure time, at home, between individuals, in the interstitial spaces of social structures. How, then, can capitalism mobilize these productive powers, which take place outside of its immediate range of control? In simpler terms, how can a company like Google mobilize the immaterial working time not merely of its workers—which it does by recreating life-like atmosphere in its offices, simulating 'life itself'—but also the working power of the whole of humanity? It is here that the full significance of digital technology—particularly Web 2.0 and social media—to capitalism becomes evident. Just as the assembly line for Ford's motor company, so is social media for the knowledge economy: they are a technology which helps construct a new model of relations between work and time, which allowed the unprecedented mobilization of life-time to the capitalist project of capital accumulation. The deep and wide penetration of digital networks to the texture of our lives allowed harnessing our thoughts, feelings, knowledge, behavior and communication to the creation of economic value.

Think about communication technologies where so much of human communication—from the most mundane romantic exchange on WhatsApp between two lovers to complex webs of emails among multiple organizations—is now taking place over private platforms. But an even more radical form of mobilization of human potentialities was made possible by this new constellation of work/time/ technology. Think about Google's search engine, Waze's navigation application, and Facebook's social networking site. These very different digital platforms can be likened to an 'assembly line' which organizes the labour of millions of users. Google's search engine offers search results of webpages based on the online behavior of millions of previous users, and billions of previous search entries. Waze renders real-time information streaming from its users' devices, such as their location, destination, and travel speed, into knowledge about traffic conditions. And Facebook is a platform that allows unprecedented access of a single media organization to human communication of all sorts in immeasurable quantities. These three companies are founded, then, not merely on the labour power and labour time of their workers but also on the labour of millions of people using their technologies. Platform capitalism (Srnicek 2016), then, can be schematically thought of as the assembly line of digital, dispersed labour; a new constellation for the mobilization of immaterial labour via media use.

Just like their formal workers, and just like the workers in Ford's factory, so are users of digital services receive remuneration for their audience work as Smythe (1981), Jhally and Livant (1986) have put it in the form of 'wages', or wages' substitute: a search engine, a navigation application, and a social networking site, accessible from virtually anywhere for free. However, just like the formal workers, so are digital media users not fully compensated for the value they produce; the surplus value they create is transferred to the capitalist. In this sense, the familiar structure and dynamics of capitalist society have not changed since Ford's days, indeed since the rise of capitalism: capitalists have a monopoly over the means of production (in the case of knowledge production: a search engine, a navigation system, a social networking site), whereas workers (or users in this case) are left with only one choice; to create the value needed to sustain their livelihood, or the reproduction of their lives (in this cases getting access to knowledge), they are forced to work for capitalists in their factories, be it Ford motors factory, or the knowledge, information, and communication factories of Google, Waze, and Facebook (Scholz 2013).

Struggling over Social (Media) Time

But this side of the coin—of an increased ability to exploit human capabilities and labour time, and mobilize them to the process of capital accumulation through digital technology—should be complemented with its opposite side. Digital technology did allow colonizing the whole of wake time (and increasingly even sleep time) to capitalist ends. On the other end it also gravely exacerbated the problem of control: the ability of capitalists to control the time of workers. Whereas Ford's assembly line achieved a dual task of making the production process more efficient while also exerting more control over workers by separating and alienating them, the communication network that Google facilitates between its workers and among its users also affords new opportunities for workers (and users) to cooperate in order to struggle for shared interests in an organized fashion. The mail client which forces workers to take care of work-related issues during dinner time or family vacation might also help them organize a large group of workers in order to protest the amelioration of working conditions, or the breech of their privacy in social media sites. In paraphrase of the classic idiom by Marx and Engels (2002): What the digital bourgeoisie therefore produces, above all, are its own grave-diggers.

A case in point is a legal battle of Facebook users against the media company over the Sponsored Stories advertising program. Sponsored Stories, introduced by Facebook in January 2011 (and halted three years later), were ads based on regular users' posts. The program allowed businesses and organizations to buy these regular posts from Facebook, which rendered them into ads. According to Facebook, by rendering posts into ads, they were 'highlighted' and given a better chance to be noticed (Facebook 2012). A Sponsored Story then was an ad, based on a post by user X that would have appeared anyway on the news feed of user Y. By rendering posts into Sponsored Stories Facebook changed both the position of the original post on the page and its graphic formatting; Sponsored Stories appeared higher in news feeds or on the right-hand side of the page, and usually featured the logo of the brand. A Sponsored Story could be created when a user did either of several actions: Like a page, Like or comments on a page's post, RSVP to a page's event, vote on a page's question, check-in to a place, use an application or play a game, or Like or share a website (Facebook 2012). Once a post has been converted into a Sponsored Story all further communication acts associated with it were then taking place within the context of the Sponsored Story. So that any comment or Like on the Sponsored Stories 'reactivates' the ad and is disseminated to the network of friends of the user clicking the Like. That means that the dissemination of a Sponsored Stories was exponential (or viral). It also means that the movement of the ad in the social network was not arbitrary: ads move organically in channels of communication which have been constructed bottom-up and spontaneously by users.

Figures 3.3 and 3.4 illustrate the visual appearance of Sponsored Stories. Figure 3.3 features a regular Facebook post. In this example, a Facebook user named Jessica is using a location-based application on her mobile phone. She checks into a Starbucks café for the second time that day with Philip, a Facebook friend. This would automatically create a post reading 'Jessica: Second time today – at Starbucks with Philip'. Figure 3.4 features this post rendered into a Sponsored Story, after it has been bought by Starbucks. Graphically, the text is a little more compact, eliminating technical information, and compressing comments and Likes of friends to the post. The bluish background of the comments box is also eliminated. The text is organized in a box-like format, and a logo of Starbucks is added.

The legal case began in April 2011 (only four months after Sponsored Stories was introduced) with a class-action lawsuit filed at the US district

Fig. 3.3 Regular Facebook post

Fig. 3.4 Post rendered into a Sponsored Story

court, Northern District of California, San Jose division. Plaintiffs, who represented the class of Facebook users in the United States, accused Facebook of using their names, photos, and identities to advertise products and services through Sponsored Stories without seeking their permission and without remunerating them. On December 2011 the court decided to partially accept plaintiffs' arguments regarding remuneration. On 25 August 2013, after extra-court negotiations, Facebook reached a $20 million settlement with its users (Fraley vs. Facebook 2011).

What concerns me here is not the result as much as the way that users sought to define the time they spend on social media as work time (Fisher 2015b, c). Users alleged that Facebook was drafting them as sponsors for commercial products and services without their consent, and without remunerating them. Users' assertion that they create economic value is backed by Facebook's own enthusiastic declarations. In their lawsuit, plaintiffs quote the public expressions of two senior managers at Facebook. Mark Zuckerberg (Facebook's CEO) announced that '[n]othing influences people more than a recommendation from a trusted friend. A trusted referral influences people more than the best broadcast message. A trusted referral is the Holy Grail of advertising' (Fraley vs. Facebook 2011). Zuckerberg highlights the value of familiarity with the person making the recommendation and links this value to advertising. And in a direct appeal to advertiser Sheryl Sandberg (Facebook's Chief Operating Officer) explained:

> [m]arketers have always known that the best recommendation comes from a friend ... This, in many ways, is the Holy Grail of marketing. ... When a customer has a good experience ... on Facebook, the average action is shared with the average number of friends, which is 130 people. This is the elusive goal we've been searching for, for a long time; [m]aking your customers your marketers. (Fraley vs. Facebook 2011)

Sandberg points to the kind of work that Facebook presumes users to be doing as marketing, and valorizes their work thus:

> On average, if you compare an ad without a friend's endorsement, and you compare an ad with a friend's [Facebook] 'Like', these are the differences: on average, 68% more people are likely to remember seeing the ad with their friend's name. A hundred percent ... more likely to remember the ad's message; and 300% more likely to purchase [the advertised service or product]. (Fraley vs. Facebook 2011)

From that users conclude 'that the value of a Sponsored Stories advertisement is at least twice the value of a standard Facebook.com advertisement, and that Facebook presumably profits from selling this added value to advertisers' (Fraley vs. Facebook 2011). Uses, then, redefine Sponsored Stories as a form of a 'factory', mobilizing the immaterial labour of millions of 'workers' (Scholz 2013). Sponsored Stories, they argue, is 'a new form of advertising which drafted millions of [Facebook members] as unpaid and unknowing spokespersons for various products' (Fraley vs. Facebook 2011). Based on this redefinition, the plaintiffs assert their entitlement to be compensated for their labour. In addition, the plaintiffs argued that while Facebook's terms of use do give the company permission to use personal information for commercial purposes, they joined the service before the introduction of Sponsored Stories, and so were unaware of the monetization of their personal information for advertising. In sum, the plaintiffs made two legal claims pertaining to their right to control what they consider to be the fruits of their labour: their right to have control over the commodification of this information (i.e. alienation), and their right to profit from that commodification (i.e. exploitation).

Users as Media Workers

While the case touches upon issues of privacy, it does that in a way that's quite uncommon to the dominant discourse by linking privacy to value and labour. Discussing previous court cases involving the 'commercial misappropriation' of online personal information, the court concluded:

> Plaintiffs have articulated a coherent theory of how they were economically injured by the misappropriation of their names, photographs, and likenesses for use in paid commercial endorsements targeted not at themselves, but at other consumers, without their consent. (Fraley vs. Facebook 2011)

The court defines the case of users against Facebook as a struggle between labour and capital over value. The argument made by the plaintiffs and accepted by the court is that by merely spending time on SNS, users create measurable economic value. The court asserts that in contrast to previous cases,

> The plaintiffs did not allege that their personal browsing histories have economic value to advertisers wishing to target advertisements at the plaintiffs themselves, nor that their demographic information had economic value for general marketing and analytics purposes. Rather, they alleged that their individual, personalized endorsement of products, services, and brands to their friends and acquaintances had concrete, provable value in the economy at large, which can be measured by the additional profit Facebook earned from selling Sponsored Stories compared to its sale of regular advertisements. (Fraley vs. Facebook 2011)

Users, then, did not launch a general critique of the use of personal information for commercial ends, but rather, a more particular critique of the commodification of their persona. The thrust of the argument was not anti-commercial per se, but went against the shift from commodifying disparate bits of personal data (such as age or browsing history) to commodifying the persona of users as a whole. The argument made by the plaintiffs (and accepted by the court) is that by merely participating in the SNS, users create a measurable economic value:

Plaintiffs assert that they have a tangible property interest in their personal endorsement of Facebook advertisers' products to their Facebook Friends, and that Facebook has been unlawfully profiting from the non-consensual exploitation of Plaintiffs' statutory right of publicity. (Fraley vs. Facebook 2011)

This alludes to the special kinds of labour (or value-creating activities) that users carry out on social media. In the first place, this labour entails the production of information: from 'Liking' a page or posting a comment, to creating meta-data regarding their activities online and offline. However, according to users, the value they create involves an even more subtle and intangible form of labour, involving their very persona, their 'human capital', in Feher's critical appropriation of the term (2009). To explain this kind of value, users liken their position in social media to that of celebrities, in whom case value emerges from being, rather than doing:

> …in the same way that celebrities suffer economic harm when their likeness is misappropriated for another's commercial gain without compensation, Plaintiffs allege that they have been injured by Facebook's failure to compensate them for the use of their personal endorsements because '[i]n essence, Plaintiffs are celebrities – to their friends'. (Fraley vs. Facebook 2011)

The time dedicated to maintaining an online persona is redefined by users as a work time, since it creates value. Users equate themselves with traditional (i.e. mass media) celebrities, appearing in advertisements, due to the fact that like celebrities, users' personas—on which they labour online and offline—is commodified.

Users' interpretation of social media is that of a productive space where value is created by them. Once their persona is mobilized for advertising in social media the users, in fact, become media personalities, or celebrities. The value they produce emerges from their mere presence in the media, a media which has become social (in that its content is produced by its 'consumers' or users) and personalized (where each user can be identified). According to users, their work and the value they create 'has concrete, measurable, and provable value in the economy at large' (Fraley vs. Facebook 2011).

Facebook counters this argument by asserting that the value that users create can only be created within the context of social media; it is value that emerges out of use of the media and is therefore entangled with it and dependent on it: '[Facebook] does not deny that [users] may assert economic injury, but insists that, because they are not celebrities, they must demonstrate some preexisting commercial value to their names and likenesses' (Fraley vs. Facebook 2011). Facebook attempts to define social media users in terms that strip them off of their mediated subjectivity. As pre-mediated social being users, so Facebook claims, have no monetary value since they are not 'celebrities' in any way.

Users, in contrast, underscore the always-already mediated nature of all celebrities. A celebrity is a mediated subjectivity, preconditioned on media exposure, since familiarity on a large scale can only occur via mass-media exposure. Likewise, the commercial value of celebrities increases the more familiar they are to the audience, that is, the more mediated their subjectivity is, *the more time they spend online.* Users, then, suggest that the personal nature of social media (in contrast to the massified nature of traditional media) redefines what a celebrity is, how it is used in advertising, and how it generates value:

> While traditionally advertisers had little incentive to exploit a non-celebrity's likeness because such endorsement would carry little weight in the economy at large, Plaintiffs' allegations suggest that advertisers' ability to conduct targeted marketing has now made friend endorsements 'a valuable marketing tool', just as celebrity endorsements have always been so considered. (Fraley vs. Facebook 2011)

According to users, social media has ushered in new opportunities for commodifying the persona of 'ordinary' people. Whereas the old era of mass media created the mega-celebrity, watched and known by the audience as a whole, the new era of mass-personalized media has given birth to a new type of micro-celebrity, watched and known by a small fraction of the audience. A generalized, mass audience gave way to highly fragmented and personalized micro-audiences. To these micro-audiences, users are assumed to be more or less known and their mediated existence—the performance of their selves and their everyday lives in social media—becomes of economic value and is commodified. What is being commodified is in fact the mutual familiarity, sociability, and friendship of Facebook users—resources that are created in traditionally free time. The court accepts the thrust of this argument and redefines mediated relationships—and hence mediated time—as inherently public, as belonging to the market and as bearing an exchange-value: 'Though Plaintiffs are not models or celebrities per se, the Court agrees that they have a vested interest in their own right of publicity' (Fraley vs. Facebook 2011).

Conclusion

Time has been a central site of contradiction to capitalism in at least three ways, giving rise, accordingly, to three distinct struggles: (1) struggles over productive time (for example, over the duration of the work day); (2) struggles over the free time/work time ratio; and (3) struggles over the arrangements that distinguish work time from free time at all. As the chapter suggests, as capitalism has become increasingly reliant on labour power deposited in so called free, non-productive time, so have struggles over time expanded further to include struggles over the very discursive distinction between productive time and nonproductive time. The legal battle over Sponsored Stories is a testament to that expansion. It is a struggle over how time should be defined in contemporary capitalism.

The legal battle over Sponsored Stories can illuminate the extent to which media audience might resist top-down media practices, even its political economy model. The importance of the Sponsored Stories legal battle lies in uncovering the degree to which the notion of work time is relevant to understanding social media not only as an objective-scientific framework, but also as a really existing, subjective, popular theory upheld by social media users. Platform capitalism, so keen on exploiting the *life time* of individuals as value-producing *work time* also creates the subjects that become reflexive of the liquidity of time, and of value extracted from time which is experienced and commonly still defined as free time, leisure time, vacation time, and so forth.

That social media users recognize the time they spend online as productive work time could be partially attributed to the very nature of the environment of digital networked technology. Audiencing and watching have been accumulation strategies for a while, since the rise of commercial mass media in capitalist societies. But listening to the radio or watching television has been socially constructed as a passive behavior—the opposite of work. In fact, a cold theoretical gaze was needed to reinterpret such leisure activity as work (Jhally and Livant 1986; Smythe 1981). But with digital media, and particularly with social media and social networking sites, the picture is very different. In fact, audiencing in the digital era is socially constructed as active: we are *using* the web (after a decade or so of *surfing* it), we *participate, share, post*, and *search*. In short—when we are online we do things, sometimes even make things. The conceptual leap from that construction to thinking about what we do online also as work is short (Fisher 2015a).

Moreover, whereas audiencing the mass media took place in a spatial and temporal space of leisure, the blurring of the boundaries between work and leisure helps this trend as well. As we use digital media—such as mobile devices or out laptop computers—the two worlds, that of work and non-work—conflate to the point where it's sometimes almost impossible to discern whether what we do is work or not. After all maintaining our online persona on Facebook might have consequences for both our private life and our work life.

The integration of life itself into the economy on the one hand, and the immersion of life into digital media on the other hand, both promise to even heighten the struggle of working people—either at "work" or online—over time.

References

Aglietta, M. (2001). *A theory of capitalist regulation: The US experience.* New York: Verso.
Bauman, Z. (2004). *Work, consumerism and the new poor.* Berkshire: Open University Press.
Boyer, R. (2002). *Regulation theory: The state of the art.* New York: Routledge.

Braverman, H. (1974). *Labor and monopoly capital: The degradation of work in the twentieth century*. New York: Monthly Review Press.

Facebook. (2012). *About sponsored stories*. http://www.facebook.com/help?page=15450007128255. Accesses June 2012 (No longer available).

Feher, M. (2009). Self-appreciation. Or, the aspirations of human capital. *Public Culture, 21*(1), 21–41.

Fisher, E. (2008). The classless workplace: The digerati and the new spirit of technocapitalism. *Working USA, 11*(2), 181–198.

Fisher, E. (2010). Contemporary technology discourse and the legitimation of capitalism. *European Journal of Social Theory, 13*(2), 229–252.

Fisher, E. (2015a). 'You media': Audiencing as marketing in social media. *Media, Culture and Society, 37*(1), 50–67.

Fisher, E. (2015b). Audience labour and sponsored stories. *Information, Communication and Society, 18*(9), 1108–1122.

Fisher, E. (2015c). Class struggles in the digital frontier: Audience labour theory and social media users. *Information, Communication and Society, 18*(9), 1108–1122.

Fraley vs. Facebook. (2011). *Order granting in part and denying in part defendant's motion to dismiss*. United States District Court, Northern District of California, San Jose Division, Case No.: 11-CV-01726-LHK.

Fuchs, C. (2014). Digital prosumption labour on social media in the context of the capitalist regime of time. *Time & Society, 23*(1), 97–123. Retrieved http://journals.sagepub.com/doi/10.1177/0961463X13502117

Harvey, D. (2007). *The limits of capital*. New York: Verso.

Jhally, S., & Livant, B. (1986). Watching as working: The valorization of audience consciousness. *Journal of Communication, 36*(3), 124–143.

Lazzarato, M. (1996). Immaterial labor. In S. Makdisi, C. Casarino, & R. E. Karl (Eds.), *Marxism beyond marxism*. London: Routledge.

Mandel, E. (1999). *Late capitalism*. New York: Verso.

Marx, K. (1993). *Grundrisse: Foundations of the critique of political economy*. New York: Penguin Books.

Marx, K., & Engels, F. (2002). *The communist manifesto*. New York: Penguin Books.

Morini, C., & Fumagalli, A. (2010). Life put to work: Towards a life theory of value. *Ephemera Theory and Politics in Organization, 10*(3–4), 234–252.

Mumford, L. (2010). *Technics and civilization*. Chicago: Chicago University Press.

Noble, D. (1984). *Forces of production: A social history of industrial automation*. New York: Knopf.
Postone, M. (1996). *Time, labor, and social domination: A reinterpretation of Marx's critical theory*. Cambridge: Cambridge University Press.
Scholz, T. (2013). *Digital labour: The internet as playground and factory*. New York: Routledge.
Smythe, D. W. (1981). *Dependency road: Communication, capitalism, consciousness and Canada*. New York: Ablex Publishing.
Srnicek, N. (2016). *Platform capitalism*. Cambridge: Polity Press.
Virno, P. (2004). *A grammar of the multitude: For an analysis of contemporary forms of life*. New York: Semiotext.

4

The Production of Algorithms and the Cultural Politics of Web Search

Paško Bilić

Google's search algorithms are contradictory artefacts. On the one hand they are used for free. On the other hand, they are proprietary technical solutions protected by patents,[1] trade secrets, copyrights and trademarks made profitable by accumulated advertising revenues for the parent company Alphabet Inc. Their contradictory existence is driven towards finding the perfect technical solution to the information needs of global users. They require extensive labour of computer scientists and engineers, and dynamic estimates of what the people (citizens, consumers and advertisers alike) are actually interested in looking for on the internet. The accumulation of data on searches, browsing histories, locations and social media use is essential for tweaking the algorithms and making them more useful, relevant and profitable worldwide. The quick searchability of global online information, coupled with the accumulation of data usage, creates an information vortex that is only possible to commodify from within the company.

P. Bilić (✉)
Department for Culture and Communication, Institute for Development and International Relations, Zagreb, Croatia

Alphabet vertically integrates the search engine, the advertising agency and the ratings system (Lee 2011)—entities previously separated in the advertising system of the mass communication era—within a single company.

Defining algorithms as analytical objects of social science and humanities inquiry is no easy task, given their proprietary nature and ownership by major corporations. The need for more transparency and accountability in the way algorithms provide interpretations and solutions to social phenomena is driving contemporary research on algorithms (e.g. Beer 2017; Bolin and Schwarz 2015; Gillespie 2014; Kitchin 2017) and search engines (e.g. Granka 2010; Hargittai 2007; Introna and Nissembaum 2000; Pasquinelli 2009, 2015; Van Couvering 2007). This chapter adds to that debate by providing a theoretical outlook grounded in the works of Herbert Marcuse, contemporary readings of his ideas, and digital labour studies.

I argue that Marcuse's works can be utilized and updated for a critical analysis of algorithms from at least four different starting points. First, he offers a critique of commodification and consumer culture. Given the proprietary nature of algorithms, such an analysis is much needed to expand our understanding of algorithms in contemporary society. Second, Marcuse develops a dialectical relation between technological domination and human values, interests and liberation. He is not dismissive of technology in itself, only of technological control and domination within the capitalist system. Such control is increasingly implemented through various solutions in algorithmic capitalism. Third, by following Marcuse, algorithms can be conceived as the expression of the Enlightenment project (Horkheimer and Adorno 1944) with the goal of rationalization, calculability, neutrality, objectivity and effectiveness in handling social affairs. They are reified forms of socially established technological control (Marcuse 1964). Finally, algorithms can be analysed as tools for global dominance and control embedded in the labour-intensive production process within the global division of search engine labour.[2]

Building on such a foundation, the goal is to look for 'contingencies' (MacKenzie 1984) and contradictions in the production of algorithms and the culture of search. Production is analysed by unpacking key layers of digital labour. The culture of search is a specific type of web search based on Alphabet's unique algorithmic solutions and definitions of information utility and relevance. These analytical standpoints are supported by an analysis of public representations of algorithms and web search, particularly within key documents such as Alphabet Inc.'s SEC filings (Form 10-K) and Search Quality Ratings Guidelines (SQRG). SEC filings explain the positioning of the company within the global search market, digital economy and technological rationality (Marcuse 1960, 1964). The SQRG documents provide empirical details on how Alphabet defines algorithmic search quality and produces algorithmic technical artefacts. The focus of this chapter is not on algorithms as ideology (Mager 2012, 2014) but, instead, on technological rationality (Marcuse 1941, 1964), which reifies, covers and hides the production process and the global division of search engine labour.

In the first section, the origins of the concept of technological rationality, its contemporary interpretations and its relevance for the study of algorithms are elaborated. Technological rationality is supported by new forms of expert knowledge, knowledge work and cultural values embedded in relations of production within algorithmic capitalism. In the second section, the global division of search engine labour is presented, along with visions of users promoted by Alphabet Inc. in its search quality rating process. The following section argues that such cultural politics of web search limits democracy and funnels human experience into preordained and calculated forms. Finally, the chapter concludes by outlining the main contradictions in the production of algorithms and the culture of web search from a Marcusean perspective.

Technological Rationality in Algorithmic Capitalism

Technical artefacts such as algorithms require mathematical, computational and rational design. They create an aura of universality of reason, an aura of calculable, efficient and truthful solutions to given problems. Algorithms are governed by calculated risks and assessments. Yet Habermas (1968) and especially Horkheimer and Adorno (1944) argue that the dominant, 'instrumental action' installed since the Age of Enlightenment produces irrational results, impoverishes human experience and ultimately leads to totalitarianism. Algorithms can be analytically conceived as a contemporary socio-historical expression of this philosophical position, although their historical limits in terms of the negative effects on society are yet to be fully determined. It would be overreaching to argue that algorithms establish totalitarian society. However, the piling up of dramatic social influence through surveillance, privacy violations, fake news and the ecological risks of high maintenance of server farms can all be attributed to the ongoing abuse of algorithmic artefacts.

In computer science, algorithms are conceived as tools for rational quantification and control. For example, Kowalski (1979, p. 424) states, 'Algorithms can be regarded as consisting of a logic component, which specifies the knowledge to be used in solving problems, and a control component, which determines the problem-solving strategy by means of which that knowledge is guided.' In a more recent work, the international Association for Computing Machinery (2017) defines an algorithm as 'a self-contained step-by-step set of operations that computers and other "smart" devices carry out to perform calculation, data processing, and automated reasoning tasks.' They further point out that 'algorithms implement institutional decision-making based on analytics, which involves discovery, interpretation, and communication of meaningful patterns in data.'

Such definitions fall short in explaining why these technical artefacts circulate and why they exert social influence. A broader understanding of digital artifacts as embodiments of technological rationality is needed to capture their contextualization within corporate structures and relations of production. In following Marcuse (1941, p. 41), I would argue for an analytical distinction between algorithms as *technics*, or technical artefacts, and algorithms as expressions of technological rationality. Translated to the contemporary digital age, we could argue that the most relevant tools, technical artefacts and *technics* are algorithms embedded within a technological rationality as a mode of production, a specific form of capitalism—algorithmic capitalism.

In some of his best-known works, Marcuse (1960, 1964) developed an understanding of technology and its enduring influence over humans and nature. He initially put more emphasis on the differentiation between *technics* and technology; while a critique of technology's control and dominance over humans and nature took a more central role in his later works. In particular he used the term reification in connection to technology. The origin of the term can be traced back to Marx's (1867) notion of commodity fetishism and Lukacs' (1972) notion of reification for describing the capitalist tendency for clouding class consciousness behind commodity forms. In Marcuse's (1964, p. 172) interpretation, technology 'is the great vehicle of reification' since the social position of the individual and his, or her, relations to others become increasingly determined by objective qualities and laws and appear as 'calculable manifestations of scientific rationality'. Such a depiction seems quite familiar within algorithmic capitalism where different profiling, surveillance and targeted advertising strategies are used to increase advertising revenues and profit rates.

It is important to note that Marcuse was not a cultural pessimist. His dialectical thinking was broad enough to offer potential solutions to control and dominance. Technology as 'the great vehicle of reification' can also be turned into a 'great vehicle of liberation' (Marcuse 1969) under the condition that technical artefacts are used in a more democratic and non-repressive manner. He argued for the importance of philosophy and art in offering alternatives to the existing repressive reality. In particular, in his late work (Marcuse 1978) he emphasized the importance of the aesthetic dimension in changing human experience.

Coming back to the notion of algorithms, the key is to understand their design features, analyse how they commodify information input/output and establish domination and/or control. By following Marcuse, Feenberg (1999) introduced the notion of 'design critique' to emphasize how social interests and cultural values influence the realization of technical principles. Different kinds of technological rationalizations are always possible, rationalizations that use the language, not of profit and power, but of responsibility for human and natural concerns. Feenberg (2010) also developed the term 'democratic rationalization', which requires technological advances made in opposition to the dominant hegemony. Understanding rationalization in such broad terms helps us to uncover socio-historical contingencies of technology and *technics*. In other words, it forces us to think about rationalization in different ways in different points in time and to conjure up alternatives to those technological realities that present themselves as the only possible solutions to social problems. Rationalizations are embedded within social relations and relations of production. Artefacts are not freefloating objects. They need to be produced, updated, managed and utilized. The materiality of labour is essential and forms a key element for a critique of technical artefacts embedded within algorithmic capitalism.

Knowledge and Culture: Key Labour Resources in Algorithmic Capitalism

The key driving force behind scientific and technological development is the rise of expert knowledge and increasingly narrow and segmented specialisations in science. New labour processes include the manipulation, not only of nature and raw material, but also of information and culture (Lazzarato 1996), knowledge, symbols and communication (Mosco 2011). As Mosco and McKercher argue (2009), knowledge work becomes increasingly differentiated in two important ways. First, there is vertical inequality between those at the top who, for example, build software and hardware systems and those at the bottom who deal with mechanical, repetitive labour. Second, there is also horizontal inequality between those who operate with content categories and those who operate with technical systems. Looking at the digital media and the internet, it is clear that 'expert knowledge' is one of the main driving forces of the global digital economy, both in terms of applying relevant knowledge to the creation of value and in terms of managing the workforce. Technological rationality, expert knowledge and knowledge work testify to how capitalism continuously reinvents itself in new shapes and forms.

New experts provide a key resource for algorithmic capitalism. Trust in such expertise and knowledge is fuelled by a contradictory mix of ideas and beliefs. Barbrook and Cameron (1996, p. 45) called it Californian ideology. It 'promiscuously combines the free-wheeling spirit of the hippies and the entrepreneurial zeal of the yuppies'. They argue that the major idea behind the global spread of Californian ideology and the expansion of Silicon Valley companies was a profound faith in the emancipatory potential of new technologies. The emerging culture combined cutting-edge technology, efficiency and entrepreneurialism with alternative notions of bohemianism (Turner 2009) and even occasional ventures into technology retreats as a form of maintaining 'digital health' (Fish 2017). It formed a novel ethos and spirit of legitimation of capitalism through promises of enhancing individual emancipation and allowing more creativity and personal expression (Fisher 2010, p. 23).

Expert, technical knowledge is essential for algorithmic capitalism. But it does not come into conflict with everyday experience in terms of creativity, expressivity and individuality. At first glance it seems that such work manages to level out the contradictions between technology and experience (Feenberg 2010) and between repressive reality and everyday life (Marcuse 1964) embedded in the modern project. Yet it fails at one key point: it does not manage to transcend the inherent technological rationalization of capitalism. Ventures into alternative behaviour and identity construction only serve the purpose of reinforcing the existing structures and profit-seeking mechanisms. They provide the cultural fuel to burn within new relations of production.

The Production of Search Engine Algorithms

Analytically, three layers of search engine labour can be identified within academic studies, search engine industry journals and other publicly available information. The first is the highly glorified knowledge work (Mosco and McKercher 2009) of engineers and computer scientists. The second is the work of so-called search quality raters. These low-skilled raters are hired via third-party companies to provide contextually relevant knowledge that is used for testing algorithmic changes and updates worldwide. They provide evidence of global value chain management, outsourcing repetitive microtasks to low-skilled workers, and of the increasing need for human evaluation of technical solutions to web-search. The third is the unpaid digital labour (Fuchs 2010) of search engine users. By using the engine and spending time searching the web, the users leave massive amounts of data traces that can be commodified and sold to the advertisers.

Top-Level Computer Science and Engineering

In 2017 Alphabet Inc., the company that owns Google, was the second largest company in the United States behind Apple in terms of market capitalization (NASDAQ 2017). In 2016 its total accumulated revenue came to US $90.2 billion, with 88 percent of that revenue coming from advertising (Alphabet Inc. 2017a). The company continuously accumulates massive amounts of data, which requires not only enormous computing power and infrastructure but also expert knowledge in computer science and engineering. Alphabet's research team is continuously on the lookout for new employees. Engineers and computer scientists are hired to innovate in areas such as security and privacy, information retrieval, machine intelligence, data mining, natural language processing and so on. Total research and development expenses for the company in 2016 amounted to $13.9 billion (Alphabet Inc. 2017a). The majority of the expenses relate to compensation and related costs for personnel responsible for the development of new products and services. Alphabet simultaneously cultivates a culture of creativity and flexibility which forms a major part of its corporate strategy. According to the market report:

> Despite our rapid growth, we still cherish our roots as a startup and wherever possible empower employees to act on great ideas regardless of their role or function within the company. We strive to hire great employees, with backgrounds and perspectives as diverse as those of our global users. We work to provide an environment where these talented people can have fulfilling careers addressing some of the biggest challenges in technology and society. (Alphabet 2017a)

This type of work blurs the lines separating research, engineering and marketing. As Hillis et al. (2013, p. 46) argued, Google occupies a hybrid position in the global internet. It generates mass audiences and huge profit while maintaining its association with non-economic imperatives, such as refusing to mix paid and unpaid advertising. The strategy helps build consumer trust and legitimacy and allows for the accumulation of economic and cultural capital. Alphabet company is driven by profit maximisation. On the other hand, top-level knowledge workers of the company offset the economic and political discussions with technical discussions and discourses of empowering the employees and improving technical affordances of the search engine.

Paid Search Quality Labour

The least transparent layer of search engine labour is the hidden labour of the so-called search quality raters. According to search engine industry reports, Alphabet performs worldwide search quality tests via companies that specialize in product localisation services (Bilić 2016). The input from search quality raters is necessary to establish the value of search information, relevance and utility in different geographical locations, language and cultural contexts. One of the major suppliers of such services is Lionbridge Technologies Inc., a company that offers translation and localisation, digital marketing, global content management, application testing and other services for multilingual content management and global growth acceleration (Lionbridge 2017a). It offers 'search relevance testing' by crowdsourcing human raters worldwide:

> When it comes to reaching prospects at the point of decision, search is critical. But for search to pay off you need to be sure that each query delivers the right result, to the right user, at the right time – a task that becomes infinitely more complex as you move into new markets. Leveraging Lionbridge BPC gives you access to the expertise, scalable resources and global reach required to verify the relevance of search data in local markets around the world. (Lionbridge 2017b)

In 2015 Google (Alphabet Inc.) accounted for 11 percent of Lionbridge's $559 million revenue (Lionbridge 2016). The exact details of the business cooperation between these companies are difficult to determine. However, Alphabet publishes and updates Search Quality Rating Guidelines (SQRG) which are used in search quality testing (Alphabet Inc 2017b). The guidelines offer some insight into the construction of algorithmic relevance. According to the latest version of the document (dated 14 March 2017), the purpose is to evaluate search engine quality around the world. It is emphasised that good search results give results that are helpful in their specific language and locale. Raters represent users in the locales that they evaluate. Page quality rating tasks consist of exploring landing pages and websites associated with URLs. The goal is to evaluate whether the page achieves its purpose. In terms of skills, the rating process requires that a rater have experience using the web as an ordinary user in his rating locale, have in-depth knowledge of the guidelines, and continually practice quality rating tasks.

Quality is determined by providing a score on a scale offering five options: lowest, low, medium, high and highest. Decisions are based on multiple factors. Some of the most important ones are the expertise, authoritativeness and trustworthiness of websites. The guidelines give special status to websites that influence 'the future happiness, health, or financial stability of users'. Such pages are called Your Money or Your Life (YMYL) pages. They include shopping or financial transactions, financial information, medical information, news articles and public information pages. The highest page quality rating standards need to be fulfilled for YMYL pages.

The YMYL category shows what Alphabet values most in terms of online content and how it constructs the image of an average user and his/her interests. Its cultural politics assigns higher value only to selected aspects of human life and experience. As a major digital advertising company it is not surprising that it highly values commercially related content. User orientation is reflected in assigning high value to health-related content. Surprisingly, though, the newest version of the SQRG (dated 14 March 2017) contains news websites in the YMYL category (Alphabet 2017c) which were not included in the earlier SQRG (dated 28 March 2016) (Alphabet 2016). This is a response to public outrage over the spread of fake news in the 2016 US presidential campaign. The company announced it will be using more than 10,000 available search quality raters to combat the rise of fake news.[3] To maintain an aura of technical innovation one of its senior engineers discarded the term fake news as too vague, and instead argued that Alphabet will be targeting 'demonstrably inaccurate information'.[4]

Regardless of the definition, the use of human raters in detecting search relevance, particularly with regard to fake news, is in stark contrast with the vision of automated algorithms. The use of humans in untangling linguistically, culturally and politically sensitive information is a highly slippery terrain for the company. The issue boils down to whether or not such tests ultimately influence page ranking. Alphabet states that they do not.[5] Yet there is no way to tell, since public scrutiny is closed due to trade secrets and patents protecting the design of the search algorithms. This is a highly contentious, contradictory and crucial point since there is no immediate way of determining the validity of such claims made by the company. According to McKenzie (1984, p. 502), 'The most obvious way to legitimate any particular design decision or choice of technique is to say it is "technically necessary"'. He argues that the claims of technical necessity disguise the extent of contingency and foster specific routines and habits for using technical artefacts. It closes the possibility for conceiving alternative, democratic rationalizations (Feenberg 2010) and technical designs (Feenberg 1999). The selected way of constructing technical artefacts serves the primary purposes of supporting and extending control and dominance (Marcuse 1960, 1964) in a specific technological rationality that sustains algorithmic capitalism. Nothing explains the position of Google search algorithms better than the fact that we are closed to the possibility of searching the web otherwise.

Unpaid User Labour

The third type of search engine labour is the unpaid labour of internet and search engine users. This unacknowledged process of value creation was previously detected within mass communication research as the time the audience spends in 'watching' (Jhally and Livant 1986) and 'buying the products' (Smythe 1981). It was taken up by digital labour scholars (Fuchs 2010; Fuchs and Sevignani 2013; Fisher 2015) and applied as a critique of digitally mediated sociality. Search engines rely on information processing, which is somewhat different from mass communication. In other words, the search engine first creates indexes of available websites by crawling the web. Top-level knowledge workers (Mosco 2011) build the algorithms that help the users find the relevant information from the indexed web. The connection between users' search intent and search results is based on algorithmic calculations of what the engineers believe might be of interest to the users. Pages are ranked based on a number of calculations and estimates and the results are returned to the users as so-called 'organic' results.

The algorithmically estimated connection between user-intent and displayed search results forms the core of Alphabet's information processing business model. Paid search results are the results that are paid for by digital advertisers who are interested in reaching the widest possible consumer pool via the connection with specific search queries and terms. Paid results are listed as ads on top of the first page of Google's search results. Without widespread global use, Alphabet's business model falls apart. The labour time of internet users is a key component in an intricate relationship between the company and the advertisers.

Limiting Democracy and Funnelling Human Experience: The Cultural Politics of Web Search

The Google search engine held a 90 percent market share for internet search services in most European Economic Area (EEA) countries in 2015 (European Parliament 2015). The European Commission has launched several antitrust investigations in the past several years on Google's comparison shopping service,[6] the pre-installation of Google's applications and services on Android OS and the restriction of third-party websites from displaying search ads from Google's competitors.[7] The point of contention with European legislation is not the fact that Google has a high market share, but the fact that its products and services stifle market competition and create barriers for the entry of new companies into multiple markets that Google is dominating. The company is quite aware of the business risks such regulation poses:

> The growth of our company and our expansion into a variety of new fields involves a variety of new regulatory issues, and we have experienced increased regulatory scrutiny as we have grown.... We continue to cooperate with the European Commission (EC) and other regulatory authorities around the world in investigations they are conducting with respect to our business and its impact on competition. Legislators and regulators may

make legal and regulatory changes, or interpret and apply existing laws, in ways that make our products and services less useful to our users, require us to incur substantial costs, expose us to unanticipated civil or criminal liability, or cause us to change our business practices. These changes or increased costs could negatively impact our business and results of operations in material ways. (Alphabet 2017a)

This statement is an example of business effectiveness and rationalization (Marcuse 1960, 1964) in managing not only technical solutions but also the political economy of the company within the global market. It reflects a specific set of beliefs and ideas (Barbrook and Cameron 1996) rooted in the company culture that values visionary engineers and resourceful entrepreneurs in the free market, liberated from intrusive government oversight and regulation.

Alphabet's algorithmic artefacts cannot be separated from political, economic and cultural contextualizations. They adversely affect public visibility and advertising revenue flow in the digital economy. The complicated political economy of the Google search engine is sustained by constant algorithmic changes in a balancing act that requires all the actors interested in digital visibility to closely follow and interpret Alphabet's new ideas of how to rank the websites on the internet. The company keeps the whole internet advertising and search engine optimization (SEO) industry on its toes in a path-dependent creation of how web search should be performed. It imposes a dominant interpretation of search relevance, utility, neutrality and objectivity, evidenced in such condensed, funnelled versions of relevance as the Your Money or Your Life (YMYL) pages. The YMYL strategy forms the core of the cultural politics of web search promoted by Alphabet Inc.

Localisation companies extend algorithmic production beyond the confines of Alphabet's organisational structures. They provide new outsourcing options by utilizing digital technologies and distributed crowd-sourced workers. While arguably promoting more usability and utility in local markets, the customization of services also creates filter bubbles (Pariser 2011) in local digital markets, reduces the visibility of all actors seeking public exposure and/or promotion of their services and impedes the flow of information and market competition. A limited company vision of human experience was blatantly evidenced in the spread of fake news and the subsequent fallback to the increased input from search quality raters. Yet this creates further contradictions and tensions between the techno-utopian visions of web search, on the one hand, and human interpretation, reflexivity and contextualized knowledge on the other. It is a contradiction that the company promised to resolve in the early days of the invention of the PageRank algorithm by Stanford's computer science PhD candidates Larry Page and Sergei Brin. So long as the myth of technical solutions to human needs remains sustainable and plausible for the general public, the company will be able to hide its algorithmic decisions, choices and profit-making mechanisms behind trade secrets and patents (Bilić 2017). Once the myth stops being convincing, the company will have to open the 'black box' of algorithms to public scrutiny, regulation and accountability (Diakopulous 2014).

At stake is not only the process of dealing with algorithmic transparency and accountability, but more importantly whether the systemic conditions can be transcended and opened up to democratic rationalization (Feenberg 2010). In 2017, the Association for Computing Machinery (ACM) issued a statement on algorithmic transparency and accountability with seven key principles. First, more awareness is needed of the potential harms and biases the algorithms can cause to individuals and society. Second, there should be enabling access and redress to regulators. Third, responsible institutions should be accountable for the decisions made by the algorithms. Fourth, systems and institutions that use algorithmic decision-making should provide explanations of the procedures for algorithmic decisions. Fifth, a description of the way in which the training data was collected should be maintained by the builders of the algorithms. Sixth, models, algorithms, data and decisions should be recorded so that they can be audited in cases where harm is suspected. Seventh, institutions should use rigorous methods to validate their models and document those methods and results.

The ACM initiative and the European Commission's investigations operate under a limited horizon of projected change in how major companies operate. More efficient transparency, accountability and market competition will not alleviate the problems that algorithmic objects are imposing on social processes. Such thinking is precisely the reason why algorithms create problems, since they operate under a notion of technological rationality (Marcuse 1960, 1964) that gives precedence to calculability, quantification and measurement over human experience, subjectivity and hermeneutic interpretation. Furthermore, such thinking does not address the relations of production, information commodification and commercialisation of human experience in the digital realm.

Conclusion

Alphabet's evolving algorithms are not just technical artefacts, or *technics* (Marcuse 1941), but also business strategies for market control and dominance of an imposed vision of technological rationality (Marcuse 1941, 1960, 1964). They are embedded in the capitalist production process and the global division of search engine labour. By looking at the production process and labour behind the production of algorithms we can create a strong critique of the technical design (Feenberg 1999) and ask for more democratic procedures (Feenberg 2010) and accountability in the cultural politics of web search. Algorithms are commodified objects whose embeddedness in market relations is reified by techno-utopian visions of digital technology and hidden human labour. The position of search quality raters is essential, since it contradicts the aura of technical solutions to information problems and uncovers the labour processes necessary for the production of algorithms.

The existence of human quality raters testifies to the complex entanglement of technological rationality with algorithmic capitalism. *Technics,* or technical artefacts, allow for a global expansion of the workforce and for companies such as Alphabet to perform search quality tests in different locations worldwide. Quality tests allow the company to fine-tune the algorithm to different locations, outperform the competing search companies and maximise local advertising revenues. Technical artefacts are also the object of labour since in-company engineers and computer scientists as well as low-skilled quality raters hired via third parties contribute to the evolving rationality of the algorithm. The algorithms operate on top of the production process sustained by multiple levels of search engine labour. The technical design ultimately promotes a specific vision of web search, a sort of cultural politics of web search condensed in the notion of Your Money or Your Life (YMYL) websites. Such complex technological rationality allows for global market dominance, commodification of internet search and the submission of local languages, lived experiences and cultural nuances into the dominant rationality of the algorithm. Alternatives are always possible, but the horizon for reaching them is being limited by the profit-making interests of major companies.

Notes

1. According to the US patent office there were 14,814 patents assigned under the name Google in June 2017 as well as 17 assigned under the new company name Alphabet Inc.
2. This term broadly relates to the international division of digital labour (IDDL) proposed by Fuchs (2013).
3. https://www.bloomberg.com/news/articles/2017-04-25/google-rewrites-its-powerful-search-rankings-to-bury-fake-news. Accessed 16 August 2017.
4. http://searchengineland.com/google-flag-upsetting-offensive-content-271119. Accessed 16 August 2017.
5. https://www.google.com/intl/es419/insidesearch/howsearchworks/algorithms.html. Accessed 16 August 2017.
6. In June 2017 Alphabet Inc. was fined a record 2.42 billion Euros for abusing its dominant position and giving illegal advantage to its own comparison shopping service. http://europa.eu/rapid/press-release_IP-17-1784_en.htm. Accessed 16 August 2017.
7. http://europa.eu/rapid/press-release_IP-16-2532_en.htm. Accessed 16 August 2017.

References

Alphabet Inc. (2016, March 28). *Search Quality Rating Guidelines* (*SQRG*).
Alphabet Inc. (2017a). *Form 10-K*. Available at https://www.sec.gov/Archives/edgar/data/1652044/000165204417000008/goog10-kq42016.htm. Accessed 16 Aug 2017.

Alphabet Inc. (2017b). *How search works?* Available at https://www.google.com/intl/es419/insidesearch/howsearchworks/algorithms.html. Accessed 16 Aug 2017.

Alphabet Inc. (2017c, March 14). *Search Quality Rating Guidelines (SQRG)*.

Association for Computing Machinery. (2017). *New statement on algorithmic transparency and accountability by ACM U.S. Public Policy Council*. Available at https://techpolicy.acm.org/?p=6156. Accessed 18 Aug 2017.

Barbrook, R., & Cameron, A. (1996). The Californian ideology. *Science as Culture, 6*(1), 44–72.

Beer, D. (2017). The social power of algorithms. *Information, Communication & Society, 20*(1), 1–13.

Bilić, P. (2016). Search algorithms, hidden labour and information control. *Big Data & Society, 3*(1), 1–9.

Bilić, P. (2017). *The hidden human labour behind search engine algorithms*. London School of Economics Media Policy blog. http://blogs.lse.ac.uk/mediapolicyproject/2017/02/21/the-hidden-human-labour-behind-search-engine-algorithms/. Accessed 16 Aug 2017.

Bolin, G., & Schwarz, J. A. (2015). Heuristics of the algorithm: Big data, user interpretation and institutional translation. *Big Data & Society, 2*(2), 1–12.

Diakopulous, N. (2014). *Algorithmic accountability: On the investigation of Black Boxes*. http://towcenter.org/research/algorithmic-accountability-on-the-investigation-of-black-boxes-2/#endnotes. Accessed 16 Aug 2017.

European Parliament. (2015). *Google antitrust proceedings: Digital business and competition*. Available at http://www.europarl.europa.eu/thinktank/en/document.html?reference=EPRS_BRI(2015)565870. Accessed 16 Aug 2017.

Feenberg, A. (1999). Marcuse or Habermas: Two critiques of technology. *Inquiry, 39*, 45–70.

Feenberg, A. (2010). *Between reason and experience: Essays in technology and modernity*. Cambridge, MA/London: MIT Press.

Fish, A. (2017). Technology retreats and the politics of social media. *Triple C, 15*(1), 355–369.

Fisher, E. (2010). *Media and new capitalism in the digital age: The spirit of networks*. New York: Palgrave Macmillan.

Fisher, E. (2015). Class struggles in the digital frontier: Audience labour theory and social media users. *Information, Communication & Society, 18*(9), 1108–1122.

Fuchs, C. (2010). Labor in informational capitalism and on the internet. *The Information Society, 26*, 179–196.

Fuchs, C. (2013). Theorising and analysing digital labour: From global value chains to modes of production. *The Political Economy of Communication, 1*(2), 3–27.

Fuchs, C., & Sevignani, S. (2013). What is digital labour? What is digital work? What's their difference? And why do these questions matter for understanding social media? *Triple, 11*(2), 237–293.

Gillespie, T. (2014). The relevance of algorithms. In T. Gillespie, P. Boczkowski, & K. A. Foot (Eds.), *Media technologies: Essays on communication, materiality, and society* (pp. 167–193). Cambridge, MA/London: MIT Press.

Granka, L. A. (2010). The politics of search: A decade retrospective. *The Information Society, 26*, 364–373.

Habermas, J. (1968/1989). Technology and science as "ideology". In J. Habermas (Ed.), *Toward a rational society: Student protest, science and politics* (pp. 81–122). Boston: Beacon Press.

Hargittai, E. (2007). The social, political, economic and cultural dimensions of search engines: An introduction. *Journal of Computer-Mediated Communication, 12*, 769–777.

Hillis, K., Petit, M., & Jarrett, K. (2013). *Google and the culture of search*. New York: Routledge.

Horkheimer, M., & Adorno, T. W. (1944/2002). *Dialectic of enlightenment: Cultural memory in the present*. Stanford. Stanford University Press.

Introna, L. D., & Nissembaum, H. (2000). Shaping the web: Why the politics of search engines matters. *The Information Society, 16*, 169–185.

Jhally, S., & Livant, B. (1986). Watching as working: The valorization of audience consciousness. *Journal of Communication, 36*(3), 124–143.

Kitchin, R. (2017). Thinking critically about and researching algorithms. *Information, Communication & Society, 20*(1), 14–29.

Kowalski, R. (1979). Algorithm = logic + control. *Communications of the ACM, 22*(7), 424–436.

Lazzarato, M. (1996). Immaterial labour. In P. Virno & M. Hardt (Eds.), *Radical thought in Italy: A potential politics*. Minnesota: University of Minnesota Press.

Lee, M. (2011). Google ads and the blindspot debate. *Media, Culture and Society, 33*(3), 433–447.

Lionbridge. (2016). *Form 10-K*. Available at https://www.sec.gov/Archives/edgar/data/1058299/000105829916000047/liox-20151231x10k.htm. Accessed 16 Aug 2017.

Lionbridge. (2017a). *About Lionbridge*. Available at http://www.lionbridge.com/our-company/. Accessed 16 Aug 2017.

Lionbridge. (2017b). *Global testing*. Available at http://www.thesmartcrowd.com/solutions/global-testing/. Accessed 16 Aug 2017.

Lukacs, G. (1972). The phenomenon of reification. In G. Lukacs (Ed.), *History and class consciousness: Studies in Marxist dialectics* (pp. 83–110). Cambridge, MA: MIT Press.

MacKenzie, D. (1984). Marx and the machine. *Technology & Culture, 25*(3), 473–502.

Mager, A. (2012). Algorithmic ideology: How capitalist society shapes search engines. *Information, Communication & Society, 15*(5), 769–787.

Mager, A. (2014). Defining algorithmic ideology: Using ideology critique to scrutinize corporate search engines. *Triple C, 12*(1), 28–39.

Marcuse, H. (1941). Some social implications of modern technology. In D. Kellner (Ed.), *Technology, war, fascism: Collected papers of Herbert Marcuse* (pp. 41–65). London/New York: Routledge.

Marcuse, H. (1960). From ontology to technology. In D. Kellner & P. Clayton (Eds.), *Philosophy, psychoanalysis and emancipation* (pp. 132–140). London/New York: Routledge Press.

Marcuse, H. (1964/2007). *One-dimensional man: Studies in the ideology of advanced industrial society*. London/New York: Routledge.

Marcuse, H. (1969). *An essay on liberation*. Boston: Beacon Press.

Marcuse, H. (1978). *The aesthetic dimension: Toward a critique of Marxist aesthetics*. Boston: Beacon Press.

Marx, K. (1867/2004). *Capital, volume 1*. London: Penguin Books.

Mosco, V. (2011). The political economy of labor. In J. Wasko, G. Murdock, & H. Sousa (Eds.), *The handbook of political economy of communication* (pp. 358–380). Chichester: Blackwell Publishing Ltd.

Mosco, V., & McKercher, K. (2009). *The laboring of communication: Will knowledge workers of the world unite?* Lanham/Boulder/New York/Toronto/Plymouth: Lexington Books.

NASDAQ. (2017). *Companies by industry; North America; Mega-Cap*. Available at http://www.nasdaq.com/screening/companies-by-industry.aspx?region=North+America&coun-try=United%20States&marketcap=Mega-cap. Accessed 16 Aug 2017.

Pariser, E. (2011, March). Beware of online filter bubbles. In: *TED conference*, Long Beach. www.ted.com/talks/eli_pariser_beware_online_filter_bubbles.html. Accessed 16 Aug 2017.

Pasquinelli, M. (2009). Google's PageRank algorithm: A diagram of the cognitive capitalism and the rentier of the common intellect. In K. Becker &

F. Stalder (Eds.), *Deep search: The politics of search beyond Google* (pp. 152–162). London: Transaction Publishers.

Pasquinelli, M. (2015). Italian *Operaismo* and the information machine. *Theory, Culture & Society, 32*(3), 49–68.

Smythe, D. W. (1981/2006). On the audience commodity and its work. In M. G. Durham & D. Kellner (Eds.), *Media and cultural studies: Key works* (Rev. ed., pp. 230–256) Malden/Oxford/Victoria: Blackwell Publishing.

Turner, F. (2009). Burning man at Google: A cultural infrastructure for new media production. *New Media & Society, 11*(1&2), 73–94.

van Couvering, E. (2007). Is relevance relevant? Market, science, and war: Discourses of search engine quality. *Journal of Computer-Mediated Communication, 12*(3), 866–887.

5

Algorithms, Dashboards and Datafication: A Critical Evaluation of Social Media Monitoring

Ivo Furman

Introduction

On March 31st 2017, Ülker—the largest confectionery manufacturer in Turkey—launched a campaign to commemorate April Fools' Day. Intended specifically for social media and television, the slogan of the campaign was 'It's hard to be the younger brother'. As part of the campaign strategy, the official Twitter account of Ülker planned to release a video, which would then be followed up by a television advert on the 1st of April. The video released on Twitter featured a cartoon figure tormented by an older, unseen brother figure in a variety of settings.[1] In one scene, an ominous sounding voice says, 'when you are coming home, suddenly flash of light shall blind you' while light bulbs explode in the background. At the end, there is a repetition of the phrase 'the first of April is coming, it is time for payback. Prepare for surprises'. While the production is amateurish on a technical level, one might deem little from the actual contents of the video to be offensive. In more ordinary times,

---

I. Furman (✉)
Istanbul Bilgi University, Istanbul, Turkey

© The Author(s) 2018
P. Bilić et al. (eds.), *Technologies of Labour and the Politics of Contradiction*, Dynamics of Virtual Work, https://doi.org/10.1007/978-3-319-76279-1_5

the video probably would have been dismissed as little more than a bad corporate gimmick trying to capitalize on April Fools' Day. However, the public reception on Twitter was anything but normal.

By the evening of the 31st, social media was hysterically abuzz with rumours about the tweeted video. A circulating rumour claimed that the video was a subliminal message calling for a coup attempt. Supposedly, the exploding light bulbs symbolized the destruction of the government (a lightbulb is the symbol of the AK Party) and the flash of light symbolized the assassination of the Turkish president. For a society still reeling from a violent coup attempt in July 2016, such a rumour was more than enough for several pro-government supporters to gather up in front of the Turkish president's Istanbul residence in the middle of the night.[2] A panicked tweet from the CEO of Ülker claiming that the company was a victim of a conspiracy exacerbated things even further.[3] By the time things were put under control, Ülker had lost more than 3% of its share value on the Istanbul Stock Exchange. Both Ülker and the creative agency responsible for the video were forced to make public apologies. The campaign was suspended indefinitely and everyone involved resigned in the days following the scandal.

What this rather surreal story shows is that we live in an era wherein it is difficult, if not impossible for professional communicators to have complete control over their public messages. A badly planned campaign can wipe millions off the public value of a corporation and destroy their brand reputation. This shift is caused by the shifting logic of engagement in the age of social media. Engagement has become a vital element of the so-called 'affective economy' in public relations as well as marketing (Jenkins 2006). Within the affective economy, emotional investments made by consumers towards a brand or product play a key role in determining their purchasing decisions (Jenkins 2006, p. 319). Therefore, the capacity to mobilize emotional commitment of consumers is crucial to the valuation of a company. Value in the global economy is 'co-created' (Prahalad and Ramaswamy 2004) through engagement and the capacity of a brand to build lasting social ties with consumers. Furthermore, entities with strong brand reputations tend to attract a much higher investor valuation on global markets in comparison to their actual earnings potential. What this suggests is that value creation, rather than just occurring through direct commodity exchange where market prices correspond to necessary labour time (see Fuchs 2010) also relies on an affective law of value, wherein the value of companies and their intangible assets are determined in relation to their ability to aggregate various kinds of affective engagements (Arvidsson and Colleoni 2012, p. 144). This transformation has been interpreted as evidence of the shift from a Fordist, industrial model of capitalism to an informational, finance-centred one wherein the value of a company is increasingly related to its ability to maintain a brand which attracts a share of the global surplus circulating on financial markets (Arvidsson and Colleoni 2012, p. 146).

Within the context of the affective economy, the emergence of interactive technologies has created an unprecedented potential to encourage new forms of engagement. In fact, the very definition of engagement itself is shifting alongside the evolution of social media platforms and their interactive features. As it has been described elsewhere, interactive features on social media afford the possibility for users to create webs of affective attachments around content, creating what has been described as the social web (Langlois et al. 2009). As interactive technologies evolve, engagement is no longer defined as simply viewing content. Instead, engagement is now characterized as usage of interactive technologies to create the conditions for a lasting social relationship to develop between the brand and the consumer (Kozinets et al. 2010). This shift has pushed brand communication strategies into mobilizing participants or online communities in chat rooms, forums and on social networks while also promoting engagement through online content marketing. Yet despite the dominance of such a paradigm, promoting engagement also runs certain risks. As the Ülker story shows, people may react in an unintended manner to engagement attempts. To reduce risks associated with such a communication paradigm, organizations both in Turkey and abroad have begun to invest in social media monitoring services that allow real-time access to online conversations.

Social media monitoring (SMM) can be defined as the continuous systematic observation and analysis of social media networks and online communities. SMM tools facilitate the listening of what people say about various topics online and enable organizations to have real-time access to customer opinions, complaints and questions. In Turkey, demand for SMM tools have led to the creation of a nascent digital public relations (PR) and online reputation management industry which focuses on offering varying degrees of control over the message put out on social media.

The case study in this chapter focuses on BoomSonar, a SMM system developed by Tick Tock Boom (TTB), an Istanbul-based digital PR agency. Founded in 2009, TTB is Turkey's oldest digital public relations agency and has over 350 clients worldwide. The agency offers a wide array of services, including application development, online monitoring services, digital marketing consultancy for brands and online reputation management. The agency defines itself as a technology company which harnesses the opportunities offered by datafication. By studying BoomSonar, this chapter seeks to answer two key questions. Firstly, what are the forms of control provided by SMM tools and how do these technologies rely on datafication? Secondly, how do SMM tools contribute to the generation of value within the contexts of the affective economy and global capitalism?

Datafication

As a term, datafication refers to the dramatic change in the ways through which we record and analyse the world around us (Floridi 2012). Our societies are now able to gather, analyse and share virtually unlimited amounts of data. The explosion in the production of data is leading some to argue that a paradigmatic transformation ('datafication') is underway in how knowledge is produced, business conducted, and governance enacted (Bollier 2010). The key mantra of this paradigmatic shift is that all social action can—and should be—quantified into data (see Mayer-Schoenberger and Cukier 2013). Increasingly, organizations are developing the capacity to create a 'data double' of all our social actions (Latour 2007). These data doubles create the capacity for organizations to reflect and act in a reflexive manner, allowing for intervention as events unfold. On one hand to develop such capacities, organizations are focusing upon developing the ability for continuous gathering of data (Kitchin 2014).

In order to do so, these actors are increasingly ditching conventional sampling-based information-gathering for continuous processes of management based on total and unremitting surveillance (Andrejevic and Burdon 2015; Ruppert 2011). On the other hand, organizations are actively recruiting data specialists who can develop algorithmic analysis techniques functioning in real-time. This is important insofar as datafication only has utility if an actor has both the capacity to extract meaning and act upon it (Uricchio 2017). In this regard, data scientists are the main purveyors of 'algorithmic culture' (Striphas 2015), as they create the capacity for institutions to analyse and react upon the possibilities offered by datafication. Accordingly, within an institutional context the datafication paradigm has led to the formation of three core elements: the capacity to aggregate large-scale datasets, the presence of professionals able to generate analytics from aggregated datasets, and an organizational structure able to react upon data analytics.[4]

Although datafication encompasses a wide range of categories including mobile phone conversations, health records, barcodes, banking transactions, electronic toll collection system and RFID technologies, data derived from social media are the most relevant (and valuable) for the mechanisms of the affective economy. This is because interactions collected from the social web are considered to be proxies for depicting social complexity. The availability of quantifiable interactivity on the social web also creates the possibility for third-party SMM applications to monitor and record certain aspects of these interactions.

BoomSonar: A SMM Technology

The following section examines BoomSonar as a social media monitoring tool. Rather than just tapping into something just existing 'out there', such tools produce measurements out of an intersection of several different technologies which capture, analyse and visualize aggregated data (Vis 2013). Within the context of SMM tools, the key technologies at work include a back-end system that can 'listen' to the Internet, a variety of data analytics (including sentiment analysis), a database for storing historical data and a dashboard (Fensel et al. 2012). Building on this observation, I focused on three technologies crucial to the services offered by BoomSonar: *listening systems, analytics* and *dashboards*. The results produced out of the intersection of these technologies enable the capacity for users to adjust their online presences in real-time and respond to emerging situations (Couldry et al. 2016).

Data for this case-study was collected over the course of a three-month period. During this time, I made numerous visits to TTB's main office. During the initial round of visits, I conducted interviews with a senior analyst who would eventually connect me with company partners and senior administration. During my third visit, I spent the afternoon discussing my research with the company partners. Afterwards, they decided to give me access to BoomSonar through an old declassified account. With this account, I had the opportunity to explore BoomSonar's dashboard, explore analytic features and gain a stronger grasp of how BoomSonar's back-end systems operated. Having prior expertise regarding SMM tools, I had an innate familiarity with operating the system. Yet, any queries about specific features were answered by the Head of Innovation in the Department of Research and Development who, in the meantime, had developed an interest in my project. Therefore, the data collection strategy for this case-study was a combination of on-site research, in-depth qualitative interviews and hands-on experience with the technology itself.[5]

Listening to the Internet

The key characteristic of any SMM tool is the capacity to gather data from many online sources and in different forms (e.g. posts, pictures, videos). For this, SMM tools need to have a well-designed and maintained listening apparatus which run in an autonomous, back-end manner. The focus of such an apparatus is defined through three dimensions:

- The channels needing to be monitored (e.g. blogs, online news portals, social networks, video and image websites, etc.),
- Countries and languages the tools provide support for; and
- The topics relevant to the company or a client.

Unless these dimensions are well defined, any monitoring system simply functions on 'hearing' rather than 'listening' mode. When on hearing mode, a system is functional but the capturing capacities are not activated. For SMM to begin, the system rather than just hearing online conversations, needs to listen in an active and focused manner. Although there are several techniques through which the listening capacities on SMM tools can be activated, BoomSonar relies on a client provided list of keywords and hashtags. Clients also have the capacity to determine the range of online spaces as well as the countries and languages that BoomSonar will listen to.[6] This range includes not only social media but also popular forums and news media portals.

BoomSonar's listening apparatus relies on application programming interfaces (APIs) to collect data from social media services. Essentially one can define APIs as interfaces which facilitate controlled real-time access to data hosted by a software service. Control is based on a pre-defined set of rules (protocols) which regulate the kinds of software that can gain access to the service. While APIs 'provide new ways of sharing and participating, they also provide a means (…) to achieve market dominance, as well as undermine privacy, data security, contextual integrity, user autonomy and freedom' (Bodle 2011, p. 320). Therefore, APIs are not just support systems for software (Puschmann and Ausserhofer 2017). They have the capacity to shape how data can be used by third-parties, and this can determine the back-end structure of SMM tools. For example, the Twitter API imposes 'rate limits' for listening systems seeking to collect data for free (see Borra and Rieder 2014). If the rate of data collection surpasses more than 1% of global tweet generation at any given moment, the API will withhold the collection software from accessing Twitter's databases. Therefore, most SMM tools must opt for premium 'Firehose' services, which give them unrestricted access to Twitter API. The Firehose service is handled by two data providers, GNIP and DataSift. Firehose access can be rather costly and constitutes a large part of the fixed costs associated with setting up a listening apparatus for Twitter. The costs can grow even further when access is expanded to a range of social media platforms with similar premium services. By being able to define the relationship between social media and a SMM tool, APIs can become powerful mediators in a datafied society (Bucher 2013).

Social Media Analytics

Other than having a listening apparatus that can capture data around topics relevant to the company or client, analytics are the other characteristic common to all SMM tools. Data analytics are algorithmic functions allowing systems to process and analyse collected material. Such functions can be broadly split into two categories. The first category of algorithms allows users to filter unwanted information (e.g. spam or duplicates) from a dataset. This category of analytics is often found within search engines as filters. The granularity of the function is often left up to the initiative of the user. For example, BoomSonar's inbuilt search engine allows users to filter collected content according to hours, days, weeks and quarters. Similarly, the system's deep filtering options allow users to filter content according to social media platforms and news portals.

Other than filtering algorithms, BoomSonar also offers the possibility to use opinion mining algorithms to extract in-depth meaning from datasets. Within the context of BoomSonar, opinion mining can be used to obtain information regarding new ideas and thoughts about a brand, find accounts on social media who can be considered as 'brand ambassadors', and pinpoint hidden social media influencers within a network. The algorithms used in opinion mining are diverse and are often drawn from a variety of scientific fields including topic modelling, social network analysis, sentiment analysis and trend analysis (Fan and Gordon 2014). Although each SMM tool uses a different assemblage of algorithms for opinion mining, sentiment analysis algorithms tend to be extremely common. Sentiment analysis aims to train computers to measure the attitude, opinion, emotional state, or intended emotional communication of a speaker or writer. On BoomSonar, sentiment analysis allows for automated classification of social web content into three categories—positive, negative and neutral. When combined with other analytics such as topic detection, it can isolate themes or issues that have caused the sentiment to develop. Sentiment analysis algorithms rely on machine learning (latent semantic analysis) and Natural Language Processing (NLP).

Sometimes called text analytics or computational linguistics, NLP refers to the process of using computers to automatically analyze the meaning of human language. Within the context of sentiment analysis and opinion mining, NLP is used to classify linguistic units into separate categories, correct misspelled words in a corpus, or detect the grammatical roles of words such as subject, object or predicates (Schütze 1998). Within the context of BoomSonar, the morphology of the Turkish language poses a key challenge. As a non-Indo-European language, Turkish has several unique characteristics which make it challenging for NLP. For example, Turkish has no noun classes or grammatical gender. The language relies on second-person pronouns to distinguish varying levels of politeness, social distance, age, courtesy or familiarity toward the addressee. These nuances are often difficult to capture with NLP techniques which have been mostly developed for Indo-European languages such as English or German. The extensive use of affixes can modify the original meaning of nouns.[7] To this end, NLP algorithms on BoomSonar use a two-tiered classification based on the etymological roots of words found in the Turkish language (Gungor and Oflazer 1995; Oflazer 1995).

In the second phase, algorithms compare classified linguistic units with words on a lexical database (wordnets). These lexical databases group words into sets of synonyms called synsets, provide short definitions and usage examples, and record a number of relations among these synonym sets or their members. Therefore, wordnets can be seen as a combination of dictionary and thesaurus (Miller 1995). Drawing from the examples given in wordnet, NLP algorithms can assign sentiments to predefined linguistic units in a corpus.

One of the principal challenges with NLP driven sentiment analysis is that it often fails to capture the dynamic and changing nature of language. Lexical databases are often lacking in words that are either new or specific to a cultural domain. One strategy to overcome this challenge is to apply machine learning to new corpuses and improve the efficiency NLP-driven processes (Ozel et al. 2011). A more practical solution is to manually annotate units that cannot be classified with sentiment analysis. For this, BoomSonar relies on a team of human annotators who review and classify the sentiments of each post.

Dashboards

The final element characteristic of all SMM tools is the presence of a dashboard. A dashboard can be defined as a user interface that organizes and presents information in an understandable manner (Tkacz 2015). The visual elements of a dashboard are designed to simplify the results of a search query or analysis through graphical representation. As such, dashboards tend to have customizable templates which include charts, timelines and graphs. Displayed information is usually interactive and can be combined with information from other datasets.

Dashboards need to be considered as diagnostic tools capable of 'sensing' or 'signalling' what is happening in the moment (Bartlett and Tkacz 2016). For example, when the volume of content produced online or when the sentiments of aggregated content cross over a certain threshold, BoomSonar's dashboard has the capacity to alert the user. As part of its diagnostic function, BoomSonar's dashboard uses a timeline to show how frequencies of chosen keywords and hashtags fluctuate in real-time. These frequencies can then be broken down according to social web platforms and other online spaces. Beneath the timeline is an unfolding feed of posts from different platforms. These posts can be accessed through the social media analytics page wherein one can filter collected posts according to sentiments (positive, negative and neutral). The types of information available on BoomSonar's dashboard are orientated towards improving the performance of an organization in real-time. This means that the user can compile content as well as the results of analytical functions into a downloadable report. Accordingly, one can argue that the goal of a dashboard is to bring aggregated data into the realm of organizational decision-making.

One unique aspect of BoomSonar's dashboard is the capacity for a user to manually flag posts and forward their contents to others. This allows users of BoomSonar to share all necessary information needed for analysing marketing campaigns, the online perception of brands, products or leaders and, social customer relationship management (CRM) within the confines of their organization. For example, if a dissatisfied customer is complaining on social media, an analyst can flag the post in real-time and send it to public relations. The public relations team can then respond to emerging situation before any kind of escalation happens. In a similar manner, BoomSonar can also be used to 'turn' potential customers from rivals. For instance, marketing departments of client organizations can use the system to pinpoint potential customers and offer them advantageous packages. One of the effects of developing such a capacity is that organizations can react much quicker to events happening online.

Discussion

For the most part, this chapter focused on documenting the three key technologies characteristic of SMM tools. By having the capacity to quantify interaction on the social web, SMM tools have become an indispensable aspect of branding communication strategies. In fact, it has become common practice to measure return on investment (ROI) on viral advertising and media campaigns by estimating their ability to change the number of mentions of a brand, the sentiment of those mentions, and the influence of the people who mention it (Andrejevic 2011). All of these measurements are done through SMM tools. By being able to mobilize affective attachments, such campaigns have the capacity to indirectly increase brand value in financial markets. Furthermore, financial analysts seem to be using similar tools to evaluate brand value. Studies show that data extracted from social media traffic are increasingly entering into the calculations of brand valuators and asset valuators on financial markets (Bowerman 2010).

By being able to measure the success of a campaign, SMM tools bring about an increased emphasis on metrics, indicators and measures. They encourage more intensified forms of monitoring and analysis. This brings up a discussion on the relationship between datafication, informational capitalism and surveillance. SMM tools are a key feature in the landscape of online surveillance and produce new markets for behavioural prediction. Yet as demonstrated throughout this chapter, these tools rely on relatively opaque mechanisms of extraction, commodification, and control that effectively exile individuals from their own behaviour, often forcing them to behave in manners contrary to the *laissez-faire* spirit of modern capitalism (Zuboff 2015). In this context, the control mechanisms offered by SMM tools are controversial insofar that in their capacity to generate value, they also undermine the historical relationship between markets and democracy (Zuboff 2015, p. 86). At the same time, through their increased presence, SMM tools change the empirical basis from which decisions are made within an organization and the criteria for what counts as a good decision. Although such tools are becoming an indispensable part of online communication strategies, the reality produced by these tools are often accepted at face value and without any critical evaluation. This is rather problematic as SMM tools offer a simulated, simplified version of reality based on data doubles, rather than objective representation.

Dashboards as Representation?

Like all visualizations of data, dashboards necessarily distort the information that they are attempting to present. On a fundamental level, visualization is a hermeneutic form of expression which excludes certain dimensions of data for the sake of clarity. As such, dashboards encourage some cognitive capacities (e.g. monitoring, comparison, pattern detection), which may marginalize other approaches to a specific problem. Furthermore, when presenting very complex and messy data in simplified forms, dashboards can cause subtle shifts to occur in how data is understood. For example, data that is consistently captured and available may become prioritized over that which might be important but can't be easily presented. A dashboard might focus on things occurring in the recent past such as responses, surges or spikes, rather than longer-term trends. Screen size, the positioning of elements on the screen, information refresh rates, and the use of colours and other visual cues all guide the user's attention to preferred interpretations of the data on display.

Data and Representation

As it has been critically assessed elsewhere, data culled from social media is generally considered to be imprints or symptoms of people's actual behaviour or moods and are as such considered to be treasured resources (van Dijck 2014). Social media interactions are at best, proxies to measure the intentions of people and should be treated as such. The affordances of social media platforms, their interfaces and interactive structures all shape the limits to human agency online. Rather than representing social relations in their totality, data culled from these platforms are just a version of the social as seen from the standpoint of the platform. Although the representationality of such data is problematic, it is nonetheless used by intelligence services to forecast nascent terrorist activity or calculate crowd control (Weerkamp and De Rijke 2012; Xu et al. 2014) or for marketers to predict whether someone is inclined towards a product or brand (Asur and Huberman 2010). In other words, organizations take real actions based on a platform-specific form of social reality.

Blackboxing and Algorithms

Data analytics and the algorithms used by such techniques can yield powerful information about who we are and what we do. Although we consider algorithms to be objective in their application, the truth is that algorithms are constructs shaped by human values.[8] Yet instead of critically discussing the human values imparted into analytical algorithms, we choose to treat algorithms as black boxes. The 'black box' problem occurs when an algorithm and its calculations are hidden and not open to scrutiny. Although calls for transparency have been discussed with respect to government production and use of algorithms (Tkacz 2012), similar calls have fallen on deaf ears in the other industries (Crawford 2016).

Conclusion

By creating the capacity to measure online engagement, SMM tools are used to manage risks associated with online communication strategies. Although risk management explains the role of SMM technologies within the context of brand valuation and financial capitalism, further research is needed into the actual companies managing SMM technologies.

BoomSonar may be TBB's principle value-creating service, yet the technology itself does not have the capacity to resolve the risks it identifies. For this, TBB has an entire array of side services which create the organizational capacity for action. Therefore, how the company defines and communicates risk play important roles for the continuation of the relationship with clients and the creation of profit. Yet at the same time, as this chapter has attempted to demonstrate, the empirical foundation upon which risk itself is measured is rather shaky. Data collected from the social web is problematic insofar as it is a simulated, simplified version of reality. As human constructs, the algorithms upon which data analytics are based are inherently biased while the design of dashboards can skewer our perception of data. In other words, the reality used by SMM tools to determine risk goes through numerous filters. In each phase of this process, certain aspects of social reality are lost while others reified. Further research is needed on the epistemological foundations of SMM as well as a critical evaluation of whether the social web can really be an accurate proxy for representing social complexity.

Notes

1. http://www.milliyet.com.tr/Milliyet-Tv/nevidyo/video-izle/Ülker-in-tartisilan-1-Nisan-reklami-r0eMXFA6Htg5.html.
2. http://www.hurriyet.com.tr/ortaligi-karistiran-reklama-Ülkerden-aciklama-40413613.
3. http://www.turkishny.com/images/stories/date/040117/economy-news/040117-2017-04-01-10-47-08-1.jpg.
4. Some categories of organizations that have embraced the datafication paradigm include governments, municipalities, corporations, technology companies and intelligence services (boyd and Crawford 2012, p. 663). Although the concerns regarding how the capacities developed by such organizations will reshape issues such as privacy (Morozov 2013) and surveillance (van Dijck 2014), ethics (Mittelstadt et al. 2016) or even social research (Beaton 2016) are pertinent, datafication has also been fundamentally misunderstood by many. For example, some have mistakenly argued that the capacity to quantify society as data will lead to what has

been notoriously called the "end of theory" (Andersson 2008). Algorithms, in their inherently computational (and supposedly objective) approach, will render obsolete more human-oriented forms of social research, thereby eliminating the biases found in such approached. As it has been criticized elsewhere, just much as theoretical paradigms, algorithms are also based around human biases and interpretation (Couldry et al. 2016). Therefore, datafication does not eliminate the human biases from any sort of analytical process but introduces new ones instead.
5. Most of the relevant content from interviews has been integrated into the narrative structure to make the chapter more readable in terms of flow.
6. For example, a client can put in a query for BoomSonar to just listen to results from google.com.tr rather than google.com.
7. For example through the usage of affixes, the word *Çekoslovakyalı* (Czechoslovakian) can be converted into *Çekoslovakyalılaştıramadıklarımı zdanmışsınızcasına* (meaning "Just like you are said to be one of those that we couldn't manage to convert to a Czechoslovak").
8. For example, the popular PageRank algorithm used by Google's search engine for ranking websites has a very specific definition of trustworthiness (Reider 2012). On a network, it tends to favor websites that are in closer proximity to a few popular websites rather than those who are popular in themselves. In other words, PageRank favors those who are popular amongst popular people. As one can easily see, such definition of trustworthiness is structured around the conditions of human experience and epistemology.

References

Anderson, C. (2008). The end of theory: The data deluge makes the scientific method obsolete. *Wired*. Retrieved from https://www.wired.com/2008/06/pb-theory/.

Andrejevic, M. (2011). The work that affective economics does. *Cultural Studies, 25*(4–5), 604–620. https://doi.org/10.1080/09502386.2011.600551.

Andrejevic, M., & Burdon, M. (2015). Defining the sensor society. *Television & New Media, 16*(1), 19–36. https://doi.org/10.1177/1527476414541552.

Arvidsson, A., & Colleoni, E. (2012). Value in informational capitalism and on the internet. *The Information Society, 28*(3), 135–150. https://doi.org/10.1080/01972243.2012.669449.

Asur, S., & Huberman, B. A. (2010). Predicting the future with social media (pp. 492–499). *IEEE*. https://doi.org/10.1109/WI-IAT.2010.63.

Bartlett, J., & Tkacz, N. (2016). *Governance by dashboard*. A policy paper. Demos. Retrieved from https://www.demos.co.uk/wp-content/uploads/2017/04/Demos-Governance-by-Dashboard.pdf

Beaton, B. (2016). How to respond to data science: Early data criticism by Lionel Trilling. *Information & Culture: A Journal of History, 51*(3), 352–372. https://doi.org/10.1353/lac.2016.0014.

Bodle, R. (2011). Regimes of sharing: Open APIs, interoperability, and Facebook. *Information, Communication & Society, 14*(3), 320–337. https://doi.org/10.1080/1369118X.2010.542825.

Bollier, D., & Communications and Society Program (Aspen Institute), A. I. R. on I. T. (2010). *The promise and peril of big data*. Washington: Aspen Institute, Communications and Society Program.

Borra, E., & Rieder, B. (2014). Programmed method: Developing a toolset for capturing and analyzing tweets. *Aslib Journal of Information Management, 66*(3), 262–278. https://doi.org/10.1108/AJIM-09-2013-0094.

Bowerman, M. (2010, December 7). Financial risk analysis 2.0: A win-win model for shareholders and communities. *Social Finance*. Retrieved from http://socialfinance.ca/2010/12/07/financial-risk-analysis-2-a-win-win-model-for-shareholders-and-communities/.

boyd, d., & Crawford, K. (2012). Critical questions for big data: Provocations for a cultural, technological, and scholarly phenomenon. *Information, Communication & Society, 15*(5), 662–679. https://doi.org/10.1080/1369118X.2012.678878.

Bucher, T. (2013). Objects of intense feeling. *Computational Culture*. Retrieved from http://computationalculture.net/objects-of-intense-feelingthe-case-of-the-twitter-api/.

Couldry, N., Fotopoulou, A., & Dickens, L. (2016). Real social analytics: A contribution towards a phenomenology of a digital world: Real social analytics. *The British Journal of Sociology, 67*(1), 118–137. https://doi.org/10.1111/1468-4446.12183.

Crawford, K. (2016). Can an algorithm be agonistic? Ten scenes from life in calculated publics. *Science, Technology & Human Values, 41*(1), 77–92. https://doi.org/10.1177/0162243915589635.

Fan, W., & Gordon, M. D. (2014). The power of social media analytics. *Communications of the ACM, 57*(6), 74–81. https://doi.org/10.1145/2602574.

Fensel, D., Leiter, B., & Stavrakantonakis, I. (2012). *Social media monitoring*. Innsbruck: Semantic Technology Institute. Retrieved from https://oc.sti2.at/sites/default/files/SMM%20Handouts.pdf

Floridi, L. (2012). Big data and their epistemological challenge. *Philosophy & Technology, 25*(4), 435–437. https://doi.org/10.1007/s13347-012-0093-4.

Fuchs, C. (2010). Labor in informational capitalism and on the internet. *The Information Society, 26*(3), 179–196. https://doi.org/10.1080/01972241003712215.

Gungor, Z., & Oflazer, K. (1995). Parsing Turkish using the lexical functional grammar formalism. *Machine Translation, 10*(4), 293–319. https://doi.org/10.1007/BF00990908.

Jenkins, H. (2006). *Convergence culture: Where old and new media collide*. New York: New York University Press.

Kitchin, R. (2014). Big data. In R. Kitchin (Ed.), *The data revolution* (pp. 48–67). Thousand Oaks: SAGE Publications.

Kozinets, R. V., de Valck, K., Wojnicki, A. C., & Wilner, S. J. (2010). Networked narratives: Understanding word-of-mouth marketing in online communities. *Journal of Marketing, 74*(2), 71–89. https://doi.org/10.1509/jmkg.74.2.71.

Langlois, G., McKelvey, F., Elmer, G., & Werbin, G. (2009). Mapping commercial Web 2.0 worlds: Towards a new critical ontogenesis. *Fibreculture*. Retrieved from http://fourteen.fibreculturejournal.org/fcj-095-mapping-commercial-web-2-0-worlds-towards-a-new-critical-ontogenesis/.

Latour, B. (2007, April 6). Beware, your imagination leaves digital traces. *Times Higher Literary Supplement*. Retrieved from http://bruno-latour.fr/sites/default/files/P-129-THES-GB.pdf.

Mayer-Schönberger, V., & Cukier, K. (2013). *Big data: A revolution that will transform how we live, work and think*. London: Murray.

Miller, G. A. (1995). WordNet: A lexical database for English. *Communications of the ACM, 38*(11), 39–41. https://doi.org/10.1145/219717.219748.

Mittelstadt, B. D., Allo, P., Taddeo, M., Wachter, S., & Floridi, L. (2016). The ethics of algorithms: Mapping the debate. *Big Data & Society, 3*(2). https://doi.org/10.1177/2053951716679679.

Morozov, E. (2013). The real privacy problem. *MIT Technology Review*. Retrieved from http://www.technologyreview.com/featuredstory/520426/the-real-privacy-problem/.

Oflazer, K. (1995). Two-level description of Turkish morphology. *Literary and Linguistic Computing, 9*(2), 137–148. https://doi.org/10.1093/llc/9.2.137.

Ozel, B., Yildirim, S., & Eren, A. (2011). Exploring tweet patterns to identify and analyse online political debates. In *Social technologies '11: ICT for social transformations*. Conference proceedings, 2011. ISBN 978-9955-19-378-4.

Prahalad, C. K., & Ramaswamy, V. (2004). Co-creating unique value with customers. *Strategy & Leadership, 32*(3), 4–9. https://doi.org/10.1108/10878570410699249.

Puschmann, C., & Ausserhofer, J. (2017). Social data APIs origin, types, issues. In M. T. Schäfer & K. Van Es (Eds.), *The datafied society: Studying culture through data*. Amsterdam: Amsterdam University Press.

Reider, B. (2012). What is in PageRank? A historical and conceptual investigation of a recursive status index. *Computational Culture*. Retrieved from http://computationalculture.net/article/what_is_in_pagerank.

Ruppert, E. (2011). Population objects: Interpassive subjects. *Sociology, 45*(2), 218–233. https://doi.org/10.1177/0038038510394027.

Schütze, H. (1998). Automatic word sense discrimination. *Computational Linguistics, 24*(1), 97–123.

Striphas, T. (2015). Algorithmic culture. *European Journal of Cultural Studies, 18*(4–5), 395–412. https://doi.org/10.1177/1367549415577392.

Tkacz, N. (2012). From open source to open government: A critique of open politics the commons and their im/possibilities. *Ephemera, 12*(4), 386–405. Retrieved from http://www.ephemerajournal.org/contribution/opensource-open-government-critique-open-politics-0.

Tkacz, N. (2015). *Connection perfected: What the dashboard reveals*. Presented at the digital methods initiative keynote address, Amsterdam. Retrieved from https://www.academia.edu/12077196/Connection_Perfected_What_the_Dashboard_Reveals.

Uricchio, W. (2017). Data, culture and the ambivalence of algorithms. In M. T. Schäfer & K. Van Es (Eds.), *The datafied society: Studying culture through data*. Amsterdam: Amsterdam University Press.

van Dijck, J. (2014). Datafication, dataism and dataveillance: Big Data between scientific paradigm and ideology. *Surveillance & Society, 12*(2), 197–208.

Vis, F. (2013). A critical reflection on Big Data: Considering APIs, researchers and tools as data makers. *First Monday, 18*(10). https://doi.org/10.5210/fm.v18i10.4878.

Weerkamp, W., & Rijke, M. (2012). *Activity prediction: A Twitter-based exploration*. Presented at the SIGIR workshop on time-aware information access, Portland. Retrieved from https://pdfs.semanticscholar.org/3b14/d03e40c3a121f5f3c1d34a69c632b735330c.pdf.

Xu, J., Lu, T.-C., Compton, R., & Allen, D. (2014). Civil unrest prediction: A Tumblr-based exploration. In W. G. Kennedy, N. Agarwal, & S. J. Yang (Eds.), *Social computing, behavioral-cultural modeling and prediction* (Vol. 8393, pp. 403–411). Cham: Springer International Publishing. https://doi.org/10.1007/978-3-319-05579-4_49.

Zuboff, S. (2015). Big other: Surveillance capitalism and the prospects of an information civilization. *Journal of Information Technology, 30*(1), 75–89. https://doi.org/10.1057/jit.2015.5.

Part II

Contradictions in Digital Practices and Creative Industries

6

Efficient Worker or Reflective Practitioner? Competing Technical Rationalities of Media Software Tools

Ingrid Forsler and Julia Velkova

Following processes of digitalisation, the material preconditions for media production in the media industries have been transformed. Software and computers have replaced most of the mechanical tools and part of the manual labour used for the creation of symbolic, cultural goods to be circulated in the global media markets. At the same time, the work of creating such symbolic goods represents a form of craft that needs to be exercised in close relations to, now, digital materials and tools.

Yet, conventional modes of production and distribution of media software have been based on the separation of technological production from technological use, and have resulted in software with overdetermined functionality and conventions about how media work is to be performed, producing what some craft theorists have described as 'a workmanship of certainty' (Dormer 1997, p. 141). Grounded in an anticipatory logic according to which programmers and technology designers envision what potential software users across diverse fields of practice may need (Frabetti 2015), the frameworks of production of media software have been thereby establishing hierarchies between different forms of knowledge –

I. Forsler (✉) • J. Velkova
Södertörn University, Stockholm, Sweden

© The Author(s) 2018
P. Bilić et al. (eds.), *Technologies of Labour and the Politics of Contradiction*,
Dynamics of Virtual Work, https://doi.org/10.1007/978-3-319-76279-1_6

practical and theoretical – and putting them at tension in relation to the dynamics of the work performed by media practitioners or producers. Such a disconnection is not dissimilar to how older mass media frameworks of production anticipated audiences, but did not really include them in media production.

This chapter discusses this tension through an analysis of three different production frameworks of software in the field of computer graphics media, and more specifically computer graphics animation. Using these frameworks as an example, we argue that each distinct framework of software production assumes a different way of knowing and understanding knowledge in relation to practice. Despite choosing a rather specialised field of media practice, we believe that the discussion that we develop is relevant for other fields of digital work, including game development and digital print media production.

Our suggestion is that different production frameworks of software tools for computer graphics are underpinned by competing visions of the media practitioners[1] and their knowledge, as shown in the Table 6.1.

These competing visions, we argue, are not inevitable or singular effects of industrialisation and capitalism. Rather, we conceptualise them as a possible object of contestation and redefinition at the level of practice, by changing the epistemological orientation of technical systems in terms of

Table 6.1 Conceptual model of software production framework in relation to knowledge in work practice

Software production framework	Technical rationality	
	Vision of the media practitioner	Prioritized knowledge
'Mass'-oriented tools for CG media production (Adobe, Autodesk)	The media practitioner as an efficient worker	Knowing-in-action
Hollywood entertainment industry (Pixar)	The media practitioner as a craftsperson in a Fordist framework of labour	Reflection-on-action
Free software creative community (Blender)	The media practitioner as a master of tool development	Reflection-in-action

their outlook towards the potential users, the media practitioners, thereby acting on the contradictions of technologies of digital work.

One of the reasons for choosing a seemingly marginal field of media production – that of computer graphics media – is related to its ubiquity across both diverse spheres of media work and everyday life. Irrespective of whether we turn on an electronic device such as a computer, a mobile telephone, a GPS navigator, a game or TV, each time we see an advertisement or just browse a magazine with housing interior or fashion we consume computer graphics. The multiple genres of computer graphics media – computer games, visual effects, user interfaces, digital comics, computer animations and simulations – have yielded some of the most financially worthy and aesthetically valued symbolic goods produced by the media industries and computer cultures in the past two decades, ranging from family entertainment films produced by studios such as Pixar, through computer games to user-produced animations as in the Machinima animation community.

The production of computer graphics media is heavily reliant on software, much of which emerged in the late 1990s. It coincided with a widespread enthusiasm about the democratic potential of new communication technologies, like the internet, and the affordability of the computer as provider of new possibilities for creative practice (e.g. Bolter and Grusin 1999). In the fields of web design, print, games and animation creation, software programs like Adobe Photoshop, Premiere, Illustrator and In-design, Macromedia Flash (now owned by Adobe) or Autodesk AutoCad, 3D Studio Max and Maya quickly became some of the key toolsets of work for an increasing number of media practitioners who aspire to engage with computer graphics in the global cultural industries. These new digital tools became popular with their relatively short learning curve, which allowed new producers of media to create good looking content quickly and efficiently. In effect, an expanding pool of freelancers aspiring for a more individualistic mode of work, as part of the new connectionist 'spirit' of capitalism (Boltanski and Chiapello 2007), could engage in producing content for broadcasting companies, advertising agencies and web design companies rapidly. These developments could be interpreted as signs of larger processes of de-professionalisation and democratisation of the mediascape through digital technologies of production and communication. These processes have been criticised for more than a decade now by political economists through the debate on free labour and online user exploitation (e.g. Andrejevic 2008; van Dijck 2009). Whereas these debates are important, we have chosen to put them aside in this chapter, and instead focus on how different modes of organizing work might exclude media producers from certain forms of knowledge. These processes, we suggest, can be identified if we take a closer look at the technical rationality embedded in the production frameworks of such software, and particularly their epistemological orientation in relation to media practice.

Methodological Considerations

Before discussing these different epistemological orientations, we wish to foreground the methodological and analytical approach used henceforth. We choose to discuss three examples of distinct frameworks of software for computer graphics media that can be broadly defined as industrial – developed by companies that specialise in either software production or in Hollywood entertainment computer graphics media, or as user-driven – developed or initiated primarily by media practitioners rather than by industrial manufacturers. Our knowledge on the latter is illustrated by a case of the 3D animation software Blender, and is derived from a larger ethnographic project on user-driven technologies for media production conducted in the period 2012–2017 (see Velkova 2016; Velkova and Jakobsson 2017). The empirical material collected in the course of this research featured qualitative interviews with 37 computer graphics practitioners engaged in work for the media industries but developing their own software tools for computer graphics, participant observation of computer graphics film production and an analysis of online and other relevant documents. In addition, we have performed one semi-structured interview with a practitioner working with off the shelf software ('Anna', p. 9), specifically for this chapter.

The goal with the interviews within the Blender community was to understand the meaning and role that media practitioners attributed to the software tools that they chose to use in their practice. The participant observation and analysis of online documents complemented and enriched this understanding by providing examples of situations in actual or documented contexts of practice that concerned the modes of development of the production software they used, Blender. All such data was initially coded in the software MaxQDA from where the categories and themes of analysis emerged. This approach was based on grounded theory methods (Glaser and Strauss 1967/2009), which main principle is that the data generates theory and that the analysis of data elicits the concepts of the researcher (Charmaz 2006, p. 3). It was thereby the collected and coded data that brought our attention to problems of knowledge embedded in the frameworks of production of software for computer graphics media. It emerged as a theme of concern that was brought up by our informants, and was present in the fieldnotes from the participant observation and document analysis. However, as sociologist Howard Becker observes, '[t]opics and problems do not "emerge" /.../ -- we "emerge them", invent them as a result of what we learn once we begin our work' (Becker 1982/2008, p. xi). This implies a movement in and out of a research environment, of collecting data and attempting to theorise it, going back to the field again, returning, theorising. After we identified the theme of epistemological outlook of production frameworks of software in our research on the Blender community, we attempted to relate it to other frameworks of production, particularly industrial ones since they emerged as a frequent point of reference by our informants from the Blender community.

Our discussion on these, industrial driven frameworks of software production, is made through the cases of the production frameworks of commercial, off-the shelf software for computer graphics, and of in-house software development practised by Pixar, a pioneer company in computer graphics entertainment. Our knowledge about these frameworks is based primarily on secondary literature from the fields of science and technology studies and anthropology that discusses computerisation of work and the entrance of computer graphics in work practices (Henderson 1999; Downey 1998); histories of software and the computer graphics industry (Sito 2013; Tai 2012; Pfiffner 2003); insights gained from the interviews with media practitioners described above as well as with one of the co-founders of Autodesk, and finally, online videos and documentation released by companies such as Pixar and Autodesk. Our reliance on secondary literature for discussing these frameworks is provoked by the general scarcity of research in this field of practice, and particularly on industrially developed software for computer graphics production. Due to practical constraints, we were not able to perform an equally in-depth qualitative research on these frameworks. Nevertheless, we attempted to enrich our understanding by performing a qualitative interview with a media practitioner who had worked only with proprietary software frameworks, as well as collected additional material available online about the current frameworks of work of Pixar (that material featured online videos of employees in which they share insights about technological development; and online documents publicly available on the website of Pixar). We added this data to our empirical bulk and attempted to establish analytical categories that would differentiate or find links in common between this material and the data collected as part of the research on the Blender community. We are aware that this approach makes our analysis of the industrial frameworks of production limited. Nevertheless, it has been helpful to form sensitising concepts (Blumer 1954) that would enable us to make the analytical distinction elaborated here. We bring up some of this material in the form of citations occasionally throughout the paper in order to illustrate, clarify and support our theoretical argument.

Using these primary and secondary sources, we have applied feminist theory of technological development (Suchman 2002), and theories of knowledge in relation to practice (Schön 2003), to delineate different kinds of knowledge prioritised by the different frameworks. The contribution of this chapter is thereby a proposal for a conceptual distinction that outlines some of the contradictions that emerge between these three different frameworks of software development in terms of distinct visions about the kind of practitioners that are supposed to engage with these tools based on their epistemological outlook.

As shown in Table 6.1, we have chosen to term these visions as imagining media practitioners in the following way: 'The media practitioner as an efficient worker'; 'The media practitioner as a craftsperson in a Fordist framework of labour' and 'The media practitioner as a master of tool development'. The concepts for describing knowledge that we use in the table are appropriated from the work of Donald Schön (2003) on the reflective practitioner, namely: knowing-in-action, reflection-on-action and reflection-in-action.

Each of the three software production frameworks, we suggest, exhibits a different technical rationality that arises on the axis between projected ideas of the end-user, their creative practice and different forms of knowledge. Our aim is not to promote one production framework over another, but rather to highlight different epistemological outlooks of technology that emerge at the intersection between production modes and actual practice.

Technical Rationality and Material Knowledge in Practice

Following broader processes of disjuncture (Appadurai 1990) and reorganisation of labour and structure of capitalism (Boltanski and Chiapello 2007), contemporary work is generally organised based on the disconnection between diverse kinds of practitioners according to specialisations. This disconnection is embedded not only in formal organisations of labour, but is also reflected in the frameworks of producing technologies that underpin such work, and that produce disconnect between practices through prioritising different forms of knowledge.

In research aiming to transcend simple dichotomies of theory and practice, the work of Donald Schön (2003) has been very influential. He points out that professional work, as implemented in Fordist frameworks of production, departs from a model of *technical rationality* that separates theoretical knowledge from engineering and practical skills. The concept of technical rationality is also discussed by philosopher of technology Andrew Feenberg (2009) as the way in which technologies represent modern forms of hegemony through which power gets established. Technologies reflect dominant ideas and ideologies of societies which get inscribed in the modes of technological development and its outlook. Technical rationality, according to Feenberg, encompasses not only technical devices and systems but also work, knowledge production and everyday communication. In work practice this has implied increased specialisation and standardisation of production techniques and frameworks to reflect largely an economic rationality of ever-increasing efficiency. Technical development, in this context, becomes an application of theoretical knowledge, as well as the basis for practical work, creating an asymmetric relationship between different kinds of knowledge. This fragmented understanding of knowledge not only values theoretical knowledge over practical skills, but also assumes that knowledge can be taken out of context (Schön 2003, pp. 21–30).

Separating knowledge from experience is in Donna Haraway's (1991, pp. 88–91) terms, a 'god-trick', an attempt to distance the knowing subject from the studied and practised Western knowledge-based production. For Haraway, knowledge is always situated and partial. Building on Haraway's discussion about knowledge, Lucy Suchman (1994) puts forth a feminist approach to technology development. It is based on erasing artificially created borders between different knowledge frameworks through establishing "working relations" between users and producers of technology. Technical expertise, Suchman suggests, is a necessary, but not sufficient, form of knowledge for the production of new technologies, and she states that 'the development of useful systems must be a boundary-crossing activity, taking place through the deliberate creation of situations that allow for the meeting of different partial knowledges' (Suchman 2002). For our enquiry this means that a separation between producers of software (engineers and programmers), and its users (media practitioners) in the context of production frameworks of technologies of work, specifically software, also represents a separation between different forms of knowledge, based on differences in the nature of their working experiences. Schön elaborates this understanding by stating that knowledge itself cannot be separated from the act of working, or practice: 'Our knowing is ordinarily tacit, implicit in our patterns of action and in our feel for the stuff that we are dealing. It seems right to say that our knowing is *in* our action' (Schön 2003, p. 49, Italics in original).

Far from being an application of a decontextualised knowledge framework, *knowing-in-action* is a bodily and sensory form of tacit knowledge, characterised by actions and judgement being carried out spontaneously, without thinking (Schön 1992, p. 5; 2003, p. 54). This kind of automated skill demands practice, or repetition. Through encountering a situation over and over again, the practitioner develops a repertoire of expectations, images and techniques that makes him or her better prepared for unexpected or uncertain situations in work practice.

Schön's work has been fairly criticised, among other things for being too individualistic and not taking social context into account (e.g. Thompson and Pascal 2012). Despite its shortcomings however, we believe that his understanding of knowledge and reflective practice are helpful to inform a discussion on how knowledge and practice can be configured through different modes of *producing the technologies* on which practice depends. In the next section we will discuss how the production frameworks of software, as the new technology for creative work, connect to problems of epistemology of practice.

The Media Practitioner as an Efficient Worker

The production frameworks of today's market monopolists of computer graphics software for animation production are conditioned by several historical developments. In part, they reflect the earlier history of software development in which, between the 1980s and 1990s, computer graphics software was conceptualised as a tool to increase the productivity of workers engaged in industrial design (Downey 1998; Henderson 1999). This position has carried an assumption of the intrinsically superior qualities that the computer and new visualisation technologies possess, echoing an instrumentalist worldview, according to which the creative worker should be empowered and made more efficient through tools that the industry provides for her.

The initial goals of companies like Adobe and Autodesk were rooted in ideas about automation of labour as a path towards greater work efficiency, and subjected to the logic of algorithms developed by engineers detached from actual practices of use. Later on, these ideas were adapted by tuning software to satisfy the needs and speed of production of specific branches of the media industries, while at the same time trying to make it into a universal tool that fits a broad range of practices. As Aylish Wood (2015, pp. 28–29) recalls, the popular 3D software Maya has been specifically developed for the productivity and expressive demands of the markets and industries dealing with visual effects, animation and games by favouring particular styles of movement, photorealism and simulations of textures. From such a perspective, the popular consumer software that became a standard component of 3D animation today was not envisioning to democratise media production, but rather to produce new efficient workers necessary for the entertainment media industries undergoing digitisation.

In effect, the production model of such software was tuned to reflect this vision, and implicitly reproduces divisions of labour and knowledge through separating producers of software and the greater majority of media practitioners using it. Embedded in proprietary frameworks of distribution, market-dominant software for computer graphics follows the general anticipatory mode of software development. Communication between media practitioners and developers of software is hierarchically organised and mediated through the figure of the 'technical support' (Downey 1998). Programmers anticipate the needs of practitioners in a relative disconnect from their actual, practical needs and problems. At the same time, the economic logic that guides technological development makes software producers strive to create products that fit the broadest possible groups of users. Henderson (1999) describes the impossibility of creating one software for computer graphics production that fits any design need, and points out how the work practices, from individual design processes to the organisation of workplaces, adapt to the software instead of the other way around. Henderson further points out that the designers of such technological systems have limited models of media practitioners and their needs, and can never fully imagine the problems that can emerge in situations of practical use of software. Instead, the media practitioner must adapt to the logic of the tool, as described in the following quote by a freelancing video editor who works with such software.

> What an editing tool looks like, is …a kind of an agreement since way back, it's a norm in its basic structure that I, as a user, simply have adapted to. The method gets kind of embodied. […] I'm not very interested in dialogue [with developers], since I find that the software I'm currently

working with satisfies my needs. Which I may be happy about… In this, competition plays an important role. If the user is not satisfied, he or she simply moves to another software. This means the manufacturer must listen, improve and renew. And I think this is working (Interview with 'Anna', freelancing video editor, April 2017)

What 'Anna', describes as an embodied method is the kind of knowledge Schön (2003, p. 54) calls *knowing-in-action*, tacit skills in using a specific tool. It is important here to note that the practitioner in this case does not oppose the technical rationality of this framework, but is herself part of an efficiency paradigm of media production that prioritises speed over innovation. That the framework prioritises *knowing-in-action* of course does not mean that other forms of knowledge do not exist within it, or that practitioners within this framework do not reflect over their practice. However, the production framework of the software which they use may or may not allow them to act on those reflections through modifying the tool. This means that if a software tool is insufficient for working with the problem set by the practitioner, he or she has to solve this in other ways, such as through often time consuming workarounds, or as this case, by changing software.

This production framework also reflects a linear and hierarchical model of knowledge according to which first engineers develop software and then it is taken by media practitioners in turn to solve problems of work. In real life professional practice however, 'problems do not present themselves to practitioners as given' (Schön 2003, p. 40). Instead, problems are invented by practitioners to solve or at least frame a problematic situation in a dynamic, problem-solving and problem-finding rhythm, as suggested by Sennett (2008). This situation can often be uncertain, confusing and contradictory, making the task of a predefined and overdetermined technical commission impossible. Instead, the process of defining decisions must depart from the production tools of the situation – in this case, software.

The distinction that is maintained between media practitioners and developers may be explained as a logical continuation of a longer history of industrialisation and reorganisation of labour in capitalist societies, as suggested earlier. However, this is not the only way in which software for computer graphics gets developed. Indeed, such a mode of development is typical for products that are aimed at being sold to the end-user market of consumer software. Other industries, such as the Hollywood entertainment production companies, favour other modes of software production that configure knowledge and practice in a different way. To illustrate the difference, we take Pixar's framework of software production as a reference point.

The Media Practitioner as a Craftsperson in a Fordist Framework of Labour

Pixar's technological production framework, as described by Tai (2012) and Sito (2013) is based on an assumption of animators, riggers and modellers employed to work on film productions as craftspeople rather than as mere efficient workers who have to be supplied with tools. As such, they have to be provided with possibilities to change the technological instrumentarium on which their work depends in ways to fit their creative ideas and the problems that they invent. This logic arguably stems from the need of the media industries to harness creativity and at the same time provide unique products on the market in order to be competitive. In this case, technology and the possibility of media practitioners to influence its development gain importance for upholding such a competitive advantage. Software is used and developed in a mode of cooperation between computer scientists, in-house programmers and artists working on Pixar productions. Representing still different fields of work, they are brought to work together in order to develop the aesthetic vision, movements, and the technology and tools for each production (Sito 2013; Tai 2012).

For pragmatic, marketing reasons this cooperation has historically tended to be veiled in a discourse of magic, emphasising that the products of Pixar, like those in other fields of the media industries, are made by the talent of exceptional artists (Catmull 2014, p. xi). As Alfred Gell (2010) writes, magic in the context of artistic work encapsulates the idea of making something with no effort or knowledge. The image of magic in popular discourse comes to represent an ideal technology and shifts attention from the tremendous role of technology in creative practice. Pixar's mode of software production in relation to the production of form – animation films – enables the company to create visual media beyond the limits of existing technological possibilities.

This mode of work frames the media practitioners as commissioners of features in a tool, but at the same time preserves the border between the professional knowledge of the developer and the media practitioner, as evident in this quote from a Ted talk where light designer Danielle Feinberg describes the process of visualising life underwater from 'Finding Nemo', where she emphasises the need to bring together science and creative development.

> We use science and the world we know as a backbone, to ground ourselves in something relatable and recognisable. 'Finding Nemo' is an excellent example of this. A major portion of the movie takes place underwater. But how do you make it look underwater? […] we're using the science — the physics of water, light and movement — to tether [the] artistic freedom (Danielle Feinberg, The Magic Ingredient that brings Pixar movies to life, Ted talk, Nov 2015)

For something to be brought together it needs to first be separated. We therefore argue that this process builds on a fragmented concept of knowledge that understands science as the foundation for art making practices. The quote also consolidates the linear view of creative work as problem-solving. Although the media practitioner in this framework, whether an animation artist, modeller, light designer or script writer, can articulate his or her needs, they must be framed as a problem – such as how to simulate underwater environment in film – in order to be understood by the developer.

Suchman (2002, p. 95) describes this organisation of labour in terms of *detached intimacy* and claims that it characterises much of what we know as technical development. Her suggestion, to reshape this mode of organisation, is to allow for partial knowledges to come together. The first step in doing so is to recognise our own position in the development process, as well as the visible and invisible work conducted, in other words a reflection upon one's own practice (Suchman 2002, p. 100). This aligns with Schön's (2003, p. 61) argument that reflection is a way to overcome the selective inattentiveness of tacit knowledge, but he also differs between different temporalities of reflection. Practitioners can think *about* their work on multiple levels: the decisions they took, what could have been done differently, how they felt in a certain situation, what tacit norms or feelings underlie a judgement or their role in an institutional context, to mention a few. Schön (2003, p. 61) calls this distanced or retrospective thinking *reflection-on-action*. In order to ask for new features in a software tool, the practitioners must be able to critically examine and articulate their professional practice and imagine new ways to do things. The view of the media practitioner as commissioner of features in a tool therefore requires some kind of such reflection-on-action. However, the media practitioners envisioned here are not, as Dormer (1997, p. 140) puts it, 'masters or mistresses of the available technology' but craftspeople situated in a Fordist framework of labour. To find the craftsperson described by Dormer, we must turn to a third production framework that both adopts and extends elements of the first two frameworks.

The Media Practitioner as a Master of Tool Development

More than a decade ago, a Dutch animation studio called Blender Institute started experimenting with crafting an alternative framework for computer graphics software production, which mimics the one in Pixar by allowing media practitioners to access and shape the software that they need according to their individual practice. In contrast to Pixar, which keeps its in-house developed software as a proprietary technology that is not made available to media practitioners broadly, Blender relies on a radical approach of sharing online software, films, computer graphics assets and training materials as a way to establish connections between producers of media (media practitioners) and producers of software (developers). Starting with de-commodifying a proprietary software for 3D animation in the early 2000s called Blender, the Blender Institute engaged in developing short animation films with the aim to extend the capabilities of this software in cooperation with media practitioners and developers (Velkova 2017). In the course of a year, a selected group of the latter worked together to develop a script and a film with high technical challenges that would require the development of completely new features in Blender (Velkova 2016). At the end of the production, the film, its data assets, as well as large parts of the technology were released online under a Creative Commons licence, and as free software. It is important to note that these projects have not been done online, nor for free by volunteers; they were made in Amsterdam, and produced by a mixture of public funding and crowdfunding that prepaid the production (Velkova and Jakobsson 2017). Using sharing online as a form of gifting that enforced relations of exchange and thereby cooperation between media practitioners and developers of software, the Blender community of media practitioners has grown to a few hundred thousand over a decade (Velkova 2016).

What is important for our argument here is the epistemological orientation that software gets when practitioners can take it and bend it to their current needs, and when this happens as a result of enforcing recursive relationships of reciprocity between media practitioners and developers through sharing code and media made with such software online. First, this approach reverses a long established superiority of engineers and programmers over the design of work processes for others engrained in software. Second, it requires a mode of reflection that transcends the articulation and afterthought needed to commission tools, and instead means thinking about a certain aspect of practice while performing it. This way of working represents *reflection-in-action* and differs from reflection-on-action in that it can lead to new decisions that might change the action that provoked the reflection (Schön 2003, pp. 62–63).

In a slow process like software development, this action can be stretched out in time over weeks or even months, but it still differs from the repertoire of past experiences used for knowing-in-action. Reflecting in a situation has little to do with tacit knowledge or skills. Instead, it is a surfacing of such automated understandings and actions that leave them open for reconsideration and critique. Reflection-in-action might occur in an unexpected situation when the conceptual frames in place are not sufficient. This means that the practitioner, in order to reflect-in-action, must not only recognise the irregular but also embrace and act upon it, an approach often attributed to artistic work (ibid). This relation between reflective practice and functionally undetermined tools is explicated by a Blender animation director in the following way:

> Free software matches very good with the artistic idea because no artist wants to be locked into what they can do—a lot of the process of making art is about making the tools (Bassam, animation director, archived blog post, 2014)

Characteristic for reflective practitioners is also how they *relate* to other kinds of knowledge. Rather than keeping the black box of her special expertise closed, the reflective practitioner allows uncertainty to be visible to others and a source for learning and development (Schön 2003, p. 300). Viewing the visual media practitioner as a master, or co-developer, of tools demands precisely this responsiveness towards the other, and her knowledge, feelings and thoughts. In the process of developing new tools for media production, this applies to both engineers and media practitioners. Through reflective practice, perhaps different forms of knowledge can be articulated, put into conversation and used to create new technology that better reflects the creative process and allows for non-linear work and uncertainty.

Conclusions: An Epistemology of Creative Digital Media Practice

In this chapter, we have suggested a theoretical model of how different production frameworks of software tools for computer graphics are underpinned by different epistemological assumptions and competing visions of media practitioners.

To begin with, approaching the media practitioner as an efficient worker builds on a fragmented concept of knowledge and demands skilled workers who can perform their tasks as they appear and without too much thinking. These media practitioners, we suggest, are envisioned by the frameworks of industrial producers of software for the mass-market as needing to possess predominantly *knowing-in-action*, the spontaneous and automated action and judgment that comes with training and repetition. This vision reflects a doctrine of productivity that has emerged since the 1980s in the United States, in which software was envisioned as a tool to increase the efficiency of workers engaged in industrial design. It builds on a fragmented concept of knowledge where creative skills are separated from other forms of knowing. Of course, some media practitioners can engage to a limited degree with modifying such software, and thereby gain access to other forms of knowledge, but our point is that this is not the dominant orientation of such production frameworks.

Other frameworks, as in the case of industrially made software by the entertainment industry, such as Pixar, focus more on invention and specificity of tools for their own production needs. We have argued that such vision understands the media practitioner as a craftsperson, who has to be able to modify her tools to fit specific production needs, rather than as a worker who is trained to use the provided and predefining tools. These modifications are not performed by the practitioner herself, but commissioned by her to a developer or a scientist. The technical rationality of this framework thus demands that the practitioner *reflects-on-action*, becomes aware of their own problem setting process, imagines alternative ways of doing the work and communicates these needs to the developer.

Although not as linear as the model of the efficient worker, the craftsperson view presupposes some kinds of causality. First, the media practitioner does some kind of work, either problem setting or creation, then reflects on it and frames this as a need. Only after that can she call for a tool or feature that answers to this need. For a more intuitive work process that includes the dynamic of the problem-solving and problem-finding rhythm (Sennett 2008), the media practitioner must be able to modify their software tools as part of the working process. This in turn calls for a holistic and isochronal form of knowledge, a conscious way of looking at one's own practice and reconsidering choices and judgements while performing them. In other words, to envision the media practitioner as a master of tool development, as in the case of Blender, *reflection-in-action* is needed.

Indeed, the third, user-driven production framework, which we discuss through the example of the free software for 3D animation Blender, borrows elements from the above two but also contests them. Blender aims to be both a tool for efficient work and a functionally underdetermined tool that allows being modified and extended in practice, as the need occurs. Its functionality and features get shaped in different work practices and production contexts by the practitioners themselves. This, we suggest, builds on a holistic understanding of knowledge that transcends the articulation and afterthought needed to commission tools and instead means thinking about a certain aspect of practice while performing it.

These three epistemological orientations of software should not be seen in terms of which is superior. From the point of view of the industries that employ them, we see all of them as necessary means to achieve certain ends. In the first case, it is to create efficient workers who can quickly supply content to subcontractors, such as broadcasters and advertising agencies. The more flexible framework of Pixar also strives for efficiency, but in the sense of making the most of the media practitioners' creative potential, and strengthening it through technological development, as well as for gaining market dominance by technological innovation. In the case of Blender, we can distinguish an attempt to make media practitioners who are outside high-end media production companies part of the media technology development process. However, these frameworks also contain a number of contradictions, such as between innovation and efficiency, linearity and messiness and situated knowledge through specific software tools versus universal knowledge through general-purpose tools.

These contradictions ultimately reflect the difference in technical rationalities embedded in the software for computer graphics media production – the different view on knowledge and role of media practitioner in relation to work. At the same time, as the example of Blender suggests, such rationalities are not inevitable, but they can occasionally be modified by media practitioners when they engage in creating software frameworks that allow them to change the software tools on which their work depends. Although not superior to other modes of production and development, only frameworks that enable such changes ultimately have the potential to act on the contradictions of technologies of digital work.

Note

1. The term media *practitioner* comes from Donald Schön's knowledge theory, used in this chapter, and is chosen over related terms such as *creator* or *user* to cover a wider range of practices and to emphasise media production as labour. However, we also occasionally employ the term *user* to note a division of media labour through specialisation.

References

Andrejevic, M. (2008). Watching television without pity: The productivity of online fans. *Television & New Media, 9*(1), 24–46.

Appadurai, A. (1990). Disjuncture and difference in the global cultural economy. In M. Featherstone (Ed.), *Global culture: Nationalism, globalisation, and modernity: A Theory, culture & society special issue*. London/Newbury Park: Sage Publications.

Becker, H.S. (2008). *Art worlds* (25th anniversary ed., updated and expanded). Berkeley: University of California Press.

Blumer, H. (1954). What is wrong with social theory? *American Sociological Review, 18*, 3–10.

Boltanski, L., & Chiapello, È. (2007). *The new spirit of capitalism*. London: Verso.

Bolter, J. D., & Grusin, R. (1999). *Remediation: Understanding new media*. Cambridge, MA: MIT Press.

Catmull, E. E. (2014). In A. Wallace (Ed.), *Creativity, Inc.: Overcoming the unseen forces that stand in the way of true inspiration*. New York: Random House.

Charmaz, K. (2006). *Constructing grounded theory: A practical guide through qualitative analysis* (Introducing qualitative methods). London: SAGE.

Dormer, P. (1997). *The culture of craft: Status and future*. Manchester/New York: Manchester University Press.

Downey, G. L. (1998). *The machine in me: An anthropologist sits among computer engineers*. New York: Routledge.

Feenberg, A. (2009). Critical theory of technology. In J.-K. B. Olsen, S. A. Pedersen, & V. F. Hendricks (Eds.), *A companion to the philosophy of technology*. Malden: Wiley-Blackwell.

Frabetti, F. (2015). *Software theory: A cultural and philosophical study*. London: Rowman & Littlefield International.

Gell, A. (2010). The enchantment of technology and the technology of enchantment. In *The craft reader* (English ed., pp. 464–482). Oxford/New York: Berg Publishers.

Glaser, B. G., & Strauss, A. L. (1967). *The discovery of grounded theory*. New York: Aldine.

Haraway, D. (1991). Situated knowledges: The science question in feminism and the privilege of partial perspective. In *Simians, cyborgs and women. The reinvention of nature*. London: Routledge.

Henderson, K. (1999). *On line and on paper: Visual representations, visual culture, and computer graphics in design engineering*. Cambridge: MIT Press.

Pfiffner, P. S. (2003). *Inside the publishing revolution: The adobe story*. Berkeley: Peachpit Press.

Schön, D. A. (1992). Designing as reflective conversation with the materials of a design situation. *Knowledge-Based Systems, 5*(1992), 3–14.

Schön, D. A. (2003 [1995]). *The reflective practitioner: How professionals think in action*. Repr. Aldershot: Ashgate

Sennett, R. (2008). *The craftsman*. New Haven: Yale University Press.

Sito, T. (2013). *Moving innovation: A history of computer animation*. Cambridge, MA: The MIT Press.

Suchman, L. (1994). Working relations of technology production and use. *Computer Supported Cooperative Work (CSCW), 2*, 21–39.

Suchman, L. (2002). Located accountabilities in technology production. *Scandinavian Journal of Information Systems, 14*(2), Article 7. Available at: http://aisel.aisnet.org/sjis/vol14/iss2/7.

Tai, P. (2012). *The principle of animation: History and theory of a social technology*. Doctoral Dissertation. University of California Irvine, Irvine.

Thompson, N., & Pascal, J. (2012). Developing critically reflective practice. *Reflective Practice, 13*(2), 311–325.

van Dijck, J. (2009). Users like you? Theorising agency in user-generated content. *Media, Culture & Society, 31*(1), 41–58.

Velkova, J. (2016). Open cultural production and the online gift economy: The case of blender. *First Monday, 21*(10). Available at http://firstmonday.org/ojs/index.php/fm/article/view/6944

Velkova, J. (2017). *Media technologies in the making user-driven software and infrastructures for computer graphics production*. Huddinge: Södertörns högskola.

Velkova, J., & Jakobsson, P. (2017). At the intersection of commons and market: Negotiations of value in open-sourced cultural production. *International Journal of Cultural Studies, 20*(1), 14–30.

Wood, A. (2015). *Software, animation and the moving image: what's in the box?* Houndmills/Basingstoke/Hampshire/New York: Palgrave Macmillan.

7

In the Golden Cage of Creative Industries: Public-Private Valuing of Female Creative Labour

Valerija Barada and Jaka Primorac

Introduction

The issue of work in general, and women's work in particular, has long intrigued sociology, whether the debate is theoretically informed by feminism or by more mainstream sociology of labour and professions. Within the two broader major topics of the labour process and the subjective meaning of work, a number of issues have been thoroughly investigated conceptually and empirically. These include issues of the shifting labour market, the changing characteristics and scope of work, the influence of technology on the type and experience of work, and the emergence of various gender-defined professions. If we set aside the defining classical works of Marx, Weber, Durkheim, and Simmel and consider somewhat more recent research into the changes of labour, it is sufficient to mention

---

V. Barada (✉)
Department of Sociology, University of Zadar, Zadar, Croatia

J. Primorac
Department for Culture and Communication, Institute for Development and International Relations, Zagreb, Croatia

© The Author(s) 2018
P. Bilić et al. (eds.), *Technologies of Labour and the Politics of Contradiction*,
Dynamics of Virtual Work, https://doi.org/10.1007/978-3-319-76279-1_7

Beck (2000), Bell (1973), Castells (2000), Rifkin (1995), and Touraine (1980 [1969]) as authors who have problematized the transformation from an industrial to a post-industrial, post-work, and information society. In such a post-Fordist society, service and no-collar work (Ross 2003) take precedence over traditional, Fordist labour, thus marking the emergence of the new economy of cognitive capitalism (Lebert and Vercellone 2007) and emphasizing information and communication technology (ICT) as the crucial agent of change in these developments.

We maintain that this list of authors should be expanded with the works of Crompton (1987), Hochschild (1989, 1997), Smith (1987), Walby (1990, 2005 [1997]), and Witz (1992), who focused on the characteristics of work performed by women. In this chapter, when discussing work carried out by women, we use the terms women's work and female work or labour, as they are expressions that are typically used when thematizing the issue of gendered work. However, since this chapter deals with the fundamental characteristics of work, it should be stated that this usual term is basically essentializing the labouring of women as inherently female, thus defining it as work that is substantially only performed by women. Walby and others found that this work is defined not only by the overall societal changes but, more specifically and thoroughly, by the gender regimes in which women live. Female everyday life is reproduced by gender (patriarchal) roles that format not only their participation in the labour market but also their off-work private time. Typically, female professions only extend the traditional caretaking roles that women perform in the society. Drawing on these authors and on the feminist standpoint theory, in this chapter we argue that, even if socio-economic changes are redefining labour as such, women's work is changing at a different pace, since it is additionally engulfed in patriarchal social relations. We argue that this is especially evident in the case of (female) creative labour, in which the line between work time and private time is continuously blurred due to technological affordances.

The question of women's labour is theoretically and empirically conceptualized through the following issues: women's entrance into the labour market and the related work – family conflict, both defined through the division between the public and the private sphere. The public sphere can simply be defined as the social life happening outside the home, most importantly paid work, while the private sphere depicts home and family life. With this working definition, our aim is not to add to the debate on the epistemological value and political consequence of the public/private dichotomy in both feminism and social science. Rather, our normative use of this dichotomy only helps to delineate the locality of female everyday life. As women began to permeate the public aspect of labour, female domestic work remained economically and politically marginalized. With the emergence of the creative industries, the new level of the public and private aspects of female labour has opened. With the intensive research and policy interest in the creative industries, the dictum was that creative labour would be emancipatory for both women and men; this has been shown to be a techno-optimistic fallacy, since working in creative industries has proved to be immensely labour intensive and time consuming.

In this chapter we will show how the technological underpinning of creative labour practices has contradictory outcomes for women and men, because women are typically faced with gender roles that require them to be the primer caretaker. This can lead to covert redomestication of female creatives, whereby we define redomestication as the literal returning of women to the home and thus the private sphere. We will show how, despite being economically independent with lucrative jobs that they consider as a personal choice, female creatives are facing the implosion of the public into the private sphere, while the social value of their work is decreasing. We stipulate that female creatives' labour encourages non-paid, underpaid, and self-exploitative practices, which place women in more precarious positions than men. Female creatives' everyday life is characterized by never-ending professional labour accompanied by family caring practices. Moreover, as the empirical evidence will show, this kind of social arrangement is the only possible one for female creatives, since they are left with few other options if they want to be successful or even to work at all in the creative industries. Thus, in this chapter we will show how female labour practices become embedded into private homes and daily activities, forged by the implosion of the public into the private sphere.

To corroborate this thesis, empirical evidence is drawn from two field research projects conducted in Croatia in the period from 2010 to 2016

(Barada 2012; Barada et al. 2016).[1] The studies focused on labouring conditions in two cultural and creative sectors: first on the area of visual communication design and second on civil society organizations (CSOs) in the area of contemporary culture and arts in Croatia. Although the research sample included various sub-samples (see endnote 1), the empirical findings support the claim that the redefinition of women's work is underway and indicate the contradictory role of technology in this process. It will be shown how certain 'professional redomestication' of female creatives undermines the social valuing of women's work, since it falls through the cracks of the public – private division. The usual conceptualization of women's work falls short of explaining the characteristics of female creatives' everyday life and opens up a new conceptual space. However, it should be emphasized that the purpose of this chapter is not to highlight the national context of Croatia but instead to use it to depict and explain the more global processes of transformation of both male and female work. For this reason the empirical data are not represented in the usual detailed way. Rather, they are retold and interpreted as supporting evidence for our conceptual claims. Our aim is to emphasize the different ramifications for women of the social implications of creative labour's transformation, since women are faced with gender-nuanced outcomes of intertwined social, economic, cultural, technological, and patriarchal labouring and everyday conditions.

Feminist Standpoint Theory and the (Re) Definition of Women's (Creative) Work

The feminist standpoint theory[2] approaches the totality of social reality from the perspective of women's experience and takes their experience as an indicator of that reality. On the level of a particular research project, one does not start with an existing sociological conceptual framework but takes the reality of women's diverse experience as an independent research standpoint (Smith 2002b [1990], pp. 320–321). The proponents of this approach have highlighted various characteristics of women's position, so we cannot speak about a unified theoretical or research approach (Olesen 2003; Weeks 2004 [1998]). Nonetheless, the point of convergence in all of these approaches is the focus on the embeddedness of women's everyday experience and knowledge in the gendered division of labour. Due to their localized knowledge and experience, the positions of those at the bottom of the social and economic hierarchy (not only women but also other marginal social categories) are considered as being fuller on the theoretical and research level as research starting points (Olesen 2003, p. 343). From a marginal position, one can see more clearly the overall power relations that intersect all the social positions of a certain society. In this chapter we use a version of feminist standpoint theory that specifically deals with the intersection of the gender division of labour and the gender order of institutions that organize and regulate the society itself (Smith 1987, p. 3).

Labour is understood here as a connection of the social structure and the individual (subjectivity), by which social relations are intertwined with that which makes individuals what they are and with that which they do (Weeks 2004 [1998], pp. 185, 190). The type of job that an individual holds determines his or her identity in taking different social positions while considering the gender division of labour that is historically and culturally reproduced (Weeks 2004 [1998], p. 185). Work is an activity that produces both individuals (subjects) and society, so it has practical as well as strategic dimensions. Women's work ensures support for men, who, in the gender division of labour, are assigned to deal with conceptual practices and intellectual labour. However, women's work still produces a certain type of social value that poses the question of how women's work practices should be recognized and rewarded (Weeks 2004 [1998], p. 184).[3] Therefore, this type of standpoint approach examines the overlap of identity, labour, and broader social relations as well as the limitation regarding the essentialization of women's position (Millen 1997), nevertheless with the affirmation of the situated experience.[4]

To translate these ideas into methodological instructions, Smith (1987, 2002a) developed so-called institutional ethnography with the help of terms such as experience, work, discourse and text, social relations of ruling, and everyday/everynight activities. By everyday/everynight Smith (2002a, p. 42) understands activities that occur every day and every night, day in and day out, routinely, in a sense that women's work in the home does not end only with daily activities. Therefore, institutional ethnography is a type of sociology that takes experience and the everyday world as its subject of interest. Everyday life is connected with that which is outside experience, because *social* stems from the local activities of people in a set specified time frame, and it is mediated by language and discourse as ways in which people speak about and describe these activities (Smith 2002a, p. 22). Every individual experience is different, but all of them are consolidated by institutions that connect, generalize, and objectify human activities through discourse (Smith 2002a, p. 22). Research based on institutional ethnography starts by choosing the main standpoint through which institutional order is to be examined, with a particular focus on an actual problem in people's lives. Through the analysis of data, one tries to decipher how people reproduce such order, which is why everyday work experience becomes crucial. Such an approach is truly beneficial in the context of creative labour, which relies very much on information and communication technology as (a form of) material embodiment of the socio-economic relations, since it facilitates the reproduction of a continuous blur between work and everyday/everynight activities.

When conceptualizing and researching female creative labour, the feminist standpoint informs us not only that female creatives have different labour experiences and professional paths from their male counterparts but that this experience is marginal or subordinated to the male experience. Creative labour is arranged by gender power relations that simultaneously mirror broader societal inequalities and produce new ones. In particular, drawing from the survey on female visual communication designers in Croatia (Barada 2012), it has been found that women started participating in the closure and demarcation of the profession (Witz 1992, p. 46) through two processes, both enabled by technology and socio-economic developments. The first process occurred in the late 1980s and early 1990s with the professional establishment and educational institutionalization of design.[5] This process temporally coincided with the introduction of market economy elements in Croatia, then part of the socialist Yugoslavia (Tomić-Koludrović and Petrić 2007), and with the widespread use of computer technology in the design profession. The second process, which occurred in the late 1990s and through the 2000s, was marked by complete prevalence of new information and computer technology that democratized the production process (Dormer 2003) and by further pluralization and commercialization of the design market (Petrić 2006). The number of women working in design increased; however, they eventually opted to work for less money though in more secure working environments that protected them from patriarchal social environments (Barada 2012). Younger female designers are prone to self-exploitation, since labouring in the design profession is thoroughly time consuming (Barada and Primorac 2014), but, as they approach their late thirties and early forties, and if they have children, they try to find less flexible and more structured job arrangements (Barada 2012). Their standpoint is such that they are included in the design profession through the educational process but then allocated to more 'female' positions that are less lucrative and less prominent. Institutionally they are incorporated into the profession, but gender-specific social roles push them into the traditional positions of being home and family bound.

Rethinking the Social Valuing of Women's (Creative) Labour. Interconnection of the First, Second, and Third Shifts

Throughout the decades women's work has been conceptualized theoretically and empirically through two key issues: women's entrance into the labour market and the work – family conflict. Beneath such conceptualizations lies the key rationale for the social valuing of work – the division between the public and the private sphere. This was and still is based on the prevailing notion of one type of work being carried out *in* the home and the other *outside* the home. The paid work performed outside the home, in the public sphere, forms a foundation for valuing female labour, because the value of domestic work for the reproduction of society is still not recognized to its full extent (Folbre 2012). Feminists have argued not only for women's entrance into the labour market but also for a more significant presence of women in the public sphere (through political or other public engagement) as well as for the recognition of invisible and unpaid domestic work. However, notwithstanding (primarily) feminist requests regarding the need for the recognition of such invisible and unpaid domestic work, the lines for the social valuing of women's labour are still 'blurred'. This blurring of the lines becomes even more complex in the context of creative labour, in which (digital, ICT) work practices contribute to the ambiguousness of the public – private division of the social valuing of work. Creative labour introduces further contradictions into the conflict between work time and free time and thus the conflict between work and family roles.

To understand this conflict better, one has to move beyond the traditional understanding of the gender roles, and the interchangeable sharing of roles among men and women should be considered, whereby men could accept the responsibility for example for childcare, the preparation of meals, or housework. Such views can be connected to the types of marriage ideologies that Hochschild (1989, p. 15) mentions in her inspirational work *The second shift: Working families and revolution at home*. The author gives three types of gender ideology (traditional, transitional, and egalitarian) that define the domain with which the person wants to be identified (family or work) and how much power in marriage they want to have. Creative professions consume the entire working individual, but it seems that male creatives have the option to identify completely with their profession, while female creatives, since they are burdened with family obligations, have to multiply their identification to both realms, public and private. Because information and computer technology has introduced the option to work from home, the domestic obligations eventually take precedence in female creatives' everyday life. This slowly leads them to fade out from the profession (Barada 2012).

In contemporary society gender inequalities are present in the expectations concerning childcare, the performance of housework, and emotional labour (Hochschild 1989). Using the theory of gender roles, differences in the conflict of work and family roles can be explained (Korabik et al. 2008, in Grujić et al. 2014). Although the majority of men and women claim that family is more important to them than work, traditional gender ideology attributes different levels of importance of family and work domains to men and women. It is expected that men will be the breadwinners of the family and spend more time at work, while for women it is important that they spend more time at home, taking care of the family, in particular the physical, social, and emotional well-being of the children. Because of this, even when working full time, women who have a partner and children spend more time on childcare and housework than their male partners (Hochschild 1989). They live by the rules and roles that identify them with motherhood, thus creating for themselves a subordinate position in the family. According to the above-mentioned theory, women will always experience wider work – family conflict, while men will experience more of a family – work conflict (Korabik et al. 2008 in Grujić et al. 2014). The difference between the male type of conflict and the female type of conflict cannot be emphasized enough in understanding the Croatian context with a traditional gender role division, which proves to be especially important for labouring in the creative industries' context. Although some generational changes are present, and one can say that the social position of women in Croatia is changing (Tomić-Koludrović and Petrić 2007), they are still expected to fulfil traditional maternal and family roles (Tomić-Koludrović and Lončarić 2007).

After returning from work, women work 'the second shift', as they are dedicated to childcare and housework more than men. Hochschild (1989, p. 38) defined the second shift as work at home, that is, the obligations that a person has at home on returning from their paid workplace: obligations such as shopping, cooking, paying the bills, gardening, and taking care of others. Furthermore, Hochschild (1997) continued by developing the concept of 'the third shift', that is defined as dealing with the emotional aftermath of the second shift. The third shift handles everything that has been collected emotionally and mentally during the second shift, carried out at home. The longer the working day, the more stressful is the time spent at home. Family time becomes precious, while the lack of time and the solutions attempting to rectify this (haste, organization, etc.) put additional pressure on women to engage in the third shift. In the context of the changing nature of work in contemporary capitalist societies, epitomized in creative labour in which all time becomes work time, we further ask how to value women's (creative) work when all the shifts have melted into one.

Women's Labour Turns Creative

The emergence of creative industries has brought a new dynamic into the conceptualization of labour. The initial much-cited definition states that 'the creative industries [are] those industries which have their origin in individual creativity, skill and talent and which have a potential for wealth and job creation through the generation and exploitation of intellectual property' (Creative Industries Fact File 2002). In the scope of the sociology of labour, this definition introduces individual creativity as the specific new element of changing work and economy. Ideally, from manual work through service work comes the creative, mostly digital work, supported by information and communication technology and embedded in the individual *per se*, setting him or her free from the existing socio-economic constraints. Information and communication technologies are a prerequisite for contemporary creative labour, and this strong interconnection of creative labour and ICT has served to a certain extent as a background to the notion that creative labour will be emancipatory for both women and men.

The now almost forgotten and heavily contested ideas of Florida (2002, 2005) were notoriously optimistic in promoting the idea of the new, creative class of mostly young professionals who create their lives and consequently economic value by talentedly using technology in tolerant and multicultural social environments. Their social impact is implicitly vast but also fragile, since this new class is highly sensitive to both culturally and economically restrictive social conditions (Florida 2005). However, this initial social but mostly technological optimism proved to be a misleading notion, because various researchers have since proved that not only the old (gender, race, class, and ethnic inequalities) but other new inequalities are reproduced in creative industries in contemporary capitalist societies (Conor et al. 2015; Hesmondhalgh 2002; Hesmondhalgh and Baker 2011; Primorac 2016; Randle 2015). Labour relations and working conditions are deeply embedded in the social and cultural context, making the changes slower but more profound. In a way, labour culturally lags behind the somewhat superficial technological and economic changes but deeply redefines social relations in the long run. Women's work turns out to be the epitome of creatively redefined labour, changing at its own pace.

This is especially evident in societies with changing but still traditional gender role division, such as the Croatian society (Tomić-Koludrović 2015). Our data and analysis show that female creatives work in propulsive jobs (Barada et al. 2016), but, with them being professionally redomesticated, their everyday life is immersed in typical gender regimes (Walby 1990). As Barada (2012, p. 201) shows, while creative labour in Croatia has been professionally modernized, the female labour experience has not significantly moved from patriarchal practices. Female creative workers are subject to the overall global professional developments, while at the same time they are under pressure from the local particularities, which in this context mean the reproduction of the traditional social and gender roles. This claim is corroborated by the fact that Croatian female creatives, although professionally successful, heading innovative and financially viable CSOs and businesses with a large number of collaborators, are underpaid, overworked, and mostly single, childless, and with neglected health issues (Barada 2012; Barada et al. 2016). If they do have families, then they have to diminish their professional involvement, since most of the housework depends on them. On the other hand, most of the female visual communication designers who do have children have moved out of Zagreb, the capital of Croatia, the most vibrant and creative cultural market. They have returned to their (usually smaller) home towns, where they can rely on help from other female relatives in sustaining family life (Barada 2012), thus bonding them more with home. Long hours of never-ending shifts of creative work collide with traditional gender roles and division of labour, contributing to the contradictory nature of redomestication.

Characteristics of Creative Labour's *Feminization*

Creative labour, albeit primarily situated in individual creativity and agency, is nevertheless reinforced by and dependent on social and cultural relations, which means that the labouring conditions in creative industries are not exempt from broader circumstances and changes in the world of work. Contemporary creatives are labouring in flexible, fragmented, project-oriented, technologically mediated work that is conducted multi-locally and often at home (Primorac 2016). This work is marked by long hours and underpaid wages, short deadlines and continuous availability for work, and self-exploitative but, conversely, highly motivated and devoted workers. Creative workers tend to be overworked, insufficiently paid, prone to having high health risks, and single. They have university diplomas, but they rely heavily on family ties and financial resources when facing a work crisis (Barada et al. 2016; Rašić Bakarić et al. 2015, p. 79). However, men and women of creative industries identify almost zealously with their vocation and profession (Barada et al. 2016, p. 130). Even when feeling overworked and overburdened (Kalleberg 2007), and with a high level of personal burnout, they maintain that they are truly satisfied with their job (Barada et al. 2016, pp. 91–94). As Ross (2008) argued, working in creative industries comes at a high price, both for men and for women. However, the social costs of working in such a profession have completely different ramifications for the everyday lives of women.

In creative jobs, the border between the public and the private sphere is constantly being erased through the continuous conflation of work (and life) practices into one timeless continuum of living to labour (Barada 2012). As previously noted through the work of standpoint theory writers, such attributes of continuous and constant work are characteristics of female everyday life. As Smith stated (2002a, p. 42), the lives of women are characterized by everyday/everynight activities. That is, for female creatives both professional and private activities are ongoing every day and every night, since women's work does not end with daily chores and does not end with the first or second shift. Everyday life is double-layered, since it is both embodied and privately localized as well as being structurally institutionalized (Smith 2002b [1990], p. 317). This means that the experience of everyday life is simultaneously subjective and objective, which makes it thoroughly gendered, since the embodied experience is female and the institutional one is male featured. However, professional women exist in both worlds at the same time, because the professional life requires more structured management and separation of embodied experience then the 'ordinary' everyday, domestic work, making women constantly experience the 'line of fault' (Smith 2002b [1990]). Their private life does not correspond to their professional life and vice versa. In the case in which the working time has engulfed the private time, as occurs in the creative industries, we can safely say that the day has been *feminized*, as its main characteristic is exactly the experience of never-ending and constant immersion in work (Barada 2012).

Hereby we use the term 'feminization' in an unorthodox way, as it usually denotes the numerical and structural change in a particular profession (Abercrombie et al. 2000). However, we use this term to emphasize the lack of borders between private and public, whereby all time is merged into one continuum of *private* and redomesticated everyday practice. As already noted, this is the characteristic of creative labour in general, but it is more evident for women's work day, colloquially described by the feminist motto 'women's work is never done'. Female creative workers are, just as their male counterparts, always available for work and engaged non-stop in work process and practices. Creative work is never done. However, unlike male creatives, female creatives are constantly involved in domestic work and are faced with family obligations expanding throughout the day (Barada 2012). Their work overlaps with their private time, and their private time spills over into work, so that, for example, female visual communication designers who are married with children tend to sleep for just a few hours a day to be able to cater to a demanding job as well as family tasks (Barada 2012, p. 150). With such daily arrangements, and ICT providing the possibility to work from any location, they eventually start choosing to work at home. With time, they become domestic creative workers, less and less visible in the profession. This is also the reason why their client pool remains limited, since they do not have the time to find and expand new professional relations (Barada 2012, p. 151). Being constantly online and working virtually does not compensate for them being literally all the time at home, within the family, confined in the house. This feeling of being 'closed in', in a 'closed off' position in the 'house/home', and in particular business circles, in time even leads to the wish to exit from the profession (Barada and Primorac 2014). Female labour practices become embedded in their private homes and daily activities, forging the implosion of the public into the private sphere. Therefore, although 'creative work is never done' for both male and female workers, creative labour results in covert redomestication of female creatives and contributes to the decrease in the social value of women's work in creative industries.

Concluding Remarks

Throughout this chapter we have shown that female creative labour is characterized by never-ending shifts of everyday – everynight professional and personal activities. To play on the old term by Weber, creative industries have become not the iron but the golden cage for female creatives. Faced, on the one hand, with 'public' redomestication of their work and, on the other hand, with the lack of acknowledgement of their house, family, and care work, these creative women find themselves carrying the multiple intertwined burdens of professional and private labour. They are productive in highly competitive and flexible professions but are also socially reinforced to maintain the traditional gender roles. As the empirical data corroborate, female creatives are economically productive and even professionally established, but they are still at risk of falling through the cracks of double invisibility: since their day is professionally feminized and also home bound, they are actually redomesticated. With this implosion of the public and private realms, female creatives' social presence and impact remain firmly confined within the private. Therefore, the social value of their work is at the least publicly elusive and subservient, while the social costs of their redomestication are privately all-encompassing.

In conclusion, it can safely be stated that the question of female creatives' work is only initially being sketched out in the scope of the sociology of labour and professions. The conceptualization and research operationalization of women's labour when considering the public – private valuing of creative labour and the feminization of working everyday life still fall short of comprehending the social conditions and ramifications of professionally redomesticated female creatives. The puzzle of their individual agency on the one side and their structural social position on the other side might be resolved by rethinking the newly re-established but old issue of *domestic* work. In the case of female creatives, this work is professional and paid but deeply embedded in the home and house (sometimes also family) routines. For them, there is no division between outside, public time and work and private, home time and work. Even though their work exists in terms of economic production and professional establishment, it remains blurred in terms of the socio-cultural reproduction of historically present and currently redefined gender roles.

The beginning of an answer to this puzzle could perhaps be discerned from the idea of Georg Simmel, who claimed that the greatest cultural achievement of women is the creation and maintenance of the home (Simmel and Oakes 1984). Homemaking is the cultural specificity of female existence, since the home is the only social space where women can create both themselves and other members of the family. All the house routines, customs, and relations are creatively produced only by women (Simmel 2001 [1911]). According to Simmel, the concept of the home does not allow the division between the objective culture and the subjective experience. When juxtaposed to the strict, male-defined objective – subjective division, the domestic realm ensures the cultural reproduction and even survival of human society (Simmel 2001 [1911]). In the case of creative labour in contemporary society, objective culture is represented by public life and subjective experience is defined by individual creativity and agency. Inspired by this controversial Simmelian thesis, it just might be proved conceptually and empirically that women in general and female creatives in particular are culturally and individually equipped and prepared for such professional redomestication.

Notes

1. The first research project was conducted in 2010 and 2011 and concentrated on the female visual communication designers in Croatia, executed by the first author of the chapter (Barada 2012). For the study, in the first research cycle, 8 expert interviews with theorists and design professionals were conducted, followed by 36 interviews with female visual communication designers combining biographical and semi-structured techniques. The interviews included designers from the 6 largest Croatian cities, thus providing a regional overview of the data. In addition, secondary and tertiary data on design and creative industries in Croatia were gathered and analysed. The second research project was carried out from 2014 to 2016, and it focused on the condition of work of employed persons in CSOs in the area of contemporary culture and arts in Croatia; it was executed by the authors of the chapter and Dr Edgar Buršić for the Kultura Nova Foundation (Barada et al. 2016). The conclusions from the materials are the authors' only and are not the official position of the Kultura Nova Foundation. For this study, two online questionnaires were con-

structed: the first one was aimed at the institutional conditions of CSOs (N=93), and the second one gathered data from employees in those CSOs (N=111). Furthermore, 22 semi-structured interviews were conducted with long-term employees of CSOs in 9 Croatian cities. To contextualize all of the data, statistical analysis of the Foundation's CSO database was undertaken. Both of these surveys used the mixed-methods approach and covered a time frame of more than 7 years, so the findings are complex and multilayered, giving a good basis for conceptualizing the changes and specific conditions of female creative work.
2. In this chapter we define 'feminist standpoint theory' as a joint term for an approach that was primarily developed by Dorothy E. Smith, Sandra Harding, Nancy M. Hartsock, and Patricia Hill Collins. Although any standpoint approach can have a more general research starting point than the position (or standpoint) from those that are researched, the adjective 'feminist' denotes that it deals with women and that it is developed by feminist authors. Such an approach researches the condition of women from women's position. Dorothy E. Smith used the standpoint to develop feminist methodology, strategy, and finally sociology, taking into account the experience and position of women.
3. Weeks relied on those standpoint theory authors who referred to the Marxist tradition of women's work practices in late capitalist social relations. These are Hilary Rose, Nancy Hartsock, and Dorothy E. Smith (Weeks 2004 [1998], p. 184).
4. By using feminist standpoint theory through women's labour, the collective subjectivity of 'a woman' is constructed and situated between the unique position of a particular individual and a spontaneous, natural community of biological women (Weeks 2004 [1998], p. 189).
5. The first professional association of designers was founded in 1983 (Kršić 2009), comprising mostly men (Barada 2012, p. 100), and the first university programme started in 1989, allowing women to participate in design professions in larger numbers (Barada 2012, p. 101).

References

Abercrombie, N., Hill, S., & Turner, B. S. (2000). *The Penguin dictionary of sociology*. London: Penguin Books.

Barada, V. (2012). *Žensko iskustvo rada u kreativnim industrijama – primjer dizajnerica vizualnih komunikacija u Hrvatskoj*. Zagreb: Filozofski fakultet

Sveučilišta u Zagrebu. Doktorska disertacija. [Women's experience of labour in creative industries – Example of female visual communication designers in Croatia. Doctoral thesis].

Barada, V., & Primorac, J. (2014). Non-paid, under-paid and self-exploiting labour as a choice and a necessity: Example of women in creative industries. In M. Adamović et al. (Eds.), *Young women in post-Yugoslav societies: Research, practice and policy* (pp. 143–163). Zagreb/Sarajevo: Institute for Social Research in Zagreb/Human Rights Centre, University of Sarajevo.

Barada, V., Primorac, J., & Buršić, E. (2016). *Osvajanje prostora rada. Uvjeti rada organizacija civilnog društva na području suvremene kulture i umjetnosti* [Defining the area of work. Labour conditions in civil society organizations in contemporary culture and art]. Zagreb: Zaklada 'Kultura nova'.

Beck, U. (2000). *The brave new world of work*. Cambridge: Polity Press.

Bell, D. (1973). *The coming of post-industrial society. A venture in social forecasting*. Harmondsworth/New York: Penguin Books.

Castells, M. (2000). *Uspon umreženog društva* [The rise of the network society]. Zagreb: Golden Marketing.

Conor, B., Gill, R., & Taylor, S. (2015). Gender and creative labour. *The Sociological Review, 63*(S1), 1–22. https://doi.org/10.1111/1467-954X.12237.

Creative Industries Fact File. (2002). *Department for culture, media and sport creative industries division*. Retrieved from http://webarchive.nationalarchives.gov.uk/+/http://www.culture.gov.uk/PDF/ci_fact_file.pdf. Accessed 15 Apr 2017.

Crompton, R. (1987). Gender, status and professionalism. *Sociology, 21*(3), 413–428.

Dormer, P. (2003). *Design since 1945*. London: Thames & Hudson Ltd.

Florida, R. (2002). *The rise of the creative class. And how it's transforming work, leisure, community and everyday life*. New York: Basic Books.

Florida, R. (2005). *The flight of the creative class*. New York: HarperBusiness.

Folbre, N. (2012). *For love and money. Care provision in the United States*. New York: Russell Sage Foundation.

Grujić, H., Šimunić, A., & Gregov, L. (2014). Konflikt radne i obiteljske uloge kod zaposlenih bračnih drugova: važnost usklađenosti stava prema bračnim ulogama [Work–family conflict among employed spouses: The importance of the compliance of attitudes towards marital roles]. *Društvena istraživanja, 23*(4), 641–659.

Hesmondhalgh, D. (2002). *The cultural industries*. London/Thousand Oaks/New Delhi: Sage Publications.

Hesmondhalgh, D., & Baker, S. (2011). *Creative labor. Media work in three cultural industries*. London/New York: Routledge.

Hochschild, A. R. (1989). *The second shift. Working parents and the revolution at home*. New York: Viking Penguin Inc.

Hochschild, A. R. (1997). *The time bind. When work becomes home and home becomes work*. New York: Metropolitan Books.

Kalleberg, A. L. (2007). *The mismatched worker* (Contemporary societies, 1st). New York/London: W. W. Norton & Company.

Kršić, D. (2009). *Designed in Croatia. Didaktička izložba. V.10.* (deplijan izložbe, Zagreb, 07.05.2009.–22.05.2009.) [Exhibition catalogue].

Lebert, D., & Vercellone, C. (2007). Uloga znanja u dinamici dugog razdoblja kapitalizma: hipoteza o kognitivnom kapitalizmu. In C. Vercellone (Ed.), *Kognitivni kapitalizam. Znanje i financije u postfordističkom razdoblju* [Cognitive capitalism – Knowledge and finance in the post-Fordist period]. Zagreb: Politička kultura..

Millen, D. (1997). Some methodological and epistemological issues raised by doing feminist research on non-feminist women. *Sociological Research Online, 2*(3). Retrieved from http://www.socresonline.org.uk/2/3/3.html

Olesen, V. L. (2003). Feminisms and qualitative research at and into the millennium. In N. K. Denzin & Y. S. Lincoln (Eds.), *The landscape of qualitative research. Theories and issues* (2nd ed., pp. 332–397). Thousand Oaks/London/New Delhi: SAGE Publications.

Petrić, M. (2006). Konteksti. In M. Mrduljaš (Ed.), *Pregled hrvatskog dizajna 040506* [A review of Croatian design 040506] (pp. 8–10). Zagreb: Hrvatsko dizajnersko društvo.

Primorac, J. (2016). Towards more insecurity? Virtual work and the sustainability of creative labour. In J. Webster & K. Randle (Eds.), *Virtual workers and the global labour market*. London: Palgrave Macmillan.

Randle, K. (2015). Class and exclusion at work: The case of UK film and television. In K. Oakley & J. O'Connor (Eds.), *The Routledge companion to the cultural industries* (pp. 330–343). New York: Routledge.

Rašić Bakarić, I., Bačić, K., & Božić, L. (2015). *Mapiranje kreativnih i kulturnih industrija u Republici Hrvatskoj* [Mapping of creative and cultural industries in Croatia]. Zagreb: Ekonomski institut.

Rifkin, J. (1995). *The end of work. The decline of the global labor force and the dawn of the post-market era*. New York: Tarcher/Putnam.

Ross, A. (2003). *No-collar. The humane workplace and its hidden costs*. Philadelphia: Temple University Press.

Ross, A. (2008). The new geography of work: Power to the precarious? *Theory, Culture and Society, 25*(7–8), 31–49.

Simmel, G. (2001 [1911]). *Ženska kultura* [Feminine culture]. In *Kontrapunkti kulture* [Counterpoints of culture]. Zagreb: Naklada Jesenski i Turk.
Simmel, G., & Oakes, G. (1984). *Georg Simmel, on women, sexuality, and love.* New Haven: Yale University Press.
Smith, D. E. (1987). *The everyday world as problematic: A feminist sociology.* Boston: Northeastern University Press.
Smith, D. E. (2002a). Institutional ethnography. In T. May (Ed.), *Qualitative research in action* (pp. 17–52). London/Thousand Oaks/New Delhi: SAGE Publications.
Smith, D. E. (2002b [1990]). The conceptual practices of power. In C. Calhoun et al. (Eds.), *Contemporary sociological theory* (pp. 315–322). Malden/Oxford/Melbourne/Berlin: Blackwell Publishing.
Tomić-Koludrović, I. (2015). *Pomak prema modernosti. Žene u Hrvatskoj u razdoblju 'zrele' tranzicije* [Moving towards modernity: Women in Croatia in the period of 'mature' transition]. Zagreb: Naklada Jesenski i Turk; Hrvatsko sociološko društvo.
Tomić-Koludrović, I., & Lončarić, D. (2007). Promjene rodnih uloga u procesima modernizacije: usporedba Austrije i Hrvatske [Changes of gender roles in processes of modernization: Comparison of Austria and Croatia]. *Acta Iadertina, 3*(3), 55–71.
Tomić-Koludrović, I., & Petrić, M. (2007). Hrvatsko društvo – prije i tijekom tranzicije [Croatian society – before and during transition]. *Društvena istraživanja, 16*(4–5), 867–889.
Touraine, A. (1980 [1969]). *Postindustrijsko društvo* [Postindustrial societies]. Zagreb: Globus.
Walby, S. (1990). *Theorizing patriarchy.* Oxford/Cambridge: Blackwell Publishing.
Walby, S. (2005 [1997]). *Rodne preobrazbe* [Gender transformations]. Zagreb: Ženska infoteka.
Weeks, K. (2004 [1998]). Labor, standpoints, and feminist subjects. In S. Harding (Ed.), *The feminist standpoint theory reader. Intellectual and political controversies* (pp. 181–193). New York/London: Routledge.
Witz, A. (1992). *Professions and patriarchy.* London/New York: Routledge.

8

Digital Inclusion for Better Job Opportunities? The Case of Women E-Included Through Lifelong Learning Programmes

Lidia Arroyo

Introduction

During the first decade of the twenty-first century, the European Digital Policies have focused on providing digital skills to e-excluded social groups, particularly women, the unskilled, and the elderly, which are also socially disadvantaged groups (Van Dijk 2005; Van Deursen 2010). These policies assume that digital inclusion also helps these social groups to overcome their disadvantaged position because of the possibilities provided by the acquisition of digital skills in improving their position in the labour market (European Commission 2010). Ensuring a digitally skilled workforce is a priority for the European policies for job creation, and it is considered particularly relevant to cushion the effects of economic crisis (European Commission 2010, 2012, 2016; McCormac 2010). However, is digital inclusion truly a driving factor behind better job opportunities? This chapter provides some insight into this question by focusing on the job search of women who acquired digital skills through a lifelong

L. Arroyo (✉)
Open University of Catalonia, Barcelona, Spain

learning training programme in Spain. To focus the analysis on these women is of particular interest because they belong to different socially disadvantaged groups.

There has been extensive literature on employment service digital platforms in the field of online job searches, but there is little empirical evidence based on the job search experience and its links with to the improvement of job opportunities (Tso et al. 2010; Kuhn and Mansour 2014). The few studies that have been carried out are mainly quantitative studies performed in the United States (Stevenson 2008; Beard et al. 2012; Kuhn and Mansour 2014). There is a particular lack of evidence regarding the online job search of disadvantaged social groups located in European countries from a qualitative perspective (Campos et al. 2014).

Studies aimed at assessing the changes introduced by the Internet for job seekers have concluded that the Internet has changed the way people search for employment. Their results show that the online job search has expanded quickly since the beginning of the present century (Stevenson 2008; Tso et al. 2010). In terms of the effects of the on-line job search there are two analytical perspectives: the studies that do not take into account social inequalities and those from a critical perspective which incorporate the influence of unequal conditions.

On the one hand, the studies that only focus on the contributions of the on-line job search without taking into consideration the social context and its inequalities highlight that the Internet reduces the costs of a job search, multiplies the possibilities of contacting different employers, and facilitates access to information regarding job vacancies (Kuhn and Skuterud 2004; Tso et al. 2010; Stevenson 2008; Kuhn and Mansour 2014). Stevenson (2008) points out that the Internet allows job seekers to apply for positions at any time of the day without leaving their home while also allowing them to learn more about the organisational culture of the companies to which they are applying. Along the same lines, Feuls et al. (2014) highlight that the Internet has combated the social isolation linked to unemployment. Similarly, Beard et al. (2012) demonstrate that the Internet job search encourages job seekers to continue searching for a job, because the large quantity of job offers challenges the idea that there are no jobs, preventing the unemployed from becoming discouraged.

On the other hand, the studies with a critical perspective examine how social inequality influences the effectiveness of the online job search. These have found that young people and those with a high level of education take better advantage of the Internet than older adults and those with a lower level of education (Green et al. 2012; Campos et al. 2014). These results have added to existing evidence from the social stratification of the Internet usage approach, highlighting that digital inclusion is not a sufficient condition for overcoming existing social inequalities. It has been shown that the further resources and opportunities made possible by the Internet are unequally distributed due to the fact that Internet use differs according to age and socio-educational level. Therefore, the existing power and social structure are reproduced in the online sphere (Gurstein 2003; Sassi 2005; DiMaggio et al. 2004; van Deursen and van Dijk 2014; Selwyn and Facer 2007; Valenduc 2010).

Moreover, there are also studies from a critical perspective that focus on gender inequalities. These researches take into account the practices and representations of women in relation to the Internet. From this perspective, women's Internet experience is influenced by the gender division of labour. This gender division of labour consists in an unequal distribution of the workload in which women are responsible for caregiving and housework – in addition to their jobs – while men are required to focus only on their work in the labour market. Given the unequal distribution of the workload, women with family responsibilities have fewer opportunities for taking advantage of the Internet (Bonder 2002; Wajcman 2004; Castaño 2008; Wyatt 2008; Casula 2011; Simões 2011). In addition, taking into account the subjective dimension, the women's inclusion perspective identifies that both digital technology and the subjectivity of women are constantly evolving and mutually influenced. It is believed that with the appropriation of technology, women adapt its use to their necessities while exploring new dimensions of themselves (Sørensen et al. 2011).

From a social stratification of Internet usage approach by including a gender perspective, this chapter seeks to analyse whether the Internet use helps women from disadvantaged groups to improve their labour position.

Methodological Approach

The results of this chapter are based on episodic interviews with adult women who had participated in a basic digital skills course in the last 10 years in Spain.

The sample comprised 32 adult women who were active in the labour market, 17 of which were unemployed and 15 of which were employed. All of them were trained in basic digital skills through a lifelong learning course linked to a public employment programme.

As shown in Table 8.1, the participants came from different socio-educational backgrounds and age groups, but there is a higher representation of women with a medium or low level of education over the age of 45. The participants' ages ranged between 26 and 61 years old, but nearly three quarters of them were 45 years old (12) or older (11). With regard to the level of studies, these were equally distributed among women with a primary level of education or below (12) and women with a secondary education (12). Only eight of the participants had a higher education level.

Focusing the analysis on this group is particularly appropriate because of their disadvantaged position in the digital sphere and labour market. Ultimately, women from older generations without a higher education have the highest digital gap. Even when they are e-included, the usage gap further contributes to the reinforcement of the knowledge gap and towards further social inequalities (DiMaggio et al. 2004; De Grip and Zwick 2005; Selwyn and Facer 2007; van Deursen and van Dijk 2014; Arroyo and Valenduc 2016).

Table 8.1 Distribution of the sample by age group and education level

	Primary education or below	Secondary education	Higher education	Total by age group
25–29	1	0	0	1
30–34	3	4	1	8
45–54	4	2	6	12
55+	4	6	1	11
Total by level of education	12	12	8	32

Another characteristic of the sample is that it also includes eight immigrant women from the following developing countries: Morocco, Armenia, the Philippines, Cuba, Bolivia and Colombia. This enables an analysis of whether the immigrant condition introduces new perspectives with regard to the Internet experience and job opportunities (Garrido et al. 2009). Furthermore, it is relevant to look into the Spanish labour market because, not only is it one of the European countries with highest levels of long-term unemployment, but it also features levels of digital inclusion above the EU average (Campos et al. 2014; Arroyo and Valenduc 2016).

The episodic interviews (Flick 2000) were structured into three parts. In the first part, the interviewees were asked about their 'digital biography' in order to learn about their Internet use trajectory and explore how they used the Internet in their everyday lives. The second part consisted of more narrowed questions focusing on the Internet as it is related to work and job searching in order to explore whether the Internet use helps these women from disadvantaged groups to improve their labour position. At this point, both the objective and subjective dimensions were explored. This included questions on the specific uses of the Internet related to the job search process and employment issues, the material changes in their labour situation since becoming digitally included and its relation to Internet use, and their subjective vision of how the Internet can help them to find a job and improve their labour situation. Finally, the interview finished with a question that posed a hypothetical situation on the recommendations that they would give regarding Internet use to an e-excluded friend.

The interviews were coded using the qualitative data analysis software ATLAS.ti by adapting the main concepts of the social stratification of Internet usage approach (Sassi 2005; Valenduc 2010) from a gender perspective (Wajcman 2004; Wyatt 2008) and the women's inclusion perspective (Sørensen et al. 2011) to the empirical material. To do this, the codes were structured in three main families: digital practices related to the job search, material changes in their labour position and a subjective dimension which includes changes in their self-representations and discourses around the use of the Internet and the job opportunities.

Practices and Results of the Online Job Search for Disadvantaged Women

In this section, it is explored what contributions and what limitations offers the digital practices related to the job search for the interviewed women in terms of material changes, discourses and self-representations. In accordance with the social stratification of the Internet usage approach (Sassi 2005; Valenduc 2010) and the gender perspective (Bonder 2002; Wajcman 2004; Wyatt 2008) the contributions of digital technologies are shaped by social context and its social and gender inequalities. As the interviewees belongs to different socially disadvantaged groups, the results offers nuanced evidence on how the different axis of inequalities influence the use and results of the Internet for the job search.

In terms of digital practices, the participants mainly used the Internet to send their CVs and to search for jobs through online platforms such as InfoJobs, Trovit, Facebook or LinkedIn. The women in the sample who were characterised as being more disadvantaged did not use the Internet to get more information on the organisational culture of the companies to adapt their job profile to offers. This result differs from the research performed by Stevenson (2008) reinforces the social stratification of the Internet usage approach.

With regard to material changes related to the use of the Internet, the online job search was only effective in five cases. These women found positions as commercial agents, school lunch supervisors, non-qualified factory workers and cleaners. In addition to the scarce job positions found, three of them reported that they rejected offers because the conditions were degrading in terms of salary or due to lack of respect:

> *[The offer] didn't interest me because I consider that it is true that there is a great need, there is a lack of jobs, but one has to be respected as a person. After all, we are all people.* (41-year-old employed non-immigrant woman with a post-secondary non-tertiary education)
>
> *But sometimes they require something and you say, 'no, no, no, I don't play this game'.* (38-year-old unemployed immigrant woman with a primary education)

In terms of discourse, some ambivalence can be detected with regard to the participants' opinions on the usefulness of the Internet in finding a job. When exploring the contributions of the online job search process, the women interviewed stressed that they believed the Internet is a useful tool for helping them in searching for a job, as the quantitative research results demonstrated (Kuhn and Skuterud 2004; Tso et al. 2010; Stevenson 2008; Kuhn and Mansour 2014). The interviewees stated that they valued the large amount of job notice boards and the information about the companies who were recruiting personnel as well as the facilities offered by the Internet to contact companies and send CVs.

Despite the positive opinions that claimed it was a useful tool for the job search process, the women interviewed also pointed out that the Internet is the only option to search for a job today. They were very critical of the fact that companies no longer accept CVs delivered by hand and that they were forced to send their CVs online. Seven of them said they preferred face-to-face interaction with employers because they believe it is important that the company meets them in person:

> *So everything is on the Internet. I don't like this very much. I liked it more before, when you went, delivered your CV by hand and they saw you in person. Now, they somehow reject you and send you messages. Some company rejects you based on what they're asking for, on your profile...In that sense, I don't like it. In the past, you went to a company and said 'I'm leaving my CV'. Not anymore. Now, they no longer accept it. Now everything has to be done via Internet... And there, you don't know if they've got it or if they delete it directly.* (35-year-old unemployed non-immigrant woman with a secondary education)

This criticism of the Internet job search process leads us to revise the conclusion of Stevenson (2008) and Tso et al. (2010) regarding the online job search preference simply because it reduces the costs of submitting a CV to employers. On the contrary, the women interviewed valued face-to-face contact as a way of ensuring that applicants are assessed according to the complete set of skills that they possess (De Grip and Zwick 2005). This may be relevant especially for women from disadvantaged groups, who are afraid of being automatically excluded from a job offer through the online selection process when the employer looks at their CV, without offering them the opportunity to meet in person.

However, while the Spanish women interviewed expressed a general preference for delivering their CVs by hand, this was not applicable in the case of the immigrant women. On the contrary, the immigrants interviewed highlighted the advantages of online communication when sending their applications. Unlike the other women, they believed that this was the best way to ensure that the company received their CV, unlike the cases when they tried to deliver it in person and were rejected directly. They believed that they had a more equal opportunity to find a job and to avoid direct discrimination because of their immigrant status with this strategy.

> *Well, you find a lot of [job] offers through the Internet, but without the Internet you can't find any. Because now you go to the company to deliver your CV and they don't take it. But with the Internet, you send it and that's it. You find this easy. You feel calmer. You say 'look, today I've sent five, for example, and I'm happy. I've sent five'. Let's see if one of the five calls me. But without the Internet, all the doors are closed. Because I've tried this. I've taken the CV and delivered it by hand to the company and I say, 'Can I leave my CV?', and they say, 'No, no, no. We don't need anyone right now'. Then you become nervous. But not through the Internet. You send it over the Internet and you feel calmer, not nervous or…or upset.* (38-year-old unemployed immigrant woman with a primary education)

Thus, although the women who identified some gaps in their profile were reluctant about online job submission and preferred face-to-face interaction to avoid direct rejection as candidates, the online job search was seen as a way of ensuring more equal opportunities in the case of immigrant women. The lack of social capital that characterised immigrant women and added more obstacles to finding a job than non-immigrants is also significant for analysing the immigrants' preference for online job applications (Garrido et al. 2009). In-line with the results of previous researches that examined job seekers with low social capital

(Campos et al. 2014), the Internet can be a good tool through which people without a social network can access employment opportunities.

In terms of social networks, Feuls et al. (2014) highlighted that the Internet helps to combat social withdrawal and dampen the mental health problems that are a consequence of long-term unemployment. In the case of the women interviewed, they reported that the reinforcement of social networks when it came to facing social isolation was more linked to their involvement in a lifelong programme in which the participants shared the same unemployment status than to their use of the Internet. For instance, one of the interviewees reported that she took training courses not only 'to retrain as a worker' but also 'to avoid staying at home'. In addition, another long-term unemployed participant highlighted that the training course for the unemployed was very rewarding because she met other women in the same situation; they 'encouraged one another and this helped a lot':

> *I took this 50-hour course…she says, 'Are you interested in this [course]?', and I say, 'Yes, to be honest', so I don't stay at home and to always refresh yourself a bit.* (59-year-old long-term unemployed non-immigrant woman with a post-secondary non-tertiary education)
>
> *The companionship helps a lot. In the Job Search [programme] we came to, and in this [Internet course], I had a good time. Not only because you learn something new, but also because you meet people…we encourage each other and that does a lot.* (51-year-old unemployed non-immigrant woman with a primary education)

And with regard to self-representations, women positively valued their Internet experience in terms of their autonomy. The interviewees with a lower level of education greatly appreciated the acquisition of digital skills because they helped them to be able to find a job on their own. As the women explored a new perspective on digital inclusion, this inclusion encouraged them to explore new dimensions of themselves that brought them more autonomy and self-esteem (Sørensen et al. 2011).

This empowerment through the acquisition of digital skills is also related to participation in a basic digital skills course linked to an employment programme. The interviewees said they valued the support of the instructors because they helped them to overcome their fear of not using the Internet properly. This also reinforces Sørensen et al. (2011) idea regarding the necessity to further develop digital inclusion public policies to assure that the entire population – particularly women with fewer advantages – acquire the proper digital skills for their emancipation.

> *We took a course in basic informatics at the Employment Agency…and the truth is that it's great because I've learned how to look for a job, how to search.* (46-year-old employed non-immigrant woman with a primary education)
> *Before, nothing. I wasn't even able to send a CV or anything. With this course, now I understand it pretty well…Now I'm able to look for a job by myself; I'm able to save my things. I've learned a lot, you know? Now I'm able to send my CV to companies. In the past, I always needed help with these little things.* (49-year-old unemployed immigrant woman with less than a primary education)

In the case of immigrant women, they also highlighted the change that the use of the Internet introduced in order to be able to find the company's address and get there by themselves. These women stressed the significant impacts that Internet use had on their autonomy and self-esteem:

> *It has changed because before, without the Internet, I didn't know how to do it. But now, now I'm good at the Internet, because I can, for example, go to a place, I search for it on the Internet, and it's easy for me. But before I couldn't, I had to ask for help, always with someone next to me. Not anymore. Now, with the Internet, I go by myself… Yes, the Internet has changed me a lot. Before, I was shy, fearful, like 'I'm scared'… But not anymore. Now I've changed a lot.* (38-year-old unemployed immigrant woman with a primary education)

After analysing the contributions and limitations of the online job search according to the women interviewed, it was found that it is necessary to consider how digital technologies are appropriated by users according their social context and opportunities (Gurstein 2003; Wajcman 2004; Sassi 2005; DiMaggio et al. 2004; Valenduc 2010; Wyatt 2008). Although the Spanish women positively valued the Internet as a good tool for the job search, they preferred face-to-face interaction with the company in order to avoid exclusion because of the gaps in their employment profiles. However, immigrant women found the online option more inclusive. In terms of autonomy and self-esteem, both the immigrants and non-immigrants expressed having a positive experience in terms of their Internet usage. Usually, it was also linked to their participation in a lifelong learning programme with other women in a similar situation.

Beyond Digital Skills: Age, Education, Gender and Labour Opportunities

In accordance with the social stratification of the Internet approach (Gurstein 2003; Sassi 2005; DiMaggio et al. 2004; van Deursen and van Dijk 2014; Selwyn and Facer 2007; Valenduc 2010), the women interviewed considered the acquisition of digital skills to be an insufficient condition for finding a job because of other inequalities that prevent them from accessing job opportunities. They stressed the added difficulties that they face in the labour market on account of their age, their education level, their lack of language skills, their family responsibilities and the scarce labour opportunities in Spain due to the economic crisis.

Age discrimination was detected by five of the unemployed women who expressed that they felt they had fewer opportunities for finding a job than younger women. Not only did the oldest women of the sample (who were over 55 years old) detect this age discrimination, but two immigrant women aged 49 and 38 also found that the job offers were targeted at younger women. In addition, one of them guessed that she was automatically eliminated from the selection processes when the employers identified her age on her CV.

> *I've never found a job through the Internet. I sent my CV and I've looked, but nothing came from it; there are no jobs. I think it's because you write your age and things like that, and my age and everything is on my CV. There are no job possibilities for me because of my age, you know? Not for me. After 40, it's more difficult to find a job.* (49-year-old unemployed immigrant with less than a primary education)

The older participants also related age with level of studies. They believed that younger people have a higher level of education and can thus count on more labour opportunities. One 59-year-old woman interviewed stated that this situation is very depressing, because there are even younger women with a higher education who have not found a job, so her expectations decreased. She said that she continuously sends CVs online, but she does not receive any replies:

> *Yes, what happens is that it's depressing now because, look, in the last course that we did here, there were young women in their thirty-somethings, forties, and they didn't find anything either. They're administrative, and they are perhaps more up-to-date…because they've just finished their university degrees and everything, and they told me that it's depressing because you send 20 CVs and they don't even answer to say, 'hey, look, we're not interested'. Of course, it's true that if they received 200 CVs they're not going to call 200 people to say no. They're not going to say no 200 times. So I, well, I keep sending, to everything I see….* (59-year-old long-term unemployed non-immigrant with a post-secondary non-tertiary education)

This quotation challenges what Beard et al. (2012) pointed out about the role of the Internet in preventing job seekers from discouragement because of the huge amount of job offers. As this women stresses, it is very frustrating to send many applications and get no answer. Therefore, not only is it important to detect job offers, but also to receive positive responses to stay encouraged.

In relation to the level of studies, there was one immigrant woman interviewed who studied a professional training programme in Business Administration in her country but was working as a domestic worker in Spain at the time of the interview. She stated that despite the acquisition of digital skills, she still needed to learn the local language to be able to improve her labour position.

> *There, I worked in an office as a receptionist… Now, I'm working as a domestic servant here. It's very different…It's very different because here you have to learn more things, learn more languages. You need to learn Catalan and it's lacking…I have to study first before changing my job.* (55-year-old employed immigrant woman with a post-secondary non-tertiary education)

In the case of non-immigrant respondents, they raised the issue of language in terms of their lack of foreign language skills such as English, French or German when looking for administrative jobs:

It's complicated. At my age it's more complicated. They require a lot of languages from you and I don't have any foreign languages. For any administrative position, you need English, German, French and perhaps I don't have the proper age...I do have the right age, but not to start studying a language... You start looking [for a job] and you say, 'This is my profile', but later, they require German, English, one thing or another and that's it. (59-year-old long-term unemployed woman with a post-secondary non-tertiary education)

Therefore, a lack of language skills in combination with the level of education can mitigate the effectiveness of the possibilities offered by digital skills in finding for these women in a labour market where communication skills are crucial (DiMaggio et al. 2004; De Grip and Zwick 2005; van Deursen and van Dijk 2014). As the social stratification of the use of the Internet approach suggests, workers with low levels of education or immigrants who are not fluent in the local language have additional difficulties in taking advantage of their e-skills in the labour market (Garrido et al. 2009; Selwyn and Facer 2007; Valenduc 2010). In addition, as pointed out by the gender perspective of Internet usage (Bonder 2002; Wajcman 2004; Casula 2011; Simões 2011), the women interviewed who have family responsibilities are only able to connect to the Internet when they finish their domestic and caregiving tasks. Thus, they admit to encountering difficulties finding a job due to their schedules and the demands of their responsibilities. For example, there was the case of an immigrant woman with children under the age of 10 who stated that she could not find a job because the working hours were not compatible with caring for her three children. In addition, there was another case of a non-immigrant woman who had to take care of her disabled son and her dependent mother and indicated that she could not find a job because of her family responsibilities.

Moreover, beyond their position in the social structure, the interviewees also highlight that there is a lack of job opportunities due to the depressed economy in Spain. This situation discourages the possibilities of finding a job despite the respondents' efforts to acquire new skills. This discouragement extended to unemployed women with every education level:

> I don't know to what extent for finding a job [through the Internet]. I haven't tried it, either, but I don't know. It's just that I know very few people who have found a job just because of something like this. Plus, the situation is very bad. (51-year-old unemployed non-immigrant woman with a higher education)

Therefore, in order to put digital skills into practice to find a job, it is first essential to have job opportunities (Garrido et al. 2012). This condition is particularly critical in the case of older women with low levels of education, immigrant women or those with family responsibilities. Thus, as gender perspective and social stratification of the Internet usage approach point out, it is important to take social and gender inequalities in the labour market into consideration to assess the extent to which digital skills improve women's labour position.

Concluding Remarks

This qualitative study focused on women who acquired digital skills through a lifelong learning training programme in Spain. The results of the study add more nuanced evidence to the contributions and limitations of Internet use in finding better job opportunities when carrying out a job search. As the profile of the sample interviewed was mainly older women with low education levels who were looking for jobs – including immigrant women – this study has contributed to the analysis by adopting the perspective of these socially disadvantaged groups.

Despite the participants' positive evaluation of the Internet for searching for jobs, few of them have found a position using this method. Many of the Spanish women claimed they prefer face-to-face interaction for delivering their CVs because they were afraid of being automatically excluded in the online job selection processes due to there being something missing in their profile. However, more immigrant women preferred online job submissions because they believed that the Internet allowed them to avoid direct discrimination and thought it could be a good resource in supplementing a lack of social capital.

In terms of subjectivity, the women interviewed valued the acquisition of digital skills in reinforcing their autonomy and self-esteem and combatting the social isolation linked to long-term unemployment, as the women's inclusion perspective pointed out (Sørensen et al. 2011). However, this positive consideration is not related to the use of the Internet in itself. Instead, it is linked more strongly to their participation in lifelong learning programmes in which they found other women in the same situation.

Although the acquisition of digital skills did help to strengthen their autonomy and self-esteem, the women interviewed highlighted that their acquisition did not ensure more job opportunities. They pointed out that there are other inequalities that hinder the possibility of finding a job, such as age discrimination, their level of studies and language proficiency, thus adding evidence to the social stratification of the use of the Internet approach (Gurstein 2003; Sassi 2005; DiMaggio et al. 2004; van Deursen and van Dijk 2014; Selwyn and Facer 2007; Valenduc 2010). In addition, the unequal distribution of work means that women are not able to take full advantage of the Internet, as the gender perspective indicates (Bonder 2002; Wajcman 2004; Castaño 2008; Wyatt 2008; Casula 2011; Simões 2011). Therefore, women with family responsibilities face added difficulties in finding a job.

This analysis adds evidence to the politics of contradiction of the implications of digital technologies in terms of labour opportunities for disadvantaged women. Although digital technologies can be a source to improve the efficiency of job search and contribute to empower the self-representations of women, the gender and social inequalities shape the potentialities of the Internet use for improve the labour position of job seekers.

These results have policy implications in two directions. On the one hand, it is crucial to continue developing lifelong learning programmes for digital skills that link employment skills to experience using the Internet and facilitate social interaction among people in similar conditions. On the other hand, digital programmes for better job opportunities must not only promote the acquisition of digital skills but also other basic skills such as knowledge of a foreign language. Moreover, these policies have to be coordinated with other social policies that avoid age, race and gender discrimination.

References

Arroyo, L., & Valenduc, G. (2016). *Digital skills and labour opportunities for low-skilled woman* (Dynamics of virtual work Working paper series 6). University of Hertfordshire. http://dynamicsofvirtualwork.com/wp-content/uploads/2015/08/COST-Action-IS1202-Working-Paper-6.pdf. Accessed 31 Aug 2017.

Beard, T. R., Ford, G. S., Saba, R. P., & Seals, R. A. (2012). Internet use and job search. *Telecommunications Policy, 36*(4), 260–273.

Bonder, G. (2002). *Las nuevas tecnologías de información y las mujeres: reflexiones necesarias*. United Nations Publications. http://repositorio.cepal.org/bitstream/handle/11362/5894/S026404_es.pdf;jsessionid=2D22538A8CAA5448DC2F073415955A7B?sequence=1. Accessed 31 Aug 2017.

Campos, R., Arrazola, M., & de Hevia, J. (2014). Online job search in the Spanish labor market. *Telecommunications Policy, 38*(11), 1095–1116.

Castaño, C. (Dir). (2008). *La segunda brecha digital*. Madrid: Cátedra. Universitat de València. Instituto de la Mujer.

Casula, C. (2011). L'enracinement social des inégalités numériques: la difficile intégration fes femmes italiennes à la société de l'information. *Tic&société, 5*(1). http://ticetsociete.revues.org/987. Accessed 31 Aug 2017.

De Grip, A., & Zwick, T. (2005). *The employability of low-skilled workers in the knowledge economy* (Unpublished manuscript). Maastricht. http://www.forschungsnetzwerk.at/downloadpub/2004_zwick_grip.pdf. Accessed 31 Aug 2017.

DiMaggio, P., et al. (2004). From unequal access to differentiated use: A literature review and agenda for research on digital inequality. In K. Neckerman (Ed.), *Social inequality* (pp. 355–400). New York: Russell Sage Foundation.

European Commission. (2010). *A digital agenda for Europe*. http://ec.europa.eu/information_society/digital-agenda/documents/digital-agenda-communication-en.pdf. Accessed 31 Aug 2017.

European Commission. (2012). *Towards a job-rich recovery*. http://eur-lex.europa.eu/LexUriServ/LexUriServ.do?uri=COM:2012:0173:FIN:EN:PDF. Accessed 31 Aug 2017.

European Commission. (2016). *A new skills agenda for Europe: Working together to strengthen human capital, employability and competitiveness.* https://ec.europa.eu/epale/sites/epale/files/a_new_skills_agenda_for_europe.pdf. Accessed 31 Aug 2017.

Feuls, M., et al. (2014). A social net? Internet and social media use during unemployment. *Work, Employment & Society, 28*(4), 551–570.

Flick, U. (2000). Episodic interviewing. In M. W. Bauer & G. Gaskell (Eds.), *Qualitative researching with text, image and sound: A practical handbook* (pp. 75–93). London: Sage Publications.

Garrido, M., Rissola, G., Rastrelli, M., Diaz, A., & Ruiz, J. (2009). *Immigrant women, e-skills and employability in Europe: The case of Hungary, Italy, the Netherlands, Romania, and Spain.* Washington, DC: Technology & Social Change Group (TASCHA), University of Washington. https://digital.lib.washington.edu/xmlui/handle/1773/16288. Accessed 31 Aug 2017.

Garrido, M., Sullivan, J., & Gordon, A. (2012). Understanding the links between ICT skills training and employability: An analytical framework. *Information Technologies and International Development, 8*(2), 17–32.

Green, A., Li, Y., Owen, D., & de Hoyos, M. (2012). Inequalities in use of the internet for job search: Similarities and contrasts by economic status in great Britain. *Environment and Planning A, 44*(10), 2344–2358.

Gurstein, M. (2003). Effective use: A community informatics strategy beyond the digital divide. *First Monday, 8*(12). http://firstmonday.org/ojs/index.php/fm/article/view/1107. Accessed 31 Aug 2017.

Kuhn, P., & Mansour, H. (2014). Is internet job search still ineffective? *The Economic Journal, 124*(581), 1213–1233.

Kuhn, P., & Skuterud, M. (2004). Internet job search and unemployment durations. *The American Economic Review, 94*(1), 218–232.

McCormac, A. (2010). *The e-skills Manifesto.* European Schoolnet. Retrieved from http://gesi.org/files/Reports/The%20e-Skills%20Manifesto.pdf. Accessed 31 Aug 2017.

Sassi, S. (2005). Cultural differentiation or social segregation? Four approaches to the digital divide. *New Media & Society, 7*(5), 684–700.

Selwyn, N., & Facer, K. (2007). *Beyond the digital divide: Rethinking digital inclusion for the 21st century.* Futurelab. https://www.nfer.ac.uk/publications/FUTL55. Accessed 31 Aug 2017.

Simões, M. J. (2011). Género e tecnologias da informação e da comunicação no espaço doméstico: Não chega ter, é preciso saber, querer é poder usar. *Configurações, 8,* 155–162.

Sørensen, K. H., Faulkner, W., & Rommes, E. (2011). *Technologies of inclusion: Gender in the information society*. Trondheim: Tapir Academic Press.

Stevenson, B. (2008). *The Internet and job search* (Working paper no. 13886). National Bureau of Economic Research. http://www.nber.org/papers/w13886. Accessed 31 Aug 2017.

Tso, G. K., Yau, K. K., & Cheung, M. S. (2010). Latent constructs determining internet job search behaviors: Motivation, opportunity and job change intention. *Computers in Human Behavior, 26*(2), 122–131.

Valenduc, G. (2010). *The second order digital divide* (Synthesis of the research report). Namur: FTU – Fondation Travail-Université. http://www.ftu-namur.org/fichiers/FTU-Second_order_digital_divide-Synthesis.pdf. Accessed 31 Aug 2017.

Van Deursen, A. J. (2010). *Internet skills, vital assets in an information society*. Enschede: University of Twente. https://research.utwente.nl/en/publications/internet-skills-vital-assets-in-an-information-society. Accessed 31 Aug 2017.

Van Deursen, A. J., & Van Dijk, J. A. (2014). The digital divide shifts to differences in usage. *New Media & Society, 16*(3), 507–526.

Van Dijk, J. (2005). *The deepening divide. Inequality in the information society*. London: Sage.

Wajcman, J. (2004). *Technofeminism*. Cambridge: Polity Press.

Wyatt, S. (2008). Feminism, technology and the information society. Learning from the past, imagining the future. *Information, Communication & Society, 11*(1), 111–130.

Part III

Contradictions in Human Interaction and Communication

9

A Recent Story About Uber

Brian Beaton

Mobile and wearable technologies with near-constant digital connectivity have been surfacing inside literary works, along with the many apps (software applications) that run on such devices. Apps have become narrative features inside our storyworlds, not just features on our smartphone, tablet, and wearable computing screens. In addition to documenting and analysing some of the recent literary expression around apps, this chapter highlights how creative workers involved in literary production have been helping to record some of the 'conflictual politics' (Schaffer et al. 2017) that gave the history of early app culture some of its structure and feel. The term 'conflictual politics' is used here to highlight tensions between capital and labour: literary works have helped to chronicle when and how early apps were part of specific political and economic contexts, as well as how early apps functioned as technologies of labour extraction. In addition to clashes between capital and labour, the term 'conflictual politics' is also used here to highlight cultural clashes (and social disconnections) that specific apps helped to facilitate or accelerate. In many parts of the world, early apps produced uncountable scenes of interpersonal conflict

---

B. Beaton (✉)
California Polytechnic State University, San Luis Obispo, CA, USA

© The Author(s) 2018
P. Bilić et al. (eds.), *Technologies of Labour and the Politics of Contradiction*, Dynamics of Virtual Work, https://doi.org/10.1007/978-3-319-76279-1_9

and contradiction as part of their growing place within everyday lived experience, human social relations, and work formations. Stories about apps produced by creative writers offer a record of such conflicts and contradictions—a rich data source about early apps and human societies for present and future analysis. A recent story about Uber is the example on which this chapter focuses, a piece of literature by the American author Colby Buzzell published under the title 'My Life Driving Uber as an Iraq War Veteran with PTSD' (2015).

Buzzell opens the story, which is autobiographical, by describing a war medal that he keeps on the dashboard of his Uber vehicle: 'It's supposed to be a conversation starter, a way to bridge the gap between the passengers who are constantly coming in and going out of my car.' Despite the gesture at connection, the Uber passengers 'spend the ride staring down at their phones,' and spend the duration of Buzzell's story ignoring the driver and his war medal. The story is organized around a persistent perceptual gap between the Uber driver and his passengers. Instead of engaging with Buzzell, or with the complexities of war and militarism, Uber passengers within the story focus largely on their mobile devices and on information and web services. Buzzell provides the reader with several variations of this observation and theme: 'They [passengers] get all dressed up and socialize with one another electronically via their cell phones,' he writes. 'While driving these people around one of the most picturesque cities in the country [San Francisco], I just see the glow illuminating from their cell phones, radiating off their faces while they text.' Buzzell's attention, according to the story, is also stuck on a screen: 'You pick up whoever the damn app tells you to pick up and you follow the thin blue line on your app that tells you exactly where to go.'

Buzzell's concerted effort to start particular lines of conversation, his attempts to use a war medal as an expressive technology to share personal history and experience, fails to find success. While in theory Ubering might afford new moments of proximity across social divides, as Buzzell portrays it the structure of such encounters and the presence of conflicting screens—one or more screen(s) for the driver and one or more screen(s) for the passenger(s)—makes certain kinds of co-present interaction and sharing extremely difficult inside Ubers, the alleged epicentre of what some call a larger 'sharing' economy. The Uber passengers in Buzzell's account are unmoved by their immediate surroundings, despite being on the move in an Uber car and facing an evocative context and a human driver looking to share accounts of war. Meanwhile, the driver in Buzzell's story has to maintain continuous engagement with a navigation app. The overall effect, according to the story, is an immersive, cocooned experience marked by near-total disconnection between the driver and passenger(s).

In many ways, Buzzell's treatment of Ubering supports a provocative line of argument made by the Toronto School media theorist Sarah Sharma. In Sharma's research on the social world of urban taxis, she argues that taxis have come to function as a 'medium' akin to something like cinema, radio, or television and that taxis offer medium-specific space-time engagements (Sharma 2008). Taxis are 'new media,' and Ubers too, and are approachable as new media, according to Sharma. Not just because multiple screens now commonly appear inside such vehicles but also because, as Sharma's critical and creative research demonstrates, of how passengers use taxis to engage in complex fantasies about interacting with specific kinds of people and places, and to act out elaborate desires for certain kinds of interpersonal exchanges (Sharma 2010)—not entirely distinct from what happens when people engage with, say, digital cinema. Buzzell's recent story about Uber reveals a similar pattern involving Uber drivers but the desire goes the other direction, with Buzzell longing for specific kinds of sharing with his passengers.

What makes Buzzell's recent story about Uber all the more important is how the story captures two distinct processes that have been happening simultaneously in both the recent past and the present day, twin processes that seem to be altering our very sociotechnical condition in fundamental ways, changing what technology means and which technologies matter. Buzzell's portrayal of competing screens inside the Uber and of app-enhanced or app-accelerated perceptual divides is anchored to the opening description of the war medal and its failure as expressive technology to capture the attention of his passengers. Ultimately, Buzzell refuses to offer a literary treatment of Uber without also attending to a concurrent technological process: the war medal's inability to stir.

In this way, Buzzell's recent story about Uber is a much-needed contribution to the growing body of contemporary literature that contains pre-installed and downloaded apps as core narrative features. When it comes to our current moment, *two* things are happening simultaneously that demand equal attention and yet few authors have figured out how to include both processes within the same work. The first process is the proliferation of 'new' digital technologies. Many of these technologies appear 'new' only because of misconceptions regarding material substrates and a general lack of knowledge regarding the genealogy of digital devices (Allen-Robertson 2017), including a lack of knowledge among many working writers.

The second process is much less documented and understood, if not also far more fascinating. One possible name for it is *technology recession:* the 'social death' of older technologies that have suddenly lost their cultural value, user communities, maintainability, or everyday legibility. Technologies are receding from our contemporary societies in dramatic fashion, nearly overnight, presumably across every sector and niche of human culture and work. Many technologies have entered a phase of their 'social life' nearing what looks to be a potential end point. The war medal in Buzzell's recent story about Uber is a textbook illustration of technology recession, an impressive example of a process far too often left out of how contemporary technology is framed and discussed.

Despite the severity of technology recession in the present day, perhaps the largest such occurrence in human history, almost nothing about the process is being systematically studied. The time and space-bound erosions of value and relevancy that so many technologies experience: left out of most accounts, both creative and scholarly. The precise timing, character, and location of a technology at the very instant it becomes démodé: largely ignored. In what settings and through what specific contexts do specific technologies lose their cultural relevance or meaning? When and how do particular technologies lose their acquired affordances or functionalities? The American author Bruce Sterling (2008) has suggested that we live in the 'Golden Age of Dead Media,' meaning that numerous media technologies are dying off in favour of digital replacements. This chapter argues that Sterling has been perhaps too narrow in his description of our recent past and present. We live in a time of mass *technology* extinction that includes media technologies, yes, but also financial technologies, retail technologies, military technologies, energy technologies, medical technologies, educational technologies, expressive technologies, and so forth. The death is everywhere; one can almost smell the technological carnage surrounding us, and that began to surround those who lived through the recent past.

In fact, technology recession could become the far more important event underway right now in human history, something even more significant than cases of 'new' technology creation—which is what still dominates much of the current writing in technology studies. The very future of (digital) technology's history is tied to an accumulation of individual technology sunsets that have yet to receive thorough investigation. What Buzzell's recent story about Uber helps us to remember is that for every storyworld that features smartphones, tablets, wearables, and apps there should also be something like a war medal in the background of the plot, setting, or characterization—*technology receding*, something concrete and specific losing some or all of its acquired charge or meaning.

Uber Technologies, Inc. and the UberMILITARY Campaign

By the time Uber launched in 2009, a rich body of transnational knowledge had been created around the concept of mixing information technology networks with personal travel services. In the early 2000s, a group of taxi companies in the city-state of Singapore began experimenting with an Automatic Vehicle Location and Dispatch System (AVLDS) that aimed to match taxi drivers and passengers based on their mutual geographic coordinates using a shared database of Singapore's streets, wireless communications systems, real-time data transmission, and a variety of new taxi request mechanisms that included special telephone hotlines and personal computing (PC) interfaces (Liao 2005). Similarly, in 2006, a group of transportation researchers in Taipei City carried out (and later publicized) an experiment with taxi 'sharing' that involved matching passengers and vehicles in Taipei Nei-Hu Science and Technology Park using the Internet, mobile devices, and a pair of algorithms that were specifically developed around the challenge of factoring personal preferences into collaborative trip-making (Tao 2007). In fact, these kinds of experiments in taxi procurement and 'dynamic ridesharing' can be traced back to the 1990s and include an assortment of other, under-remembered efforts in not only Asia but also Europe and the United States (dynamicridesharing.org 2015).

Building on these earlier ideas and experiments, the Uber app described in Buzzell's story made a number of different things possible. For passengers, the app personalized travel to places that were previously un- or underserved by existing public transportation infrastructures and traditional taxis, as well as provided transportation services along established travel routes. Through the Uber app, prospective passengers could arrange individual trips to less-traveled (or un-traveled) destinations, opening up whole areas to personal traveling that were previously inaccessible. In this way, the Uber app greatly eased travel within areas where it was cumbersome, as well as made travel 'ungrid-able' (Myers 2016) from standardized travel pathways and schedules. More than merely duplicating pre-existing transportation infrastructures, recursively covering the same terrains as older forms of public and private transportation, Uber and apps like it quickly expanded personal travel in cities, suburbs, and rural areas worldwide. The Uber app also promised to expand tourism. Truly personalized travel made thinkable the idea of totally tailored tourism decoupled from historical patterns of sightseeing and voyaging. Apps like Uber personalized wayfinding, disentangling it from previous travel options that came over time to privilege only certain types of destinations and only certain ways of getting to them.

Uber's software stack would help to coordinate each trip and transaction—including rider-driver matching, payment, and records creation. Uber drivers like Buzzell would then 'share' their own vehicles to provide Uber passengers with rides. These 'sharing' drivers, as was widely noted in popular press coverage of Uber by the time Buzzell was writing about it, typically lacked not only traditional labor relations but also personally shouldered the risk and expense of driving 'with' Uber. Drivers had to buy or lease their own vehicles, and they also had to maintain levels of insurance dictated by Uber Technologies, Incorporated. In addition, drivers had to pay for their own vehicle registration, vehicle maintenance, operating equipment, and fuel. According to the 'Terms of Service' (ToS) that came with the app at the time Buzzell was writing about it, Uber went so far as to exclaim (in all capital letters): 'UBER DOES NOT PROVIDE TRANSPORTATION OR LOGISTICS SERVICES OR FUNCTION AS A TRANSPORTATION CARRIER' (Uber 2015). The company, according to the ToS, merely provided a software stack that was used by others to provide personal transportation services.

Yet critical to understanding Buzzell's recent story is how Uber targeted specific communities in its driver recruitment efforts, something that often goes under-noted in accounts of Uber's labour practices. At the time Buzzell crafted 'My Life Driving Uber as an Iraq War Veteran with PTSD,' Uber Technologies, Incorporated was running a large-scale 'UberMILITARY' campaign specifically designed to recruit US troops and recent veterans as new Uber drivers. Waves of US soldiers were returning from wars in Iraq and Afghanistan looking for work; Buzzell was part of a much larger, coordinated workforce scheme to convert US soldiers returning from war into instant 'entrepreneurs.' The UberMILITARY campaign, which was announced in September of 2014, initially aimed to recruit 50,000 US service members as new Uber drivers, along with military spouses and recent veterans.

As explained in the UberMILITARY campaign's recruitment and promotional literature, the impetus behind the effort was to combat the high rates of unemployment and under-employment among US veterans. In short, Uber offered instant jobs. Another impetus behind the UberMILITARY campaign was a prediction made at the time 'that over the next five years we can expect to see 300,000 service members transition to the civilian workforce every year' (Gates and Kalanick 2014). It was anticipated that more US soldiers would be returning home from wars overseas, on top of those already looking for work, and on top of those engaged in work perceived to be mismatched to their knowledge and skill base. What driving 'with' Uber was represented as offering, then, was a new type of solution not just for getting people from one place to the next but a solution to a broader (and recurring) labour problem.

Military and defence experts in the US call this particular labour problem 'transitioning'—when US soldiers have to re-enter everyday life and have to find pathways to self-sufficiency, wellness, functionality, and steady wage work. For many soldiers, working in the military offers relatively clear and straightforward career pathways. But when someone leaves the military, authority is far more indirect and can often take the form of enforced self-reliance rather than direct commands and orders. In this regard, 'transitioning' is the imagined problem-space of journeying from a military subject position to a civilian one, of moving from structured to unstructured living, and of possibly confronting new kinds of contingencies and uncertainties in the disorganization of everyday American life and work. 'Ordinary' Americans (non-soldiers) daily negotiated these same contingencies and uncertainties but the rationale underpinning soldier 'transitioning' discourse, at least as it came to be espoused by 2015, was that one's quotidian survival tactics can become rusty and obsolete from the experience of working in such an administered, structured organizational form like the US military. Put simply, the rationale behind 2010s military 'transitioning' discourse was that soldiers forget how to be everyday Americans. Despite all the ambient militarism that pervaded US society at that moment in time, American life and military life were totally unalike, according to most 'transitioning' discourse.

That Uber was presentable as a viable 'transitioning' program was part of larger shifts in 'transitioning' schemes that occurred over the course of several decades. Official 'transition assistance' programs for US soldiers first began in the early 1990s, in the aftermath of the cold war. By 2015, when Buzzell was writing, returning soldiers were not only required to develop an 'Individual Transition Plan' but also required to attend multi-day workshops and training sessions about how to apply their military skills to the non-military workforce, how to pursue further education, and how to start businesses (United States Government Accountability Office 2014). In addition to the 'transitioning' resources provided by the Department of Defense, numerous organizations in the NGO sphere (e.g., Hire Heroes USA, American Corporate Partners, Return to Work Incorporated) had also begun to develop and provide 'transition assistance' programming to help recent soldiers navigate and move through everyday experience. NGOs of this sort began to provide 'career coaching' and mentoring to soldiers, as well as began to broker relationships between individual soldiers and large US corporations like Disney, Fidelity Investments, Intel, and more.

Formalized inside the US military a quarter-century ago, but broadened over time to include a host of other institutional actors, the soldier 'transitioning' process by the 2010s had come to involve a lively assortment of stakeholders and employment vehicles. By February 2015, Uber was publicly reporting that 10,000 UberMILITARY drivers had been recruited and that UberMILITARY drivers were providing rides in 120 US cities. By May of 2015, Uber was publicly reporting that UberMILITARY drivers were earning more than US$1 million per week and had collectively earned US$35 million since the launch of the UberMILITARY campaign just eight months prior. Buzzell published his story about Uber the following month, in June of 2015.

Co-present Disconnections and App-Enhanced Interconnections

The existence of the larger UberMILITARY campaign makes Buzzell's recent account of Ubering all the more essential reading. The UberMILITARY's participation numbers, as promoted by Uber, suggest that thousands of other Uber drivers in this same period of history may have been temporarily sealed inside their Uber vehicles, unable to connect with their passengers across competing screens, with war medals and allied props rusting on their car dashboards. Encouraged to live by 'Individual Transition Plans' and to think entrepreneurially, Buzzell's treatment of Uber suggests that 'transitioning' in the 2010s, for some US soldiers and veterans, took on entirely new qualities that involved engaging with not just 'new' technologies of labour but also with new kinds of mediated experience that blurred the lines between space, time, screen technology, physical movement, human sociality, timekeeping, financial exchange, and personalized access to competing information, web, and travel services.

Throughout the story, Buzzell catalogues some of his different Uber passengers in a mode reminiscent of *Chatroulette*: the Russian website that became famous for facilitating webcam conversations between strangers, which started in 2009, the same year as Uber. The majority of the chats in Buzzell's story (or 'spins' in *Chatroulette* lingo) fail to move beyond trivialities. According to Buzzell: '[M]ostly my passengers spend the ride staring down at their phones, treating me like a machine[.]' The author's frustration and loneliness is palpable across the story: 'A robot could do my fucking job. Most of the time I'm completely invisible to the people I drive.'

This pervasive sense of invisibility, and associated dehumanization, is a core part of the 'conflictual politics' that creative workers involved in contemporary literary production have been helping to record in relation to early apps and their histories. People in physical contact with early app users, like Buzzell when driving his Uber vehicle, were beginning to feel backgrounded. Had our digital worlds already become bigger and more interesting than embodied life? This is one of the questions clearly informing Buzzell's dismay at how his Uber passengers choose to spend their time in his car, as readers are shuttled across the story, riding along on various Uber trips.

The story is also noteworthy for how it documents early apps as catalysts within everyday cultural clashes and social disconnections. Apps that could bring people together for fixed periods of time—examples beyond Uber, in 2015, would have included apps like Meetup, Grouper, Tinder, or Scruff—typically brought people together who each, as individuals, possessed levels of digital connectivity that made it possible for those same individuals to perceptually 'leave' co-presence by accessing and engaging with other information and web services. What Buzzell notices about early apps is how they could bring people together but also separate or divide co-present groupings of people by enabling those who were co-present to shift their attention to digital worlds.

Yet contrary to Buzzell's stormy and pessimistic account, his passengers were also potentially engaging with their surroundings in deep and what were then still radical ways, not at all disengaging from place or person as Buzzell presumes. Themes of space and location were key features of early app culture (Mowlabocus 2016). Building on this idea, Buzzell's passengers might have just as easily been using apps in their driver's presence that provided tremendous levels of still-novel, location-specific data about local restaurants and bars (Yelp, Urbanspoon, OpenTable), local neighborhoods (Dwellr, AroundMe, WalkScore), local sights (Detour, PocketGuide, TourPal), local events (BandsInTown, Applauze, Eventbrite), local people (Wiith, Peoplehunt, Grindr), local government (PublicStuff, SeeClickFix, UP2CODE), and local resources (UrbanSitter, Library Finder, Find a Health Center).

What Buzzell mistakes for disengagement from people and place, as vacuous disinterest on the part of his passengers, was actually a new culture of 'being there' having only just recently started to coalesce. What many early apps encouraged was a form of location-based interconnection with one's immediate surroundings for which few historical precursors come to mind, unless you go back to antiquity, the period before the Middle Ages. Although Buzzell frames his passengers' behaviour as a practice of difficult dialogue dodging, as a type of thoughtlessness or obliviousness to the complexities in their driver's head (or in the surrounding city), many of his passengers were just as likely doing something special to early app culture: for many users of early apps 'being there' had come to involve a vivid software layer for ingesting and digesting the world immediately around them. In addition, many early app users had also begun to digitally create and share running stories about themselves and their lives through various social media platforms, enrolling concrete place and time to manufacture digital content for other app users like themselves. Buzzell's recent story about Uber is a remarkable record of what that looked like in early app culture, even if Buzzell himself remains critical of such cultural practices throughout the story. Engaging with place is exactly what many early apps promoted, and engaging with people.

Something else special to early app culture was the rise of what might be termed computing socially, for lack of a better descriptor. Although Buzzell frames his passengers as relatively asocial, the process of talking to someone co-present while simultaneously engaging with information and web services (digital culture) via mobile and wearable technologies was quickly normalizing across a range of settings. In addition to a new culture of 'being there' arose a new culture of 'being with' others in the era of early apps. Building on this point, one key flaw or mischaracterization in Buzzell's recent story about Uber is the author's failure to acknowledge that co-present conversations were routinely happening over competing screens by the time the story was written and published, including many difficult and painful conversations. Nothing about his passengers' behaviour, at least by 2015, would have actually precluded Buzzell from launching into a conversation about war. In this aspect, the story runs deeply conservative. Its portrayal of sociotechnical mores drifts into old-fashioned traditionalism. Buzzell nostalgically idealizes device-devoid interactions, co-present conversations unencumbered by competing screens.

Whether the thousands of other UberMILITARY drivers working alongside Buzzell held similar viewpoints on 'new' technology remains unknown. Also unknown is what other kinds of expressive technologies the thousands of other UberMILITARY drivers potentially mobilized inside their Uber vehicles in the hopes of prompting specific lines of conversation about war. Were those technologies, like Buzzell's medal, also losing aspects of their acquired functionality? What other forms of technology recession were underway in this precise domain?

Conclusion

Apps now populate not just our networked devices but also our literary cultures, thanks in part to creative workers like Colby Buzzell. Stories about Uber are appearing as everything from self-published poetry to driving diaries. Each of which add a different kind of value to the historical records that cover the social, political, and economic manifestations, or stakes of, digital technology and culture. What makes Buzzell's recent story about Uber especially notable is its heavy emphasis on the 'conflictual politics' surrounding a particular app in its specific contexts of use. The story is one of capital and labour. The story is also about contradictions in human interaction and communication. In fact, this latter point becomes so salient across the story that Buzzell (the character within the story, not necessarily the person) misrecognizes certain forms of passenger behaviour and likely misses opportunities to engage in the very kinds of sharing that he purports to desire. 'Being there' and 'being with' are moving objects, in 2015 just as today, something that Buzzell seems to overlook throughout the story, while stuck following the 'thin blue line' on his own screen, Uber's navigation app.

In addition, Buzzell's recent story about Uber helps to chronicle a larger process of technology recession that coincided with the era of early apps. Lurking inside Buzzell's story is a subplot about the 'social death' of certain things. The death in question: Buzzell's war medal. Its symbolism: bidirectional. War medals were markers of individual pasts but also of futures not yet lived; the very presumption that underpins making and bestowing one is a future, physical need to remember, acknowledge, and decorate. Many war medals, like the one in Buzzell's story, in fact came to be made and given out at critical junctures in people's lives, during moments of 'transitioning' from soldier to civilian-inflected subjectivities. War medals validated past choices and experiences, even those doubted and questioned after the fact by those complicit in terrible events. War medals often arrived at the absolute darkest moments in people's lives, when it could seem that nothing mattered and all was meaningless. A reliable, if not enthusiastic, source of appreciation for someone's very existence it will be interesting to see what the world looks like without war medals. For what Buzzell captures so well in his recent story about Uber is that war medals are undergoing technology recession, like so many other technologies, losing efficacy and purpose as part of a world-historical event that few seem to be noticing or documenting. Item by item, thing by thing, 'social death' is everywhere. What might come to replace war medals will be interesting to see. If only the same could be asked of war.

References

Allen-Robertson, J. (2017). The materiality of digital media: The hard disk drive, phonograph, magnetic tape and optical media in technical close-up. *New Media & Society, 19*(3), 455–470.

Buzzell, C. (2015). My life driving Uber as an Iraq War Veteran with PTSD. *Vice* [online]. Available at: https://www.vice.com/en_us/article/zngv39/driving-uber-as-an-iraqi-war-veteran. Accessed 15 June 2015.

Dynamicridesharing.org. *Dynamic ridesharing projects, current, past, and proposed* [online]. Available at: http://dynamicridesharing.org/projects.php. Accessed 2 July 2015.

Gates, R., & Kalanick, T. (2014). How Uber is helping veterans. *Politico* [online]. Available at: http://www.politico.com/magazine/story/2014/09/robert-gates-uber-veterans-111039. Accessed 10 July 2015.

Liao, Z. (2005). Real-time taxi dispatching using global positioning systems. *Communications of the ACM, 46*(5), 81–83.

Mowlabocus, S. (2016). 'Y'all need to hide your kids, hide your wife': Mobile applications, risk and sex offender databases. *New Media & Society, 18*(11), 2473.

Myers, N. (2016). *Ungrid-able ecologies: Cultivating the arts of attention in a 10,000 year-old happening*. Available at: https://www.youtube.com/watch?v=8BFmf7GTFoc

Schaffer, S., Serlin, D., & Tucker, J. (2017). Editors' introduction [Political histories of technoscience]. *Radical History Review, 127*, 1–12.

Sharma, S. (2008). Taxis as media: A temporal materialist reading of the taxicab. *Social Identities, 14*(4), 457–458.

Sharma, S. (2010). Taxi cab publics and the production of brown space after 9/11. *Cultural Studies, 24*(2), 183–199.

Sterling, B. (2008). The life and death of media. In P. D. Miller (Ed.), *Sound unbound: Sampling digital music and culture*. Cambridge: The MIT Press.

Tao, C. C. (2007). Dynamic taxi-sharing service using intelligent transportation system technologies. In *Wireless Communications, Networking and Mobile Computing, 2007* (pp. 3209–3212). Shanghai: IEEE.

Uber Technologies, Inc. (2015). *Terms and conditions* [online]. Available at: https://www.uber.com/legal/usa/terms. Accessed 11 July 2015.

United States Government Accountability Office. (2014). *Transitioning veterans: Improved oversight needed to enhance implementation of transition assistance program* (pp. 5–8). Washington, DC: GAO.

10

Protocols of Control: Collaboration in Free and Open Source Software

Reinhard Anton Handler

Introduction

Peer to peer (p2p) production is a way of organising digital labour that is owed to the possibility of people collaborating in computer networks. Arguably, p2p is an alternative to capitalism for it promotes an egalitarian mode of collective self-organised production where volunteers choose when and from where to work and it additionally allows free usage of its innovative products (Bauwens 2013; Rigi 2013; Söderberg 2012). This mode of production has also been coined 'cyber communism' (Barbrook 2000) or 'commonism' (Dyer-Whiteford 2007) as it is theorised to be linked with the production of commons instead of commodities. The demarcation line between the commodity and commons production models is drawn not only by the possibility to monopolise a resource or a product. As peer-to-peer implies, this model also offers a specific form of organising and controlling labour, hence the name of the concept *commons-based peer production* (Benkler 2006).

R. A. Handler (✉)
Karlstad University, Karlstad, Sweden

© The Author(s) 2018
P. Bilić et al. (eds.), *Technologies of Labour and the Politics of Contradiction*,
Dynamics of Virtual Work, https://doi.org/10.1007/978-3-319-76279-1_10

This chapter looks at control in the production in free and open source software (f/oss), one of the prime examples of p2p. It adds to existing research on governance, hierarchies and power laws in p2p-production (Crowston and Howison 2006; O'Neil 2009; Shaw and Hill 2014) by discussing flexible forms of control in the collaborative production of f/oss. The existing empirical findings will not be summarised. Rather, the chapter's focus is on the specific characteristics concerning the ethic of collaboration and organisation of production in f/oss. The goal is to show that tracking work activities by computers has not only led to a reorganisation of labour and labour management but is also fundamental for the collaborative production of free and open source software. Hereby, I will argue that while a computational logic has specific features and repercussions it can operate differently depending on the social and cultural contexts. Tracking, embedded in the collaborative ethic of f/oss, offers close control of a collaborative flexible production process but also allows exit points of this control. Additionally, it lies at the centre of social networks, which in turn starts to change how software programmers collaborate.

Control

In *The new spirit of capitalism*, Luc Boltanski and Eve Chiapello (2007) analyse the transformation of the organisation of work towards non-hierarchic networks. They show that new organisational models have emerged in the early 1970s that discarded the hierarchic regimes of production traditionally associated with industrialised and standardised mass production. This novel form of organisation, they argue, is founded on decentralisation and immanence. Such transversely organised networks are generally unstable and require that the members engage in active and permanent collaboration. The architecture of distributed networks can be understood as a new social order system that is constructed on values like flexibility, mobility, creativity, and self-initiative. It is conceived to be a new organisational model that consists of project work, egalitarian distribution and cost-effective control mechanisms.

Boltanski and Chiappelo identify Deleuze as a key figure in capturing this new spirit. They argue that the figure of the rhizome developed by

Deleuze and Guattari (1987) makes the network the central form of organisation in capitalism; it is neither market nor hierarchy, neither teamwork nor autonomous producer, it offers leanness instead of an inflated bureaucratic machinery, and managers become coordinators who lead projects rather than a work force. Workers are not assembled in factories anymore but rather function as self-organising units that are connected with each other without representing a collective. This novel form of organisation does not come without control though. Deleuze (1992) outlined these in a short piece titled *Postscript on the societies of control*. In a technological world, for Deleuze, control is directly linked to freedom. The societies of control evolved from Foucault's (1995) disciplinary society whereby the latter's closed environments are replaced by sophisticated networks of entangled systems. Control of labour is not performed in enclosed spaces such as the factory anymore where workers are geographically linked to the production and would self-discipline themselves because of the possibility of being watched by managers. Computer technology provides mobility and flexibility, and forms of free-floating control replace the old disciplinary forms: 'Control is short-term and of rapid rates of turnover, but also continuous and without limit, while discipline was of long duration, infinite and discontinuous.' (Deleuze 1992) Thus, control is not necessarily visible and disentanglement is not possible. While flexibility and mobility provide a sense of freedom, control societies are not more free than disciplinary societies.

New forms of surveillance have been discussed thoroughly starting from Deleuze's societies of control (Andrejevic 2007; Bauman and Lyon 2013; Lyon 2007; Van Dijck 2014). The shifts in the organisation of work and economic constellation because of the crisis of traditional enclosed environments, especially in the cultural industries, has gathered quite a significant amount of academic attention as well (Fisher 2010; Hesmondhalgh 2013; Hesmondhalgh and Baker 2011; Lovink and Rossiter 2007). Both these developments originate from a computational logic that Agre (1994) conceptualised as the *capture model*. He argues that practises of applied computing have led to a fundamental change of organising labour as they allow to track human activities all the time. While the *surveillance model* is characterised as centrally organised watching by a bureaucratic organisation, the *capture model* in contrast is a decentralised process that reconstructs activity by assimilating human activities 'to the constructs of a computer system's representation languages' (p. 107). Deleuze's characterisation of the control societies echoes in Agre's distinction between surveillance and capture but the latter's focus on applied computing adds an extra layer to understand how commodified information is controlled in digital networks.

Deleuze's and Agre's conceptualisations of decentralised control that discuss control societies and commodified information are compared with f/oss, a collaborative production of digital commons, along four lines of inquiry. The aim of this comparison is not to take sides in a debate between commons and commodities or commonism and capitalism. Rather, these four lines attempt to show the embeddedness of computational systems in a specific socio-technical context.

Collaboration

The first line addresses a central question in f/oss – and peer production in general – which is understood as people working together in an egalitarian manner. Already mentioned at the beginning of this chapter, studies of these communities show hierarchical conflicts and power laws. The difference is that power in peer communities is not necessarily executed as a repressive but rather as a generative force (Meng and Wu 2013). But still, there are power struggles in peer production that are maintained at both organisational and discursive levels (Bergquist and Ljungberg 2001; Weber 2004).

In f/oss, participation depends on learning how to share and on peer-review. The level of knowledge and socialisation result in a meritocratic model that classifies participants as newcomers or experienced. Additionally, distinctions are made between peripheral participants that are contributing in an irregular manner, and key members that ultimately act as decision makers (Berdou 2011). Collaborative practices seem to adopt models of authority and decentralised self-governance, such as sanctioning mechanisms, to resolve conflicts in order to maintain the activities (O'Mahony 2005). One form of such sanction is the 'shun', a refusal to collaborate with a user after they have broken a certain norm

(Weber 2004). Not only does the collaborative production of free and open source software consists of complex relations and social organisational forms, it also includes practices that require special skills. Hackers, coders, and programmers can be understood as software craftpersons (Hoover and Oshineye 2010; Mancuso 2015; McBreen 2002; Velkova 2016). Their collaborative practices are based on sharing and peer-review but they also include competition, and they entail and sometimes even thrive on conflict, disagreements and negotiations. Conceptualising the production of free and open source software as democratic, non-hierarchical, free from control, conflict and governance does not explain these practices in their entirety.

A concept that is more adapt to describe collaborative f/oss production is *free cooperation* by Christoph Spehr (2007). He contrasts free cooperation with forced cooperation. Most of the cooperative relations we engage in, he argues, are in fact forced cooperations whether that is family life, labour, or civic duties. Forced cooperations have three defining features: First, their hierarchies, rules, and protocols are neither negotiable nor flexible. Their second defining feature is that they never stop even if an actor's problem is unsolved. Thirdly, forced cooperations cannot be left without considerable consequences for the abandoner. Free cooperation offers an opposing triad of features: (1) All rules in the cooperation can be questioned by everybody; (2) All participants can quit, limit or condition their cooperative effort in order to impact on the rules of cooperation, both individually and collectively; (3) The price for leaving the cooperation is equal and bearable for all parties.

Collaboration in f/oss is not exclusively based on consensus and egalitarian processes. It involves conflicts, arguing and the possibility of not reaching a decision. A f/oss project involves constant negotiations between contributors who mostly have never met in person and a project's assets cannot be claimed as property of a single owner as a project cannot be shut down unilaterally (Fogel 2013). In order to solve conflicts, numerous open-source software development teams include a meritocratic decision-making process that relies on a person's status within a project. Some projects have even vested a person with the title 'Benevolent dictator for life' (BDFL). These people, usually the founder of a project, have the ultimate say in project discussion. Perhaps the best known example of this model is Linus Torvalds and his role in the Linux Kernel project. Torvalds, the originator of Linux, has the last say. Small specialised teams work on a specific part and release trial versions that anybody can comment on. These comments may lead to changes and adjustments and then the proposal is voted on. All community members have one vote or can take part in the discussion but the final say is reserved for the benevolent dictator who can make a decision contrary to the majority of the community members. However, this requires communication skills and an understanding of the community to ensure that the project will not run out of contributors.

F/oss offers a different organisational model than proprietary software production but that does not necessarily mean that it is free from control. Neither does finding generative forces that exert control in those flexible and modularised organisational forms mean that f/oss maintains forced cooperative forms of production. Contributors to f/oss projects can always question the development of a project, and they can stop collaborating but control still exists. Spehr's differentiation between free and controlled cooperation is useful as it helps to highlight the shift from hierarchies to control which Deleuze described. F/oss shows, tough, that hierarchies and control are not mutually exclusive as it includes meritocratic hierarchies and control as well as democratic elements. Looking at the technological-organisational level of production it becomes further clear how important control mechanisms are for software production.

Version Control

The second line concerns the technological-organisational level of software production by focusing on the importance of control in decentralised networks. Alexander Galloway (2006) has described the importance of including the technical infrastructure to analyse the control society. He shows how networks are managed by protocols. The Internet's protocols that have replaced hierarchies are only seemingly a structure that is out of control. Contrarily, the Internet, he argues is a 'massive control apparatus that guides distributed networks, creates cultural objects, and engenders life forms' (p. 243).

The collaborative production of free and open source production can be understood as one massive control apparatus. Version control is crucial for software production. It documents project development and facilitates the coordination of collaboration. Version control lets developers track the changes that are made to the code as well as easy backtracking of the changes. In case of a mistake, contributors can compare several versions of the code which helps them in fixing the mistake quicker. Software development is based on these control processes. Version control provides this but requires discipline from the programmers. Every step needs to be documented, the code needs to be backed up and brought into agreement with other collaborators. Thus, version control systems are integral to software production in general. A version control system provides a complete log of changes of every file; every change made by anyone is automatically recorded, introduction or deletion of files included. Such a system disciplines programmers as not every version control software handles renaming and moving files perfectly. A contributor is also supposed to add a short note to their contribution to explain other the intention of the changes made. Versioning is a vital process when various programmers work on the same project. Not only does it allow them to easily share files, it also makes sure that they do not work simultaneously on the same issue and overwrite code changes. Two practices are central here: Branching and merging. In rough terms, branching means that code is copied and two teams work parallel on the same code on different branches independent from each other. Merging reconciles different branches or integrates a branch into the main line of development. Such production processes are even more diverse as the teams collaborating are agile which means they are self-organised and working on the same project. Multiple teams can work in parallel without immediately affecting each other. In order to control these cross-functional processes, controlling the versions is key. If several development teams work on the same codebase, the risk of intersecting or overlapping needs to be minimised. At the end of each iteration the aim is to have a clean, releasable version at the end of each iteration (Kniberg 2008). A branch is a separate line of development that is independent, yet it shares a common history with another line at same point in the past. If the resulting codes do not conflict, branches can be merged or a branch can be merged back to the original code (the tree). In order to work on an extra feature for a software project, also a branch is needed to avoid disturbing the development of the main line or other branches. Branches are also important to release one candidate and continue the development on another and a team with multiple projects divides the work into teams and each of them works in their own branch. Connected to this control systems are rules and policies. If one team merges their branch back into the main line, the other team has to merge these changes into their branch to avoid a conflict in code. To avoid extra work, branching has a core policy that asks for an estimate of the work that has be put into a branch. A branch should only be started if the cost of branching and merging is lower than keeping to work on the main line.

By sketching some of the main practices of coding in teams, it should have become clear that version control is highly standardised. All contributors need to use the same main line all the time in order to avoid conflicts. Additionally, there are many different rules that assure that a projects stays coherent and, as discussed before, some of them are not necessarily democratic such as the rule that 'each branch has an owner and a policy' (Kniberg 2008). Version control is set up to guarantee a stable software package hence the rigid control mechanisms. Sure, hierarchies and an uneven power distribution amongst the contributors do exist but these two realms are very much connected. Continuous contributions, keeping in line with version control without breaking the social and organisational rules and writing good code are valued amongst software programmers.

Forking

The third consideration of control in f/oss combines version control and free cooperation by presenting the option of forking a software project. To understand forking, it is best to think of it as a fork in the road. When a user copies a software repository and makes changes, it becomes different from the original version. This right to start a new development path is central to f/oss. If someone wants to contribute to a project, they can make a full copy of a certain version. If someone wants to use a project's version as a starting point for their own they are also allowed to do that. Thus, basically, a copy that is changed and not to merged back with the original project is what constitutes a fork.

While the f/oss production is based on different versions of control that ought to guarantee a production process as seamless as possible, discussion and arguments are an integral part of the production process. Following Spehr's model of free collaboration f/oss contributors cannot only question a project's rules, they can also quit their cooperative effort and leave the cooperation. F/oss is so interesting because its openness also includes forking, the possibility to copy the source code from a software package and start independent development on it. Forking code has previously often been portrayed as detrimental for f/oss. It was viewed a 'bad thing' because 'forks tend to be accompanied by a great deal of strife and acrimony between the successor groups over issues of legitimacy, succession, and design direction' (Raymond 2000). In this context forking is understood as splitting a community into rivalling factions and it is considered 'the cardinal sin of OSS' (Ågerfalk and Fitzgerald 2008). Further, it is claimed that the most common outcome of a fork is its death (Wheeler 2015). However, there are arguments that this negative view on forking is based on an outdated definition of the term and that it actually 'represents the single greatest tool available for guaranteeing sustainability in open source software' (Nyman and Mikkonen 2011).

GitHub has played a central role in the changed perception of forking. The button for forking has been placed prominently and a copy of a project can be made with one click. The process is also transparent as the author of the original project is automatically notified. Probably, the original owner will receive an improved version. Thereby, forks not only foster participation, they also affect the governance of f/oss projects as contributors can avoid to be overruled by the owner of a project or a branch if they think that the latter is wrong or did not show the necessary communicative skills to hold a team together while overruling the majority. Forking also guarantees the possibility of remixing by making the combination of projects available. However, forking an open source project also allows to lock a copy of a project in and sell it in the original version or – more commonly – in a slightly modified version that is tailor-made for a customer. Also, open source facilitates crowdsourcing project development to a community of programmers while the company decides what is sold. Open innovation is directly linked to open business models and companies have learned quickly how to integrate common-based peer production in their product development in order to harness the advantages offered by participation, i.e. highly motivated contributors who work for free.

Free and open source software collectively represents an alternative approach to software development that cannot be explained exhaustively by a refusal to monetarisation. The reason behind this is, first and foremost, that business models for free software and open source software exist (Hecker 1999; Okoli and Nguyen 2016; Perens 2005) – also for the theoretically anti-commercial free software. Generally, free software and open source software rely on the same idea: software should be free to use, copy, modify and share. They differ however in terms of political values and philosophy. According to the Free Software Foundation (Free Software Foundation 2017) a free software license means that users run, copy, and change the software as well as distribute the changed versions. It is not important if the software is commercial or non-commercial, the crux of the matter is that users always have access to the source code. The ultimate aim of free software is to avoid copyright, hence the invention of copyleft, a license that attempts to ensure that code remains freely available. Code that is obtained from a free software license needs be released as free software. Free access to the source code is also a key feature for open source software but it also allows that modified versions of a code that is derived from an open source license do not necessarily be redistributed under an open source license. Open source intents to allow commercialisation of code by removing the restrictions of free software license. Open source was founded as an alternative to free software in order to avoid 'ideological tub-thumping' and to use it as 'a marketing tool for free software' (Open Source Initiative 2006). The business of open source software has proven to be successful. The most prominent example is Red Hat, a company that offers the software as open source but charges for tailor-made modulations as well as for support, training and certifications. Mozilla's Firefox browser, which is produced and maintained with the help of a large group of volunteers and offered without charge, earns money by signing deals with search engine companies that makes it the default search engine in a specific area of the world.

While there are philosophical differences between free software and open source software and advocates for each of them (Perens 1999; Stallman 2016) both philosophies are exemplary for a culture of collaboration that is not free from control but that offers a model for open innovation that renounces copyright and allows the sharing of knowledge. Part of the fundament for this is version control, a tracking of the collaborative production.

Social Coding

The last line attempts to approach control in f/oss by resorting again to Agre's (1994) *capture model*. The short summary given before needs to be expanded a little bit. In contrast to centrally organised surveillance, Agre describes how human activity in networks is tracked by computer systems. Capture means that human activity is aligned with a language a computer can process. This language comes with an accurate grammar that decides how activities are arranged into a computer system; Agre calls this a *grammar of action*. Computer system also force these grammars upon the users who have to organise their actions so that the computer can process it. Social network platforms, computational systems by their nature, also impose their grammars of action upon the user. A heart on Twitter reduces many different forms of activity (thanking someone, agreeing with someone, etc.) into a processing unit. Social network platforms for software production such as GitHub or Stack Overflow have not only become an important channel of communication between coders, but they have also adapted them as a new social tool. A new participatory culture emerges in software engineering (Storey et al. 2014) as the meritocratic thinking, technological practices, and control in production are reassembled on social network platforms that follow the same computational logic by capturing human activities.

This new culture of software engineering, also called *social coding*, is epitomised by GitHub. It is the most popular platform for exchanging and developing software. In April 2017, GitHub reported to have 19 million users and to host 57 million repositories (a storage location for a software package). It is a hybrid of a social media platform and version control software: The version control system Git has been augmented with 'social coding' elements such as starring or watching other users and projects, capturing and displaying user activities and progress of projects as well as management tools for collaborative production (Fuller 2017). It is a repository for software that allows contributors to work on projects without having to share a common network. To put across how social and technical control mechanisms in software production are inseparable from each other and need to be understood as socio-technical performances, it is useful to look at GitHub.

Software revisions are stored on the servers of GitHub and are accessible for those who are registered as users. GitHub builds on Git, a version control system that is run under a free software license. It was developed by Linus Torvalds to configure the contributions from a multitude for programming the Linux kernel. Torvalds himself gave to Git the epithet *The stupid content tracker*. Stupid it might be but it proved to be so quick and versatile that it has become the standard system for storing and sharing source code. With Git small distributed software development projects can be handled as well as the largest projects. Based on Git as a version control software, GitHub has added elements similar to social network platforms. GitHub declares in its mission statement to build social applications in order to foster collaborative coding. Those applications allow users to follow each other and the activities of others as well as track the progress of projects in a very transparent and easy way. The social network features on GitHub are well received and people make a variety of inferences from the activity of users and the progress of projects that is displayed (Dabbish et al. 2012). As Dabbish et al. have shown users felt audience pressure because their activities are visible on GitHub and they adjusted their behaviour in order to create a portfolio. By contributing to specific projects or engaging in a certain activity, the users want to show what type of programmer they are and what code they write. Because of the fast updates on GitHub and the feed that is offered, users on GitHub do not wait for a release of a project they need in their work. They rather make other aware of their needs by highlighting bugs or suggesting their patches. The possibility to track people on GitHub, look at their activities and history makes it easy for users to learn from more experienced programmers. Not only code is visible to everyone also a history of all the projects a person worked on. In this sense GitHub functions as an archive that offers tutorials by emulating experts. Experienced programmers with high reputation act as tutors without actively teaching others and their behaviour becomes an example of best-practice for others.

The sociotechnical practices that rely on the control that GitHub offers, i.e. the possibility to track users activities and projects, are further emphasised by the research of Tsay et al. (2014). They found that decisions on which contribution to include in a project are based both on the technical standard as well as on the strength of the social connection between the contributor and the project manager. Both merits are the result of sharing and community building as well as the easily accessible data that illustrates the strength of social connections, technical knowledge and commitment that make up a user's reputation. Marlow et al. (2013) came to the conclusion that GitHub users seek out the additional information that is offered through tracking the activities about each other. They form impressions around other users by evaluating the history of activity, collaborations with high status projects and users with high reputation in the community. All in all, users on GitHub combine control-related practices which are enforced by tracking applications that enhance visibility and transparency. They use control for coordinating projects, improving their coding skills as well as managing their own status.

Conclusion

Technology, media technology in particular, is often perceived as a tertium non datur, something that is part of 'the given preconditions for media production' (Löwgren and Reimer 2013). Yet as the computer has turned into a universal machine, software has become a universal language (Manovich 2013). Thus, software is not a neutral tool. The 'softwarization of society' (Berry 2015) not only transforms industries along computational processes it also activates the imagination of society with a computational logic of decentralised networks. Society is understood through software and digital decentralized networks.

As this chapter has shown, decentralised networks do not function without control. Control is a significant part of digitality as a cultural logic (Franklin 2015). Exploring the structures of f/oss in order to ask for the forms of control contributes to the endeavour of determining the possibilities of a digital society. The socioeconomic transformations that started in the twentieth century are inextricably linked with computer technologies. They reflect new forms of organising groups, whether that is a workgroup in a company or whole societies. F/oss shows how contradictory these new forms can be: discussions are vital but not all decisions are made in a democratic manner; participants can drop out of projects – usually without major consequences. But it also includes hierarchies and shows control mechanisms that are not only inseparable from computer networks but also inform the imagination of collaborative work. F/oss transcends a lot of distinctions and dichotomies including that between commons and commodities. Following De Angelis (2017), f/oss is not just about producing common goods. It rather is a field of power relations which are negotiated constantly on different levels: social, philosophical, political, economic, technological, practical; these levels cannot be understood in isolation from each other and are all transformed by the specific logic of computer networks.

References

Ågerfalk, P., & Fitzgerald, B. (2008). Outsourcing to an unknown workforce: Exploring opensourcing as a global sourcing strategy. *MIS Quarterly*, *6*(1), 385–409.
Agre, P. E. (1994). Surveillance and capture: Two models of privacy. *The Information Society*, *10*(2), 101–127.
Andrejevic, M. (2007). *ISpy: Surveillance and power in the interactive era.* Lawrence: University Press of Kansas.
Barbrook, R. (2000). Cyber-Communism: How the Americans are superseding capitalism in cyberspace. *Science as Culture*, *9*(1), 5–40.

Bauman, Z., & Lyon, D. (2013). *Liquid surveillance: A conversation*. Cambridge: Polity Press.

Bauwens, M. (2013). Thesis on digital labor in an emerging P2P economy. In T. Scholz (Ed.), *Digital labor: The Internet as playground and factory* (pp. 207–210). New York: Routledge.

Benkler, Y. (2006). *The wealth of networks: How social production transforms markets and freedom*. New Haven: Yale University Press.

Berdou, E. (2011). *Organization in open source communities: At the crossroads of the gift and market economy*. New York: Routledge.

Bergquist, M., & Ljungberg, J. (2001). The power of gifts: Organizing social relationships in open source communities. *Information Systems Journal, 11*(4), 305–320.

Berry, D. M. (2015). *Critical theory and the digital*. New York: Bloomsbury.

Boltanski, L., & Chiapello, È. (2007). *The new spirit of capitalism*. London: Verso.

Crowston, K., & Howison, J. (2006). Hierarchy and centralization in free and open source software team communications. *Knowledge, Technology & Policy, 18*(4), 65–85.

Dabbish, L., Stuart, C., Tsay, J., & Herbsleb, J. (2012). Social coding in GitHub: Transparency and collaboration in an open software repository. In *Proceedings of ACM 2012 Conference on Computer Supported Cooperative Work* (pp. 1277–1286). New York: ACM Press.

De Angelis, M. (2017). *Omnia sunt communia: On the commons and the transformation to postcapitalism*. London: Zed Books.

Deleuze, G. (1992). Postscript on the societies of control. *October, 59*, 3–7.

Deleuze, G., & Guattari, F. (1987). *A thousand plateaus*. Minneapolis: University of Minnesota Press.

Dyer-Whiteford, N. (2007). Commonism. *Turbulence, 1*. Retrieved from http://turbulence.org.uk/turbulence-1/commonism/

Fisher, E. (2010). *Media and new capitalism in the digital age the spirit of networks*. Basingstoke: Palgrave Macmillan.

Fogel, K. (2013). *Producing open source software: How to run a successful free software project*. O'Reilly Media. Retrieved from http://producingoss.com/en/producingoss.pdf

Foucault, M. (1995). *Discipline and punish: The birth of the prison*. New York: Vintage Books.

Franklin, S. (2015). *Control: Digitality as cultural logic*. Cambridge, MA: The MIT Press.

Free Software Foundation. (2017, March 20). *Selling free software*. Retrieved April 23, 2017, from https://www.gnu.org/philosophy/selling.html

Fuller, M. (Ed.). (2017). *How to be a geek: Essays on the culture of software*. Cambridge: Polity.

Galloway, A. R. (2006). *Protocol: How control exists after decentralization*. Cambridge, MA: MIT Press.

Hecker, F. (1999). Setting up shop: The business of open-source software. *IEEE Software, 16*(1), 45–51.

Hesmondhalgh, D. (2013). *The cultural industries*. London: SAGE.

Hesmondhalgh, D., & Baker, S. (2011). *Creative labour: Media work in three cultural industries*. London: Routledge.

Hoover, D. H., & Oshineye, A. (2010). *Apprenticeship patterns: Guidance for the aspiring software craftsman*. Cambridge, MA: O'Reilly.

Kniberg, H. (2008, March 31). *Version control for multiple agile teams*. Retrieved April 21, 2017, from https://www.infoq.com/articles/agile-version-control

Lovink, G., & Rossiter, N. (Eds.). (2007). *MyCreativity reader: A critique of creative industries*. Amsterdam: Institute of Network Cultures.

Löwgren, J., & Reimer, B. (2013). *Collaborative media: Production, consumption, and design interventions*. Cambridge, MA: The MIT Press.

Lyon, D. (2007). *Surveillance studies: An overview*. Cambridge: Polity.

Mancuso, S. (2015). *The software craftsman: Professionalism, pragmatism, pride*. Upper Saddle River: Prentice Hall.

Manovich, L. (2013). *Software takes command: Extending the language of new media*. New York: Bloomsbury.

Marlow, J., Dabbish, L., & Herbsleb, J. (2013). Impression formation in online peer production: Activity traces and personal profiles in GitHub. In *Proceedings of the 2013 Conference on Computer Supported Cooperative Work* (pp. 117–128). New York: ACM Press. Retrieved from http://dl.acm.org/citation.cfm?doid=2441776.2441792

McBreen, P. (2002). *Software craftsmanship: The new imperative*. Boston: Addison-Wesley.

Meng, B., & Wu, F. (2013). COMMONS/COMMODITY: Peer production caught in the web of the commercial market. *Information, Communication & Society, 16*(1), 125–145.

Nyman, L., & Mikkonen, T. (2011). To fork or not to fork: Fork motivations in sourceforge projects. In S. A. Hissam, B. Russo, M. G. de Mendonça Neto, & F. Kon (Eds.), *Open source systems: Grounding research* (Vol. 365, pp. 259–268). Berlin: Springer. Retrieved from http://link.springer.com/10.1007/978-3-642-24418-6

O'Mahony, S. (2005). Nonprofit foundations and their role in community-firm software collaboration. In J. Feller (Ed.), *Perspectives on free and open source software* (pp. 393–414). Cambridge, MA: MIT Press.

O'Neil, M. (2009). *Cyberchiefs: Autonomy and authority in online tribes*. London: Pluto Press.

Okoli, C., & Nguyen, J. (2016). *Business models for free and open source software: Insights from a Delphi study*. Retrieved March 14, 2017, from https://ssrn.com/abstract=2568185

Open Source Initiative. (2006). *Frequently asked questions. How is 'open source' related to 'free software'?* Retrieved December 1, 2016, from https://web.archive.org/web/20060423094434/http://www.opensource.org/advocacy/faq.html

Perens, B. (1999). The open source definition. In C. DiBona, S. Ockman, & M. Stone (Eds.), *Open sources: Voices from the open source revolution* (pp. 171–188). Sebastopol: O'Reilly.

Perens, B. (2005). The emerging economic paradigm of Open Source. *First Monday, Special issue 2*. Retrieved from http://firstmonday.org/ojs/index.php/fm/article/view/1470/1385

Raymond, E. S. (2000). *The Jargon File (version 4.4.7)*. Retrieved from http://www.catb.org/jargon/html/index.html

Rigi, J. (2013). Peer production and Marxian communism: Contours of a new emerging mode of production. *Capital & Class, 37*(3), 397–416.

Shaw, A., & Hill, B. M. (2014). Laboratories of Oligarchy? How the iron law extends to peer production. *Journal of Communication, 64*(2), 215–238.

Söderberg, J. (2012). *Hacking capitalism: The free and open source software (foss) movement*. London: Routledge.

Spehr, C. (2007). Free cooperation. In G. Lovink & T. Scholz (Eds.), *The art of free cooperation* (pp. 65–180). Brooklyn: Autonomedia.

Stallman, R. (2016, November 18). *Why open source misses the point of free software*. Retrieved 3 April 2017, from https://www.gnu.org/philosophy/open-source-misses-the-point.html

Storey, M.-A., Singer, L., Cleary, B., Figueira Filho, F., & Zagalsky, A. (2014). The (R)evolution of social media in software engineering. In *Proceedings of Future of Software Engineering* (pp. 100–116). New York: ACM Press.

Tsay, J., Dabbish, L., & Herbsleb, J. (2014). Influence of social and technical factors for evaluating contribution in GitHub. In *Proceedings of the 36th*

International Conference on Software Engineering (pp. 356–366). New York: ACM Press.

Van Dijck, J. (2014). Datafication, dataism and dataveillance: Big data between scientific paradigm and ideology. *Surveillance & Society, 12*(2), 197–208.

Velkova, J. (2016). Free software beyond radical politics: Negotiations of creative and craft autonomy in digital visual media production. *Media and Communication, 4*(4), 43–52.

Weber, S. (2004). *The success of open source*. Cambridge, MA: Harvard University Press.

Wheeler, D. A. (2015, July 18). *Why Open Source Software / Free Software (OSS/FS, FLOSS, or FOSS)? Look at the Numbers!* Retrieved February 4, 2017, from https://www.dwheeler.com/oss_fs_why.html

11

Playbour and the Gamification of Work: Empowerment, Exploitation and Fun as Labour Dynamics

Raul Ferrer-Conill

Introduction

The notion of play is often portrayed as a blissful manifestation of fun and freedom. Similarly, contemporary popular culture tends to portray the figure of labour as a recurrent antithesis of play. Accordingly, Marcuse (1933/1973, p. 14) uses the concept of play as 'a counter-concept to determine labour.' Such an understanding is so rooted in modern western societies that Sutton-Smith felt compelled to actively state that the opposite of play is not work, but vacillation or depression (2001, p. 198). Whether play and labour are antagonistic figures or not, the discursive conflation of both concepts can blur notions that seemed well established until recently.

While the attempt to make work enjoyable is not a new phenomenon, in recent years, the trend of incorporating playful thinking and game elements within working processes has gained popularity among organizations and businesses. The rhetoric behind this trend is anchored in promised sources of worker empowerment, self-realization for employees

R. Ferrer-Conill (✉)
Karlstad University, Karlstad, Sweden

and turning labour into a fun and enjoyable experience. Only by adopting a narrative that promotes work as a fun form of empowerment can organizations influence the discursive approaches to labour and play. However, the intricate structures of power that steer labour dynamics tend to demarcate work as a complex assemblage of organizational goals, social interactions, and technological affordances; an assemblage that hardly can nurture genuine playful attitudes.

Yet, the parallel technological advances of digital gaming, as well as the digitization of labour process, conflate to create an environment where game mechanics can easily be deployed within tools of digital labour. These technologies make use of processes anchored in constant datafication, surveillance, and feedback loops while automating patterns of control and motivation that are concealed behind playful interfaces. Thus, the material configurations of gamified working technologies appropriate the socio-cultural power of play to serve the commercial goals of labour.

This chapter concerns itself with the active attempt to reverse the established understanding of labour as the antithesis of play. By studying the way in which games and playful thinking are being incorporated into labour processes, I argue that organizations incur in a paradoxical reconfiguration of labour where working practices are disguised as game-like activities. This contradiction lies in the friction between the promise of empowerment and free will of play, and the tactics of control and for-profit determinism of capitalist ventures. The contradiction is embodied in the set of technologies that conform playbour or gamification systems. As socio-technical constructs, they push forward business' objectives under the disguise of game-like features and playful narratives. As the boundaries between play and work are increasingly being blurred, the need to disentangle the processes in which this trend is being promoted becomes urgent.

Play Versus Labour

When Huizinga proposed that 'play is more than a physiological phenomenon or a psychological reflex' (1949, p. 1), he strategically situated play as a quality that predates human culture. Yet its primal disposition becomes a function of culture. Research indicates that play is a vital conduit for socialization in young children (Juul 2000) that helps establish cultural traits in members of society. Play is thus a social function that ascribes meaning into actions as a form of expression and communication (Sutton-Smith 2001). Sicart (2014) goes further to consider play as a mode of being. An ontological disposition of confronting existence that resembles the Hegelian ontological conceptualisation of labour. In such an ontological perspective, play and labour are conditions of the human existence, formed by praxis. Yet, adopting playfulness as a choice provides play with its most vital characteristic: the agentic notion of free will. Huizinga (1949) proposed that place, space, and the material converge by creating playgrounds enabling temporary worlds of play within the ordinary world. The material temporality of play is embodied by spaces that separate play rituals from everyday life. Caillois (1961, p. 6) proposes that 'play must be defined as a free and voluntary activity, a source of joy and amusement; a game which one would be forced to play would at once cease being play.' Thus, play is an activity that occurs naturally and cannot be enforced, but at the same time can be placed on a continuum stretching from unstructured and spontaneous playful performances to structured and ritualized games.

Caillois' statement introduces a challenging conceptual clarification: the distinction between play and game, as well as the use of play as both noun and verb. Furthermore, the complex relationship between play and games complicates the distinction. Salen and Zimmerman (2003) propose the entanglement resides in two relationships: (a) games are a subset of play, and (b) play is a component of games. Untangling both concepts entirely is an effort that often finds contentious results. For the purpose of this chapter, I understand play as 'free movement within a more rigid structure' (Salen and Zimmerman 2003, p. 300). Such a broad understanding of play allows for analytical scrutiny of three dimensions of play: game play, ludic activity and being playful. These different dimensions ascribe the noun/verb dichotomy as they explain different dispositions of play. Similarly, I adopt Salen and Zimmerman's definition of game as 'a system in which players engage in an artificial conflict, defined by rules, that results in a quantifiable outcome' (2003, p. 113). The conceptual distinction revolves around the free will of the player and its agency while engaging in the system and it becomes useful when addressing how play or games seep into labour and working contexts.

Considering contemporary labour as the remnants of a hierarchical industrial social configuration, the economic necessity by which capitalistic societies operate, situates labour as a systemic endeavour that revolves around a mutual understanding. The agreement occurs between the employee and the employer to generate value through productive processes (Thompson 1989). The productive nature of labour may be the first antagonistic characteristic between play and labour. As Caillois (1961, p. 10) notes, play is an activity which is essentially unproductive, 'creating neither goods, nor wealth, nor new elements of any kind.' Additionally, the organization of work remains a predominantly structured daily activity based on organisation, hierarchy and control. As such, play and labour seem to differ in the fundamental underpinnings of their own performativity. The diametric understanding of play as agency, and labour as coercion, signifies as Fuchs (2015) contends, that labour is a human condition that cannot be played. On a similar note, Bataille considers work a response to utilitarian needs and care for the future, while play focuses on the experience of the instant (as cited by Richardson 1994). The explicit opposition of play and work inherently means that the regime of labour denies the affirmation of play. Pfaller goes even further by stating 'it is the very nature of labour to be the negative of play' (as cited by Fuchs 2015). Marcuse (1933/1973, p. 15) arguing against the Marxist teleological view of labour, understands play as a 'breaking off from labour and recuperation for labour.' His perspective approaches play as a form of escapism and self-distraction that palliates the implicit burden of labouring processes.

The apparently dichotomous understanding that scholars brandish on the theoretical separation of play and labour seems much less binary in practice. The instrumentalisation and commodification of play during the expansive rise of leisure in the post-industrial era have been based on deconstructing play and embedding it in various social practices. Culture in the 'Ludic Century', as Zimmerman (2015, p. 20) calls it, is expected to become more systemic, modular, customizable, and participatory, and the 'ways that people spend their leisure time and consume art, design, and entertainment will be games'. A society that broadly adopts play and games as a form of culture and enjoyment quickly assimilates the positive parallels of play. Already in the 60s, Caillois (1961) recognized tendencies of perversion and corruption of play as it becomes institutionalized within the structures of society. Consequently, the structures of power attempt to reify play and devise it as a mechanism for capitalist production (Rey 2015).

Traditional analogue forms of labour and play tended to occur independently as different spaces of burden and recuperation (Marcuse 1973). Digital technologies merge those spaces, as several devices can be used both for play and for work. Here is where technology acts as an amplifier of the process that merges the seemingly separate worlds of play and labour. The rise of digital and networked labour not only has signified a revolution on labour dynamics in the developed economies, but has also shaped the interactions between portions of society that are now unknowingly labouring, simply by interacting with the digital world. The Internet and the newfound capacity to organise labour through algorithms have opened up opportunities for new spaces of empowerment, as well as new spaces for exploitation, which often conflate in the same contradictory systems (van Dijck and Poell 2013). Such contradictions in how human interaction and digital labour dynamics are being shaped by the social construction of technology, is exemplified by Scholz's (2013) metaphor of the internet as playground and factory.

Playbour and Digital Free Labour

The surge of networked technologies shows its strongest expression in the adaptability of digital media, spearheaded by social media. These new forms of media tend to afford several different forms of expression that are usually offered to users seemingly for *free*. The apparent contradiction of offering services without a monetary transaction contributed to its major adoption by users know often are unaware about how these services are sustained (van Dijck 2013).

The decoupling of providing services from actual monetary transactions opens the terrain for various contradicting strategies for empowerment and exploitation. On the one hand, the facilitation of use and self-expression, the empowerment of the user to participate in the online world is often viewed as a positive development (Jenkins and Carpentier 2013). On the other hand the strategies of constant datafication, surveillance and exploitation (Fuchs 2014a) hint patterns of control that perpetuate the neo-liberal political economy within the digital mediascapes (McChesney 2013).

The opaqueness in which value-creation and monetization tactics operate complicates the calculation of user labour's worth. Users are often unaware of the value their work generates and are not economically compensated, which defines their work as free labour (Van Dijck 2009). In order to maintain users interested and productive, several service providers have opted to embed playful approaches and game-like rewards and incentives within the experience. This appropriation of play for labour and commercial purposes is not entirely new. However, the technologies used to automatically track, quantify and analyse consumer behaviour bring to the fore concerns about the way in which engagement, motivation and labour politics are understood.

The concept playbour (Kücklich 2005) emerges as a way to conceptualize free digital labour and the industry-driven shift towards an economy combining engagement and digital rewards. Its coinage departed from the modification and production of digital games by fans whose emotional connection with the games led them to engage with the product. The engagement signified the expansion, for free, the original game, thus expanding the value of the product. This hybrid form of play and labour articulates redefined cultural and social connections to digital games and their potential to unpack broader developments in contemporary culture (Sotamaa 2007) while predominantly remaining within the confines of free labour (Goggin 2011). The structural need to keep consumers engaged and part of the production process sparks new forms of enticing free labour.

The historical narrative behind the free labour ideology is more complex than a binary distinction between paid and non-paid forms of labour. As Steinfeld (2001, pp. 14–18) notes, within the dynamics of labour relations, all workers are subjected to various degrees of coercive pressures. Yet, as western forms of labour converge in a cultural and digital economy, the proliferation of immaterial labour has decoupled the notion free labour and wage labour (Lazzarato 1996). According to Terranova (2000), the digital world affords a broad set of practices that, while largely unpaid, they generate sources of value that can be appropriated and capitalized by other actors. Such production of value is what qualifies those practices as cultural and digital labour, and the fact that there is not an economic reward attached to them, labels them as free. Though often ephemeral and complex to quantify, free labour, argues Terranova, is 'structural to the late capitalist cultural economy' (2000, p. 53).

Without coercion or pay, free labour must endow itself with alternative forms of pay; usually anchored in immaterial, emotional and affective connections. This substitution of modes of rewarding labourers has signified two major developments. First, it has accelerated and strengthened the process by which consumers are incorporated into production processes. The case of media consumers, such as fans, is particularly telling, as entire platforms are dedicated to allowing users to create and share their own content. Without their labour, the platforms are irrelevant, so the business model is sustained by their involvement and engagement with the system (De Kosnik 2013). Second, it opened room to contest claims of exploitation (Scholz 2017). If users are rewarded with the pleasure of using the service and a sense of ownership to that service, the notion of labour is veiled by connotations of joy and empowerment; the dual agency of co-creation and co-production (Bruns 2007).

This is exemplified by what Jenkins (2006, p. 319) calls affective economics, which represents a 'new discourse in marketing and brand research that emphasizes the emotional commitments consumers make in brands as a central motivation for their purchasing decisions'. To Jenkins, the negotiation of the emotional capital accumulated by the user vis à vis a brand or service, questions the way in which user labour has usually been dichotomized. By incorporating the consumer into the production processes, the degree of participation and engagement with a brand can be beneficial to all parties. However, as Andrejevic (2011) points out, the notions of participation and engagement need to be understood as modes of interactivity, rather than traditional political empowerment. While affective economics recognize the power embedded in emotional capital, free labour dynamics manage to capitalize even more on heightened degrees of engagement. Thus, whether willingly or not, whether knowingly or not, the user adheres to new productive roles, such as data provider or data labourer (Manovich 2012).

To exemplify the notion of playbour, the geo-location social media platform *Foursquare* is particularly useful. Foursquare allowed users to check-in as they visited different places during their daily activities. Users were placed in a heavily gamified interface where they received badges, coins and the opportunity to become the 'mayor' of that particular venue, in competition with friends and other users. The check-in service is offered as a free-to-play model in which the key to the monetization strategy is the creation and development of a dataset that can be strategically commercialised and exploited by advertisers and marketers (Wilken 2016). There are several reasons why users choose to use Foursquare, such as fun, exploration and coordinating with friends (Lindqvist et al. 2011). Thus, 'separating "play", "expressive", and "utilitarian use" is not always possible' (Cramer et al. 2011, p. 64). Even though Foursquare uses gamification as a way to attract its user base, it constitutes an example of playbour, as its users are not in a contractual relationship with the company. However, as they play and engage with the system (whether knowingly or not), they generate data that is collected, stored, and commercialized. The output of their play is the source of revenue for the company, and while the users are not part of the work force of the company, they are the producers of the data. The degree of freedom of the user remains high, but the emotional attachment with the gamified system becomes the internal negotiation point by which personal enjoyment and exploitation coexist.

Whether playbour can be considered a form of playful exploitation (Rey 2012), or a constructed ideological concept that pretends to point at a higher unity of play and labour (Lund 2014), what seems clear is that free playbourers are endowed with a degree of agency. Disengaging from the playbour system could be done with a relative ease.

Gamification of Work and the Appropriation of Play

Broadly defined as the use of game elements and game design techniques in non-gaming contexts (Deterding et al. 2011), gamification has been increasingly popular in service applications from education and health, to personal performance and entertainment. Gamification implements game mechanics with the intent to increase user motivation to perform a given activity. The game mechanics being deployed can take various configurations, such as points, badges and leaderboards the most common.

It may be useful to point out that gamification is in itself a commercial term (Zackariasson 2016) that potentiates the use of digital games techniques to commodify personal data, as well as streamline commercial processes. It is the marketing moniker for a set of technologies intended to enhance user engagement, consumer loyalty, and induce social habit (Paharia 2013; Werbach and Hunter 2012).

The main difference between playbour and the gamification of work in the fact that playbour targets processes anchored in free labour practices, whereas gamification of work applies game thinking within working processes. Therefore, actual waged employees are considered to be in a gamified system instead of free labourer engaging with a system. This has serious implications in terms of free will and enjoyment that sustain the discourse of gamification of work. Whether playbourers participate in processes that they freely choose, gamified employees are embedded in systems that often veil production processes with the promise of fun. The capacity to opt-out in playbour environments is often present while within gamified working processes it is usually limited, or non-existent.

Thus, the popularity of gamifying working practices lies in the promise of motivating and engaging employees. The celebratory rhetoric that promotes gamification is based on the potential to turn labour into a fun and enjoyable experience (Herger 2014). The discursive narratives behind its application vow to positively empower and self-realize employees. However, gamification proponents will explicitly advertise that fostering motivated workers leads to higher productivity and profits (Zichermann and Linder 2013). The public discourse hails gamification as a mode of worker empowerment, the sales discourse grounds gamification in business maximisation.

These two sets of discourse are not necessarily mutually exclusive. Indeed motivated employees tend to perform better, which leads to higher productivity. This is what the technologies that support gamification attempt to do. A gamified system relies on processes that automatically quantify working activities and behaviours. It then offers feedback to the employees a playful representation of their performance with the aim of boosting motivation (Werbach 2014).

The appropriation of play occurs when a purely commercial and productive process is infused with the positive representations and emotions employees associate with play. The behavioural and sentiment data collected, stored, and analysed by the system is presented as a game-like experience trying to stimulate fun. The technology in itself takes the role of interacting with the workers and providing them with automated feedback that is expected to enact intrinsic motivators, similar to the experiences derived from playing digital games (Przybylski et al. 2010).

The contradiction emerges only when comparing the discourse of empowerment with the enactment of gamification. The processes of datafication and visualization require technological assemblages that are anchored in constant, automated surveillance, and that serve as bearings for patterns of control and exploitation (Conway 2014). Here the labour dynamics become problematic, as the worker is embedded in a system based on sociotechnical norms that incorporate all employees and their daily tasks, often without the possibility of an opt-out alternative. Once a system is implemented, it is only effective if workers use it, as it provides performance data to the employer.

A good example to examine is RedCritter, a gamified project management software that introduces different types of rewards and incentives to the employees of the organizations that use the service. The RedCritter system awards employees with points and badges to employees for their performance. Most rewards are visual representations of usual work activity, but others are the outcome of a competition among employees. While the company advertises the software as a mode to motivate and empower employees, a thorough investigation of the rewards shows exploitative practices in the shape of badges awarding employees who work during their lunch break, during the weekend, or work more hours than anyone in their team (Ferrer Conill 2016). Once a system like RedCritter is in place, employees have to conform to it, as there are no viable operations outside of the system, while all working processes are automatically quantified and used by management as a source of performance indicators.

Enterprise data-drive gamified systems combine labour with play with the aim to increase employee motivation by incorporating constant surveillance techniques that measure and display employees' performance (O'Donnell 2014; Whitson 2013). Such a negotiation between business objectives and employee well-being allows for practices bound in control and exploitation, which have been called Taylorism 2.0 by DeWinter et al. (2014).

Conflicting Logics and Technologies of Contradiction

The rise of gamification can only be understood by a combination of technological innovation (extended internet connectivity, networked devices, algorithmic power, and advanced interfaces), a cultural acceptance of digital games and media convergence, and a group of active popular champions who extract potential meanings and applications of its use and who push to further the gamification agenda. The deployment of gamification and game-like approaches to labour practices results in both playbour and the gamification of work, and responds to different logics that converge in the implementation of the system. The fact that these logics usually have different and conflicting underpinnings does not imply that they cannot coexist and overlap. However, the context in which gamification is introduced usually sets the frame for the logic that will eventually predetermine the outcome of the system.

The considerable degree of hype in the industry was confirmed and spurred when the first studies on gamification considered it to be an effective method to attract the attention and engagement of users in various domains (Deterding et al. 2011). The champions of gamification push forward the celebratory rhetoric of gamification, with a large body of popular science literature, hailing gamification as a viable solution to empower users, generate social inspiration, and overcome the limitations of tedious tasks (Duggan and Shoup 2013; McGonigal 2011; Zichermann and Linder 2010). This approach constitutes the public discourse of gamification (the discourse of empowerment) which would be accomplished by the meaningful implementation of game mechanics and playful thinking. The pleasurable and empowering goal of gamification is guided by its *hedonic logic*. A hedonic interface aims at inducing enjoyable experiences, used for entertainment-oriented leisure purposes, considered to be enjoyable in itself (Hamari 2015, p. 11). This logic prioritizes different motivations for implementation, such as gratifications, pleasure, enjoyment, or value to foster user engagement (O'Brien and Toms 2010).

When analysing how the champions of gamification market their services to organizations, the logic seems to shift. Whether is contextual (e.g. sell, exercise, learn, work) or instrumental (e.g. motivation, persuasion, habit formation, behaviour modification) for achieving the context activity, the consistent feature behind gamification is a *utilitarian logic*. The utilitarian logic of gamification is not only guided by what is being gamified (context) but also why something is being gamified (instrument). In the context of business, commercial outcomes are the guiding beacon of the utilitarian logic. The business of gamification prioritizes business objectives. The decision to gamify working processes is often taken by management, not employees. Sales, revenues and profit are the logic that supports the enterprise. Thus, the utilitarian logic of a gamified system is understood as the antithesis of the hedonic logic.

These two logics operate similarly in both playbour practices and the gamification of work. Play, embodied by the hedonic labour, and labour, embodied by the utilitarian logic are separated by the dimension of freedom. Following Marcuse's (1933/1973, p. 31) argument, by using Marx's notion of the 'realm of freedom', the human existence in labour is directed to reach 'realm of freedom', where necessities are met and play can unfold. To Marcuse, the distinction was so fundamental that labour and play could not coexist, as play resided in the 'realm of freedom' in which labour had no place. While in the praxis of labour, play only existed as a mode of escapism or break of labour. The irruption of digital labour has given the opportunity for organizations to veil labour praxis as if it were the 'realm of freedom' and celebrating labour as if it was play. This is, of course, more problematic in the gamification of work, simply because the employee is placed in a system of empowerment that also acts as a system of control, and does not have the freedom to simply stop using the system.

As the celebratory discourse has been exposed to its contradicting rhetoric, a more critical strand of literature has emerged (Bogost 2015; Conway 2014; DeWinter and Kocurek 2014; Fuchs et al. 2014; Kopeć and Pacewicz 2015). These contradictions are of course translated to the technological assemblages that support gamification. On the one hand, even for an organization that is truly concerned about the well-being of the workforce, the endgame of their *engagement* strategies is to maximize productivity and keep performance inventory of its human resources. An interface will be embedded with the playful hedonic logic of gamification, prioritizing values that foster autonomy, mastery, and relatedness (Przybylski et al. 2010). Empowerment through meaningful, gameful experiences is supposed to foster user agency (Nicholson 2015). On the other hand, the interface is supported by other technologies based on surveillance and quantifying human behaviour, specifically designed to optimize working objectives (Ferrer-Conill 2017). Therefore, when the game is not a choice but a chore, user agency cannot be enacted. In fact, as Conway (2014) supports, a diminished agency caused by coercive participation endangers the notions that the very game mechanics attempt to generate. The way the system works and what tasks are being rewarded are designed by managers, which questions autonomy; competition and performance is distributed among employees generating conflicts in labour dynamics, which questions relatedness; the need to constantly achieve objectives might bring the feeling that succeeding is out of reach, questioning mastery. The precedence of priorities is usually biased towards metrics and performance that satisfy business objectives rather than satisfaction and self-realization.

Conclusions

The ramifications of infusing playful thinking and game-like elements to labour processes are complex and should only be assessed on a case-by-case basis. However, this chapter has brought to the fore how such a socio-technical assemblage can substitute working human interaction by incorporating technologies that automatically quantify, compute, and visualize labour performance.

The complexity is exacerbated by a two-sided rhetoric surrounding playbour and gamification: on the one hand, the employee empowerment narrative in which tedious working tasks will be redefined to make labour enriching and fun; and on the other hand the promise of a more motivated workforce, higher productivity rates, and bigger profits. These two forms of rhetoric signify the contradicting logics upon which gamification is built in relation to the tensions and friction between organizational goals and the employees well-being. The former articulates the hedonic logic of gamification, which entices a meaningful approach incorporating reflection, exposition, choice, information, play, and engagement (Nicholson 2015). The latter is driven by the utilitarian logic, which enforces business objectives as the prevailing feature of the system.

Whether the system is anchored in the playbour frame or as gamification of work the friction between technology and labour dynamics are more than apparent. While the user of the system only interacts with the playful visualizations that either entice actions, reward activities, or represent performance, the metrics and behaviours captured by the algorithmic surveillance and the automation of emotions that are evoked by the system remain within a black box approach (Pasquale 2015). The processes in which the technology, enabled and installed by the organization capitalizes on data to attain business objective remain unknown to the employee.

As Fuchs (2014b) proposes, gamification is establishing its ideological bearings on labour processes that are rooted in the ruling system by the use of unconscious motivational conducts. The prevalent established neo-liberal economic principles and routines are promoted and expanded in exchange for a promise of fun. Thus, the traditional frictions between work and play are mediated by contradicting labour dynamics embedded in a technological assemblage that attempts to both empower and exploit the employee, whose only choice is to play or revolt.

References

Andrejevic, M. (2011). The work that affective economics does. *Cultural Studies, 25*(4–5), 604–620. https://doi.org/10.1080/09502386.2011.600551

Bogost, I. (2015). Why gamification is bullshit 2. In S. P. Walz & S. Deterding (Eds.), *The gameful world: Approaches, issues, applications* (pp. 65–80). Cambridge, MA: MIT Press.

Bruns, A. (2007). Produsage: Towards a broader framework of user-led content creation. In *Proceedings: Creativity & Cognition 2007: Seeding Creativity: Tools, Media, and Environments* (Vol. 6, pp. 99–106). Washington, DC.

Caillois, R. (1961). *Man, play and games*. Chicago: University of Illinois Press.

Conway, S. (2014). Zombification?: Gamification, motivation, and the user. *Journal of Gaming and Virtual Worlds, 6*(2), 143–157.

Cramer, H., Rost, M., & Holmquist, L. E. (2011). *Performing a check-in: Emerging practices, norms and "conflicts" in location-sharing using foursquare* (pp. 57–66). ACM Press. https://doi.org/10.1145/2037373.2037384

De Kosnik, A. (2013). Fandom as free labor. In T. Scholz (Ed.), *Digital labor: The internet as playground and factory* (pp. 98–111). New York: Routledge.

Deterding, S., Khaled, R., Nacke, L., & Dixon, D. (2011). From game design elements to gamefulness: Defining "gamification" In *Proceedings of the 15th International Academic MindTrek Conference: Envisioning Future Media Environments* (pp. 9–15). Tampere: ACM. https://doi.org/10.1145/2181037.2181040

DeWinter, J., & Kocurek, C. A. (2014). Games, gamification, and labour politics. *Journal of Gaming and Virtual Worlds, 6*(2), 103–107.

DeWinter, J., Kocurek, C. A., & Nichols, R. (2014). Taylorism 2.0: Gamification, scientific management and the capitalist appropriation of play. *Journal of Gaming & Virtual Worlds, 6*(2), 109–127.

Duggan, K., & Shoup, K. (2013). *Business gamification for dummies* (1st ed.). Hoboken/Chichester: For Dummies.

Ferrer Conill, R. (2016). Feeding the red critter: The gamification of project management software. In M. Dymek & P. Zackariasson (Eds.), *The business of gamification* (pp. 21–40). London: Routledge.

Ferrer-Conill, R. (2017). Quantifying journalism? A study on the use of data and gamification to motivate journalists. *Television & New Media*. https://doi.org/10.1177/1527476417697271

Fuchs, C. (2014a). *Social media: A critical introduction*. Los Angeles: SAGE.

Fuchs, M. (2014b). Gamification as twenty-first-century ideology. *Journal of Gaming and Virtual Worlds, 6*(2), 143–157.

Fuchs, M. (2015). Total gamification. In M. Fuchs (Ed.), *Diversity of play* (pp. 7–20). Lüneburg: Meson Press.

Fuchs, M., Fizek, S., Ruffino, P., & Schrape, N. (Eds.). (2014). *Rethinking gamification*. Lüneburg: Meson Press.

Goggin, J. (2011). Playbour, farming and labour. *Ephemera: Theory and Politics in Organization, 11*(4), 357–368.

Hamari, J. (2015, February). *Gamification. Motivations & effects*. PhD, Aalto University, Aalto.

Herger, M. (2014). *Enterprise gamification: Engaging people by letting them have fun* (Vol. 1, 1st ed.). Los Altos: CreateSpace Independent Publishing Platform.

Huizinga, J. (1949). *Homo ludens: A study of the play-element in culture*. London: Routledge & Kegan Paul.

Jenkins, H. (2006). *Convergence culture: Where old and new media collide* (Updated and with a new afterword). New York: New York University Press.

Jenkins, H., & Carpentier, N. (2013). Theorizing participatory intensities: A conversation about participation and politics. *Convergence: The International Journal of Research into New Media Technologies, 19*(3), 265–286.

Juul, J. (2000). *What computer games can and can't do*. Presented at the Digital Arts and Culture Conference, Bergen, Norway.

Kopeć, J., & Pacewicz, K. (Eds.). (2015). *Gamification. Critical approaches*. Warsaw: The Faculty of "Artes Liberales", University of Warsaw.

Kücklich, J. (2005). Precarious playbour: Modders and the digital games industry. *Fibreculture, 5*(1). http://journal.fibreculture.org/issue5/kucklich_print.html

Lazzarato, M. (1996). Immaterial labor. In S. Makdisi, C. Casarino, & R. E. Karl (Eds.), *Marxism beyond Marxism* (pp. 133–147). London: Routledge.

Lindqvist, J., Cranshaw, J., Wiese, J., Hong, J., & Zimmerman, J. (2011). *I'm the mayor of my house: Examining why people use foursquare – a social-driven location sharing application* (p. 2409). ACM Press. https://doi.org/10.1145/1978942.1979295

Lund, A. (2014). Playing, gaming, working and labouring: Framing the concepts and relations. *tripleC: Communication, Capitalism & Critique. Open Access Journal for a Global Sustainable Information Society, 12*(2), 735–801.

Manovich, L. (2012). Trending: The promises and the challenges of big social data. In M. K. Gold (Ed.), *Debates in the digital humanities* (pp. 460–475). Minneapolis: University of Minnesota Press.

Marcuse, H. (1973). On the philosophical foundation of the concept of labor in economics. *Telos, 1973*(16), 9–37. https://doi.org/10.3817/0673016009

McChesney, R. W. (2013). *Digital disconnect: How capitalism is turning the Internet against democracy*. New York: The New Press.

McGonigal, J. (2011). *Reality is broken: Why games make us better and how they can change the world* (Reprint ed.). New York: Penguin Books.

Nicholson, S. (2015). A RECIPE for meaningful gamification. In T. Reiners & L. C. Wood (Eds.), *Gamification in education and business* (pp. 1–20). New York: Springer International Publishing.

O'Brien, H. L., & Toms, E. G. (2010). The development and evaluation of a survey to measure user engagement. *Journal of the American Society for Information Science and Technology, 61*(1), 50–69.

O'Donnell, C. (2014). Getting played: Gamification, bullshit, and the rise of algorithmic surveillance. *Surveillance & Society, 12*(3), 349–359.

Paharia, R. (2013). *Loyalty 3.0: How to revolutionize customer and employee engagement with big data and gamification*. New York: McGraw-Hill Professional.

Pasquale, F. (2015). *The black box society: The secret algorithms that control money and information*. Cambridge: Harvard University Press.

Przybylski, A. K., Rigby, C. S., & Ryan, R. M. (2010). A motivational model of video game engagement. *Review of General Psychology, 14*(2), 154.

Rey, P. J. (2012). *Gamification, playbor & exploitation*. Retrieved October 24, 2015, from https://pjrey.wordpress.com/2012/12/27/gamification-playbor-exploitation/

Rey, P. J. (2015). Gamification and post-fordist capitalism. In S. P. Walz & S. Deterding (Eds.), *The gameful world: Approaches, issues, applications* (pp. 277–295). Cambridge, MA: The MIT Press.

Richardson, M. (1994). *Georges Bataille*. London/New York: Routledge.

Salen, K., & Zimmerman, E. (2003). *Rules of play: Game design fundamentals*. Cambridge: The MIT Press.

Scholz, T. (Ed.). (2013). *Digital labor: The Internet as playground and factory*. New York: Routledge.

Scholz, T. (2017). *Uberworked and underpaid: How workers are disrupting the digital economy*. Cambridge/Malden: Polity Press.

Sicart, M. (2014). *Play matters*. Cambridge, MA: The MIT Press.

Sotamaa, O. (2007). On modder labour, commodification of play, and mod competitions. *First Monday, 12*(9). https://doi.org/10.5210/fm.v12i9.2006

Steinfeld, R. J. (2001). *Coercion, contract, and free labor in the nineteenth century.* Cambridge/New York: Cambridge University Press.

Sutton-Smith, B. (2001). *The ambiguity of play* (2. printing, 1. Harvard University Press paperback ed). Cambridge, MA: Harvard University Press.

Terranova, T. (2000). Free labor: Producing culture for the digital economy. *Social Text, 18*(2), 33–58.

Thompson, P. (1989). *The nature of work.* London: Palgrave Macmillan. Retrieved from http://link.springer.com/10.1007/978-1-349-20028-3

Van Dijck, J. (2009). Users like you? Theorizing agency in user-generated content. *Media, Culture, and Society, 31*(1), 41.

van Dijck, J. (2013). *The culture of connectivity: A critical history of social media.* Oxford: OUP.

Van Dijck, J., & Poell, T. (2013). Understanding social media logic. *Media and Communication, 1*(1), 2. https://doi.org/10.17645/mac.v1i1.70

Werbach, K. (2014). (Re)defining gamification: A process approach. In A. Spagnolli, L. Chittaro, & L. Gamberini (Eds.), *Persuasive technology, LNCS 8462* (Vol. 8462, pp. 118–136). Cham: Springer International Publishing.

Werbach, K., & Hunter, D. (2012). *For the win: How game thinking can revolutionize your business.* Philadelphia: Wharton Digital Press.

Whitson, J. R. (2013). Gaming the quantified self. *Surveillance & Society, 11*(1/2), 163–176.

Wilken, R. (2016). The de-gamification of Foursquare? In T. Leaver & M. Willson (Eds.), *Social, casual and mobile games. The changing gaming landscape* (pp. 179–192). London: Bloomsbury Publishing.

Zackariasson, P. (2016). Old things – New names. In M. Dymek & P. Zackariasson (Eds.), *The business of gamification* (pp. 219–226). London: Routledge.

Zichermann, G., & Linder, J. (2010). *Game-based marketing: Inspire customer loyalty through rewards, challenges, and contests* (1st ed.). Hoboken: John Wiley & Sons.

Zichermann, G., & Linder, J. (2013). *The gamification revolution: How leaders leverage game mechanics to crush the competition.* New York: McGraw-Hill Professional.

Zimmerman, E. (2015). Manifesto for a ludic century. In S. P. Walz & S. Deterding (Eds.), *The gameful world: Approaches, issues, applications* (pp. 19–22). Cambridge, MA: The MIT Press.

12

Audience Metrics as a Decision-Making Factor in Slovene Online News Organizations

Aleksander Sašo Slaček Brlek

Introduction

Digitalisation has significantly increased the amount of available data about audiences, and audience metrics are already significantly reshaping the functioning of online newsrooms around the globe. Editors and journalists can follow a potentially endless amount of data about audience behaviour. They can follow what audiences are viewing, follow their paths through their websites, see how long they stay on a news item and learn how long they continue watching a video as well as the sources of traffic to their sites and shares on social media. The reliance on analytics in editorial decision-making is on the rise in the USA and Europe (Cherubini and Kleis Nielsen 2016), a trend that is also confirmed by studies on Slovene online newsrooms (Vobič 2014). While not yet widespread, computer algorithms are beginning to be used as a substitute for human choice in editorial decision-making (Thurman 2011; Thurman and Schifferes 2012) as well as to analyse, predict and manipulate demand from audiences: 'In this big-data era, media organizations have an ever

A. S. Slaček Brlek (✉)
University of Ljubljana, Ljubljana, Slovenia

© The Author(s) 2018
P. Bilić et al. (eds.), *Technologies of Labour and the Politics of Contradiction*,
Dynamics of Virtual Work, https://doi.org/10.1007/978-3-319-76279-1_12

expanding supply of data on audiences' media consumption patterns and preferences to draw upon, and algorithms play a central role in extracting actionable insights and producing decision outcomes from these data stores' (Napoli 2014, p. 34).

While this overabundance of data might seem like a boon at first glance, we are witnessing several worrying trends. Newsworkers are threatened by deskilling and the loss of their professional autonomy, as media companies are experimenting with content farming, crowdsourcing or even fully automated news production as ways to 'rationalise' newswork (Cohen 2015, p. 99). The privacy of audiences, on the other hand, is being eroded by the spread of 'surveillance capitalism' (Mosco 2014, p. 10), as the surveillance of internet users is coming to play an ever-increasing role in capital accumulation (cf. Allmer 2011; Andrejevic 2007a, b; Turow 2006a, b; Usher 2013; Zuboff 2015). It is therefore not enough to view the impact of audience metrics merely through their impact on the relationship between news producers and consumers. We must take into account their potential to empower advertisers and media managers in their pursuit of profit at the expense of both newsworkers and audiences as well as how audience metrics shift power relations inside news organisations in favour of the rising numbers of analysts and consultants (Napoli 2011, p. 73) that gather, analyse and interpret these data. Historically, the implementation of new technologies within news production has tended to reinforce the control of capital over labour in 'a long historical process that has served to naturalize the dominance of technology over journalism' (Örnebring 2010, p. 69).

The literature on audience metrics, however, reveals the shortcomings of research on technology and journalism in general. The first is that the scholarship on technological innovation in journalism tends 'to consider the problems of journalism scholarship from the point of view of the journalism profession' (Anderson 2012, p. 1007), leading to research that is not grounded in broader social theory. Apart from this, such a focus is reflected in the fact that, with some notable exceptions (for example Bucher 2017; Dörr 2016; Gynnild 2014; Linden 2017), research is focused almost exclusively on journalists and changes to the process of content creation. However, other groups of workers in the value chain of producing and distributing news are often ignored; these include 'internally publishers, news managers, developers, business people in media companies, and externally advertisers, the general audience or specific groups within it, producers of data as well as middlemen between data producers and users' (Linden 2017, p. 126). Such a narrow focus is characteristic of the research on analytics, as most of it focuses on its use in editorial decision-making and the potential impact of metrics on news selection and placement as well as on the ways journalists are negotiating their professional roles in the presence of metrics (Lee et al. 2012; MacGregor 2007; Tandoc 2015; Vu 2013; Welbers et al. 2016; Zamith 2015), only rarely extending the analysis to other relevant groups such as consultants and executives (cf. Anderson 2011).

To fully understand the role and impact of (new) technology, we must situate it in the socioeconomic context in which it operates. To this end, we must ground the analysis of technology in theoretical terms, specifically in the 'concept of *labour* as a lens through which we can see the relationship between journalism and technology' (Örnebring 2010, p. 59; emphasis in the original). While Örnebring suggests drawing on labour process theory to this end, we should not forget that the labour process is but one stage in the process of valorisation of capital. While the (historically neglected) exploration of journalism as labour is indeed necessary and productive, the labour process perspective can itself benefit from a broader focus on the 'full circuit of capital' in order to 'to build up a fuller picture of the capitalist enterprise' (Thompson 1990, p. 103).

Therefore, I explore audience metrics as a symptom of capitalist surveillance by extending my focus beyond the newsroom and questions of professional autonomy and the technologically aided degradation of newswork to include the role of audience metrics in selling and buying the audience commodity. Much of the existing research on the use of audience metrics in newsrooms has the shortcoming that it does not sufficiently take into account the broader social and political–economic contexts and the ways the introduction of metrics into the labour process is bound up with logics of the 'rationalisation' of newswork, both in the sense of producing more news in a shorter time at a lower cost but also by increasing revenues by more effectively monetising the audience commodity.

This study aims to address this shortcoming by focusing on a large part of the commodity chain of news production to include not only newsrooms but also the marketing of advertising space and media planning. In this way the implementation of audience metrics within the newsroom is connected to the business models of media organisations, their relationships with advertisers and their modes of monetising audiences.

Audience Metrics and Capitalist Surveillance

Audience metrics must be understood in their double economic role as a currency that facilitates the sale of the audience commodity (cf. Napoli 2003, 2011; Buzzard 2012) as well as a source of information for marketers to be able to manipulate demand for products. The first function – that of a currency – is due to the fact that the audience commodity is peculiar on account of its intangibility. Transactions between the sellers and buyers of audiences must therefore necessarily be based upon a representation of the audience and its characteristics, on more or less imperfect measures that are accepted by both parties in the transaction. In this sense the term currency carries a double meaning: 'First, it refers to what method is currently in use by the dominant ratings services, but it also refers to the use of ratings as a form of currency or money by which to buy and sell an otherwise invisible product' (Buzzard 2012, p. 1).

The second role arises from the more general problem of surplus absorption under capitalism, of creating sufficient demand to support an ever-expanding production of goods and services, which is expressed in historically specific ways. In this respect the resolution of the crisis of Fordism in the 1970s is particularly important to the spread of capitalist surveillance. As Streeck (2016, p. 98) argues: 'capital's answer to the secular stagnation of markets for standardized goods at the end of the Fordist era included making goods less standardized'. Instead of one-size-fits all mass production came customisation and product differentiation 'in an effort to get closer to the idiosyncratic preferences of ever-smaller groups of potential customers' (Streeck 2016, p. 98). Corresponding to this shift in production is a shift in circulation, reflected in the intensified tendency of marketing to target specific consumer segments and in commercially driven fragmentation of media channels (Turow 1997). As the reliable identification of profitable consumer segments requires increased information gathering, this shift also heralded a rising significance of surveillance for capitalist accumulation.

The significance of capitalist surveillance has only gained importance with the emergence of digital information and communication technologies. Advertisers have at their disposal an increasing amount of data about sociodemographic characteristics of potential customers, their online behaviour and even their lifestyles and psychological profiles, which they are able to utilise to more effectively target audience segments and to distinguish 'targets' from 'waste' (Turow 2012, p. 103). Furthermore, in the process of a 'seeping commodification' (Amon Prodnik 2014) increasingly more social relations are being mediated by (capitalist) communication technologies, far extending the range of potential information that can be gathered – from browsing histories to 'likes' on social media sites and even private emails sent to family and friends.

Consequently, the game of buying and selling the audience commodity has been thoroughly transformed. The digital age has produced not only new players but an entirely new class of player: digital platforms, foremost Alphabet and Facebook, have had stunning success in attracting advertisers by leveraging their ability to gather data about their users. The business models of these organisations are unprecedented in that they largely eschew the activity of content creation in favour of strategic placement in the process of circulation (as a search engine, news aggregator or through 'sharing' by users), utilising the free labour of users and other content creators for this purpose. By some estimates Google and Facebook have 'accounted for 20% of global advertising expenditure across all media in 2016' and have 'captured 64% of all the growth in global adspend between 2012 and 2016' (Zenith 2017).

The news industry is having a hard time adjusting to the changing circumstances and is struggling with a double crisis – one of civic adequacy and the other of economic viability (Blumler 2012). These structural pressures combined with the availability of metrics have the potential to significantly impact the workings of newsrooms. One part might be on the side of revenue, namely attempting to more fully utilise metrics to become more competitive in the pursuit of digital advertising revenue. It is hard to imagine, however, how news media could be able to match Facebook and particularly Alphabet in terms of surveillance. The other option could be to increase the rate of exploitation and control of the workforce, as news media companies are experimenting with content farming, crowdsourcing or even fully automated news production as ways to 'rationalise' newswork (Cohen 2015, p. 99). Metrics could also contribute to the deskilling of newsworkers, increased management control and the blurring of the editorial-marketing divide, similar to the broader trends of deskilling and segmenting the white collar workforce:

> Although some are given permission to think, increasing efforts are being made to translate *knowledge work* into *working knowledge* where what is in the minds of employees is captured and codified in the form of digital software, including online manuals and computer programs that can be controlled by companies and used by other often less skilled workers. (Brown et al. 2011, p. 66; emphasis in the original)

Audience metrics can therefore not be conceptualized simply through a struggle between professional judgement of journalists and the desires of audiences. The choices regarding which data will be gathered, how it will be analysed and presented reflect certain interests and power relations. That is why the introduction of metrics into the labour process of newsrooms does not simply expose journalists to the democratic will of the audience, but to a particular representation of the audience that is more likely to be aligned with the commercial interests of the owners than with a desire to democratise the public sphere.

Research Goal and Methods

The research focuses on three distinct spheres in the value chain of the audience commodity: journalistic content production, the marketing of advertising space and media planning. The goal is to discover the ways and degree to which metrics are impacting the work of journalists as well as to focus on the way power relations and dominant business concerns manifest in the use of metrics in Slovene online newsrooms.

The analysis focused on the three most visited online news portals at the time of the study (24ur.com, operated by Pro Plus; siol.net, operated by TSmedia; and rtvslo.si, operated by the public broadcaster RTV SLO), on the marketing of advertising space at Pro Plus and TSmedia and on the two largest media planning agencies in Slovenia in terms of revenue (Media publikum and Pristop media). The representative of the third largest media agency (Omnicom media group) was contacted but refused to participate in the research. The public broadcaster was included in the research not only because of its reach but also to contrast the two commercial news portals in the sense that potential differences in the ways or degree to which audience metrics are integrated into the newsroom of rtvslo.si in comparison to 24ur.com and siol.net might indicate the significance of market pressures in promoting the use of metrics in newsrooms.

A two-step qualitative research design was adopted, consisting of document analysis in the first phase and in-depth semi-structured interviews in the second. In the first phase, documents for analysis were chosen with the aim to understand the business situation of the analysed media organisations and their sources of revenue, competitive pressures and business strategies. For this purpose several sources were used: annual reports published on the website of the Agency of the Republic of Slovenia for Public Legal Records and Related Services as well as various documents addressed to investors, available on the websites of the analysed organisations, comprising mostly reports, presentations and fact sheets. For the public broadcaster, annual reports and plans available on its website were analysed.

This first phase contributed to the construction of interview guidelines for three specific groups of interviewees: journalists and editors, marketers of advertising space and representatives of media agencies (see Table 12.1).[1] These interviews can be regarded as 'expert interviews' since interviewees were chosen on the basis of their 'technical process oriented and interpretive knowledge referring to their specific professional sphere of activity' (Bogner and Menz in Flick 2009, p. 166). Consequently, most of the questions were focused on interviewees' professional experience with the use of audience metrics and their judgment in regard to the

Table 12.1 The interviewees

Date of interview	Role in organisation	Organisation	Duration of interview
26.5.2014	Editor-in-chief	TSmedia	1:00:52
27.5.2014	Editor-in-chief	Pro plus	1:27:59
29.5.2014	Daily editor	RTV SLO	1:18:21
30.5.2014	Daily editor	TSmedia	55:31
2.6.2014	Daily editor	Pro plus	48:40
4.6.2014	Daily editor	Pro plus	46:24
5.6.2014	Daily editor	TSmedia	1:07:37
18.6.2014	Daily editor	RTV SLO	54:07
18.5.2015	Media planner	Media publikum	52:16
21.5.2015	Director	Pristop media	44:59
25.5.2015	Head of internet marketing	Pro plus	44:04
28.5.2015	Head of marketing	TSmedia	47:08

impact of metrics on their respective fields (journalism, marketing of advertising space and media planning).

The different methods were combined to achieve complementarity and also to a lesser degree triangulation. While, for example, interviews with media planners provided information that could not be accessed from the interviews with editors or from the analysed documentation (and in this sense the different methods are complementary), interviews with different actors in a large part of the commodity chain connected to the news media industries allowed me to check for consistency, especially regarding the nature of interactions between different actors and to probe interviewees regarding these inconsistencies.

The Analysed Organisations

The three most visited online news portals were included in the analysis, which are (in this order) 24ur.com, siol.net and rtvslo.si. Their online audience share is very stable, while the number of unique monthly users of all three organisations is rising slowly (see Figs. 12.1 and 12.2).

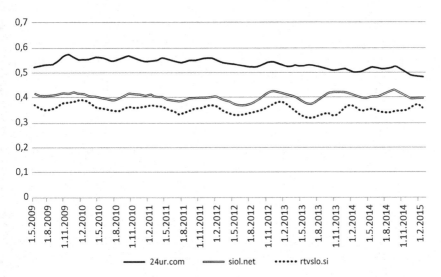

Fig. 12.1 Share of active internet users of the three most visited Slovene news websites (three-month sliding averages; Source: Slovene Chamber of Advertising)

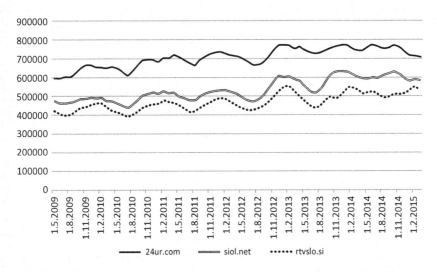

Fig. 12.2 Number of monthly unique users of the three most visited Slovene news websites (three-month sliding averages; Source: Slovene Chamber of Advertising)

It is important to take into account the financial constraint that the analysed organisations face, because it can significantly impact the pressure towards increasing advertising revenue. More in-depth analyses of media business models in Slovenia are available only for media that have ventured into the online world from print (see Vobič 2011, 2013), but these findings cannot be generalised to the organisations analysed here. Print media are in a specific position for several reasons. First of all the revenues of print media are significantly lower than those of broadcasting, limiting their ability to finance technological innovations in the digital sphere. Secondly, they have faced a steep decline in circulation, especially since the onset of the Great Recession, which hit Slovenia in 2009, further limiting their ability to offset even temporary losses in the digital sphere. As attempts to establish paywalls have largely proved ineffective (Vobič 2013) and the share of online advertising in Slovenia remains rather small, with estimates ranging from five to up to fifteen per cent[2] and with Alphabet and Facebook probably capturing around half of that revenue, print media that venture into the online sphere are caught between a rock and a hard place. The three analysed organisations on the other hand have more reliable sources of income that can help finance their expansion into the online world and can compensate for the relatively weak online advertising market.

The most visited news website, 24ur.com, is operated by Pro Plus, which is part of Central Media Enterprises and operates the most viewed television channel in Slovenia. Companies that are part of Central Media Enterprises have had a 79 per cent share of television advertising in Slovenia in Q1 of 2014 (CME 2014) and have been increasing incomes from tariffs and fees (CME 2014).

The website siol.net is operated by TSmedia, a subsidiary of the state-owned telecommunication company Telekom Slovenije. TSmedia operates a number of channels that it is able to market to advertisers, among others the only telephone directory (online and print) ; bizi.si, a site aggregating business oriented information; the search engine najdi.si as well as outdoor digital screens (TSmedia 2013). As TSmedia is a subsidiary of Telekom Slovenije, for which it represents 'a selling channel through which it can advertise its products' (Editor-in-chief, siol.net), it can survive operating at a loss for some period of time. The losses in 2012 are, according to their annual report, 'the result of planned investments in the new television business, which will generate income in the years to come, and was planned in advance' (TSmedia 2012).

Finally, rtvslo.si is the most specific of the three, since it is the online news portal of the public broadcaster, which generates the majority of its income through the license fee. In 2013 the license fee represented 71.1 per cent of all income for the public broadcaster (RTV SLO 2014). Nonetheless, advertising revenues are not irrelevant, since the broadcaster had a 15 per cent share of television advertising in Q1 2014 (CME 2014), and advertising is the second largest source of income for the public broadcaster after the license fee, representing 10.2 per cent of all income in 2013 (RTV SLO 2014). However, the public broadcaster is not free from financial constraints, especially at a time of ubiquitous financial consolidation (cf. Vobič and Slaček Brlek 2014).

All of the above does not mean that the analysed organisations are free from financial pressures, merely that those pressures are not as acute as for newspapers, which are struggling with monetising online audiences while at the same time facing steeply declining print readership. The most specific case is certainly rtvslo.si. The public broadcaster derives the majority of its income from non-market sources and is therefore much more independent from advertising revenue. Furthermore, it has a specific purpose in that it is bound to perform 'a public service in the areas of radio and television activity – with the purpose of satisfying the democratic, social and cultural needs' (RTV SLO 2014) of citizens of the Republic of Slovenia and other groups.

Audience Metrics and the Labour Process in Newsrooms

All of the interviewed editors claimed that audience metrics are an important factor in their decision-making. Especially daily editors use them when deciding on news item placement and when choosing a title or photograph. The daily editors have pointed out that the number of clicks is the most important metric that they use in their day-to day work. All three newsrooms have access to specialised software that enables the visualisation of these data in 15-minute intervals. It seems that the nature of the labour process in online newsrooms is an important factor that inhibits the use of a broader range of metrics. The interviewees pointed out that speed is a crucial requirement for their work. In this context it is understandable that they need a metric that is simple, at least seemingly unambiguous, and available in real time and that does not demand further analysis to become operational. The number of clicks meets all these criteria, while the introduction of additional metrics (like time spent on the website, number of comments, number of shares and so on) would require additional analysis and would inevitably raise the question of how much weight should be assigned to each of them. While the analysed online newsrooms have access to a broader range of metrics, they are not integrated into the workflow to a degree comparable to the number of clicks. When asked about the range of data that journalists have access to in their daily work, one interviewee replied,

> We get these data afterwards. We can see in fifteen minute intervals how much it is read, but we don't even follow the other stuff. We don't bother with it as we go. If we were to wait for these data, it would all be over by the time we got them. The website is so dynamic, the news items keep shifting so rapidly that you don't have time to analyse things. You work in this workflow and you use your intuition and a bit of those first metrics. (Daily editor, 24ur.com)

If daily editors believe that a certain news item is not reaching an appropriate number of clicks, they decide between three options: moving it to a more prominent position, changing the title or changing or adding multimedia content (especially photographs):

> If a news item that I think is important is not receiving the attention it deserves, I can give it a more attractive photo, give it a better or more telling title, but it must not be deceptive. That is where I draw the line. /.../ You can bump the thing up on the portal, you can change the title, you can add a photo, but all in the confines of responsible reporting. (Daily editor, rtvslo.si)

The interviewees claimed that they do not face pressures to increase the number of clicks, but the editors of the two commercial sites said that there is at least an implicit expectation that the number of clicks is increasing or at least not decreasing in comparison to competitors. But they claim that they have no set goals with regard to the number of clicks, reaching certain target groups and so on. They also seem not to be aware of the process of monetising audiences, as none of the interviewees could answer the question of how advertising space was being marketed to advertisers and how they are being billed.

It is therefore not surprising that all interviewees, those from the public broadcaster as well as those from the commercial websites, saw the availability of metrics as a generally positive thing that does not encroach upon their professional autonomy. They generally saw it as a question of the right measure: while a logic of blindly chasing clicks would be at odds with their professional judgment, they believe that they are able to exercise professional judgment so that the availability of this metric contributes to rather than inhibits the quality of their work. The goal seems to them to find the proper balance so that clicks are given proper attention but that one does not succumb to their temptation:

> I don't think that an item that is not clicked is of the highest quality. Maybe the case is that it is not that good. You have to find an optimal balance between what people are interested in and not crossing the line of decency if I can put it like that. /.../ I'll give you an example: that time when that father jumped with that little girl.[3] We cannot pretend that it did not happen. But we did say 'look, we won't go and take pictures.' It was five minutes away, and we could have gone, and this would have gotten a huge amount of clicks. Guaranteed. If you write: 'we have photos, one dead and I don't know what, two ambulances.' But we have agreed that this is a line we will not cross. (Daily editor, siol.net)

The editors at rtvslo.si were slightly more critical of clicks and pointed out the specific status of the public broadcaster in this respect, which frees them from the need to chase clicks so that 'this is not our only criterion, but can provide welcome help' (Daily editor, rtvslo.si). Nevertheless, they too saw the number of clicks as a metric that journalists should give serious consideration to, since it is generally associated with journalistic quality:

> I am interested in clicks to see whether a news item is good. If it contains all the information or if something is missing, for example. /.../ And if I believe something to be important and I believe that it has not received enough attention from readers, then I absolutely go and check the news item to see whether we have missed some information or it needs to be upgraded. (Daily editor, rtvslo.si)

Based on the statements of the interviewed editors, audience metrics are not a factor that negatively impacts their professional autonomy. The interviewees were much more pessimistic about increasing workloads, which some of them pointed out as a decisive factor that is impacting the ability of journalists to fulfil their obligations to the public. The editor-in-chief of 24ur.com pointed to this factor as the main cause of errors in reporting: 'This is connected with other things, because there are not enough journalists, because journalists are working on three or four topics at a time. When they finish a news item they simply don't have the time to think about it anymore, because they are working on one or even two others at the same time.' The editor-in-chief of siol.net was similarly pessimistic: 'As I said earlier, it is obviously impossible for media in Slovenia to survive by doing good work – not just work or a lot of work, but professional work.'

Both editors-in-chief pointed to another worrying trend, namely native advertising. The editor-in-chief of siol.net referred to native advertising as a 'packet project' and predicted it would become the dominant way of monetising audiences. When asked whether he knew how advertisers are being billed, he explained:

> I don't want to go into details here because I am not that familiar with this subject. In general I would say: the advertiser wants their content to be seen by X thousands of readers and is prepared to pay a price of Y for that. The other model, which is in my view becoming dominant, is the packet project: 'I have a project, I want to produce content about ozone holes because I have discovered a cure for them. Can we do this project together?' (Editor-in-chief, siol.net)

Barriers to the Integration of Metrics into Newsrooms

It is certainly possible that interviewees downplayed the impact of clicks on their work since too strong of a reliance on this metric is considered by them a violation of professional norms. While this remains a possibility, I believe it is unlikely that their answers fundamentally misrepresent reality for three reasons. The first is that answers from interviewees from the three newsrooms are largely consistent with one another. The second is that the interviewees spoke rather frankly about how journalistic standards were being lowered on account of increasing workloads as well as the increasing trend of native advertising. The third is that there exist a number of structural factors inhibiting the full integration of audience metrics into the labour process of newsrooms. It is to these barriers to the integration of metrics I now turn, also drawing on interviews with marketers and media planners.

The first barrier was mentioned already in the previous part of this chapter, namely the difficulty of translating metric targets into the workflow of newsworkers in online newsrooms. While news organisations may be able to gather an ever-increasing amount of audience data, the task of incorporating it into the fast-paced daily routines of online newsrooms that call for quick decisions is no simple task. While the number of clicks has proven to be a metric that is fit for this purpose because it is easily understandable, available in real time and seemingly unambiguous, the introduction of additional or more complex metrics might decrease the productivity of online newsrooms by burdening editors and journalists with additional software tools or might lead to additional costs if it means investing in the analysis of the data.

Furthermore, the metric that is integrated into the daily routines of journalists and editors (the number of clicks) is rather crude from a marketing perspective, since a larger number of clicks do not simply translate into higher advertising revenues. The head of marketing of TSmedia pointed out that a pursuit of clicks at all costs might even alienate some premium advertisers, who might fear that their brand image would be damaged if their ads were to appear next to 'naked breasts, buttocks and superficial content' as he put it.

This brings us to the second structural barrier, namely the relation between costs and benefits. The costs of gathering and analysing data about audiences make sense only to the degree that advertisers are willing to pay an adequate premium for reaching more narrowly defined consumer segments. As Slovenia is a very small market with a total population of roughly two million people, advertisers are hesitant to invest in segmenting an already small market: 'big data is a sort of a problem, because it is a big cost but you cannot monetise it. If we had a bigger market, it would pay off' (Head of marketing, TSmedia). The director of Pristop Media pointed to the same factor when commenting on behavioural targeting: 'we know these techniques in Slovenia, and there are some providers, but in the end everybody will tell you that the market is too small, that the law of big numbers doesn't work here.' However, as I am writing this chapter, TSmedia is marketing behaviourally based advertising solutions. They claim to be 'the only Slovenian publisher' providing this service (TSmedia 2017).

The third structural barrier is the availability and feasibility of alternative modes of monetising audiences. As already discussed in the previous chapter, native advertising is one of those modes. While it is hard to imagine news media being able to rival Alphabet in terms of their ability to gather and process data about users, they do have a competitive advantage in that they produce their own content. According to the head of digital marketing at TSmedia, the company has a separate advertorial newsroom where four persons with journalistic skills collaborate with advertisers on the production of native advertising.

This competitive advantage can also be used as an alternative means of segmenting audiences according to interests. Instead of gathering the behavioural data of users and targeting them in real time, publishers can create interest-based channels to attract the appropriate consumer segments (a specialised website for home repairs, interior decorations, food, fashion, young parents and so on), and offering connected advertorial services to advertisers can prove effective even without extensive data gathering. The head on online marketing at POP TV noted how these 'microsites' are more appropriate for collaboration with advertisers in the form of product placement or sponsored content: 'If someone comes with an idea for a sponsored competition – this sort of less serious content – that is possible. But for this the microsites are appropriate.'

Finally, the implementation of audience metrics into online newsrooms can be impacted by the overall business strategy and the role of online newsrooms in this strategy. Pro Plus is a telling example, since their dominant position in the television market gave them an important advantage when entering the online world: the website could be promoted on the television channels, and video content produced for television is often recycled on the website, while their position in the television market strengthens their bargaining position with advertisers. The website remains of secondary importance for the company: 'Since we are a television organisation, we have the support of shows, big sponsorships; we have big advertisers, who get reach through television and then they use the internet to support that and to share some specific information' (Head of digital marketing, Pro Plus).

Conclusion

I have focused on audience metrics in the context of their economic role in capitalist surveillance, where their role is segmenting audiences for more effective sales for advertisers. I have found that the number of clicks is the dominant metric present in newsrooms and that journalists and editors generally do not feel the availability of this information to undermine their professional autonomy. It seems that the segmentation of audiences through targeted content as well as collaboration with advertisers on native advertising are the primary means through which news organisations attempt to increase their advertising income.

My analysis reveals that there are effective functional equivalents to the gathering of data that news media organisations are utilising to remain competitive in the digital world. They attempt to do this by leveraging their competitive advantage vis-à-vis Alphabet and Facebook, which is the fact that they produce their own content. Segmenting audience members through specialised interest-based channels, closer collaboration with advertisers on native advertising and adapting editorial policy to focus on news stories that are attractive to advertisers are all possible examples of this strategy.

Contemporary discussions on the impact of automation on newswork tend to overlook indirect effects arising from the sphere of circulation that are by no means inconsequential. As Linden (2017, p. 127) claims: 'Where journalism jobs have been disappearing, the reasons are to be found in changing consumer behaviour and media business models, not in automation.' The pauperisation of journalism is primarily the consequence of changes in circulation, because as part of the 'stagnant sector' it has traditionally had a low degree of substitution between capital and labour, and competitive pressures are producing a 'creative destruction of journalism making it much more productive but less and less – journalism' (Splichal and Dahlgren 2016, p. 9). My findings are in line with this claim, since the nature of the labour process has emerged as an important barrier to a fuller implementation of audience metrics that could maximise advertising revenue or increase the productivity of journalists. In this situation competitive pressures are not leading to technological innovation that increases the productivity of newswork. It seems that digital technologies are not restructuring newswork into a high-tech utopia (or dystopia, for that matter) but bringing back rather primitive methods of increasing surplus value through lower wages, precarious working arrangements and longer working hours.

Notes

1. Parts of the interviews with journalists and editors were previously analysed and published in Slaček Brlek (2014).
2. The lower estimate is almost certainly inaccurate, since it relies on 'published price lists of media units' (Mediana 2017) and it consequently significantly underrepresents online advertising because of two factors: it does not include Facebook and Alphabet, which are estimated to account for about half of online advertising revenues, and it does not take into account differences between published price lists and actual prices paid (discounts).
3. A man had committed suicide by jumping through the window of his apartment with his daughter in his hands.

References

Allmer, T. (2011). Critical surveillance studies in the information society. *triplec: Communication, Capitalism & Critique, 9*(2), 566–592.

Amon Prodnik, J. (2014). A seeping commodification: The long revolution in the proliferation of communication commodities. *triplec: Communication, Capitalism & Critique, 12*(1), 142–168.

Anderson, C. W. (2011). Between creative and quantified audiences: Web metrics and changing patterns of newswork in local US newsrooms. *Journalism, 12*(5), 550–566.

Anderson, C. W. (2012). Towards a sociology of computational and algorithmic journalism. *New Media and Society, 15*(7), 1005–1021.

Andrejevic, M. (2007a). *iSpy: Surveillance and power in the interactive era*. Lawrence: University Press of Kansas.

Andrejevic, M. (2007b). Surveillance in the digital enclosure. *The Communication Review, 10*(4), 295–317.

Blumler, J. (2012). Foreword: The two-legged crisis of journalism. *Journalism Practice, 4*(3), 243–245.

Brown, P., Lauder, H., & Ashton, D. (2011). *The global auction*. Oxford/New York: Oxford University Press.

Bucher, T. (2017). Machines don't have instincts. *New Media and Society, 19*(6), 918–933.

Buzzard, K. (2012). *Tracking the audience: The ratings industry from analog to digital*. New York/London: Routledge.

Cherubini, F., & Nielsen, R. K. (2016). *Editorial analytics: How news media are developing and using audience data and metrics*. Retrieved from http://www.digitalnewsreport.org/publications/2016/editorial-analytics-2016/

CME. (2014). *Investor presentation*. Retrieved from http://www.cetv-net.com/file/u/presentations/cme_q1_2014_investor_presentation.pdf

Cohen, N. S. (2015). From pink slip to pink slime: Transforming media labor in a digital age. *The Communication Review, 18*(2), 98–122.

Dörr, K. N. (2016). Mapping the field of algorithmic journalism. *Digital Journalism, 4*(6), 700–722.

Flick, U. (2009). *An introduction to qualitative research* (4th ed.). London: Sage.

Gynnild, A. (2014). Journalism innovation leads to innovation journalism. *Journalism, 15*(6), 713–730.

Lee, A. M., Lewis, S. C., & Powers, M. (2012). Audience clicks and news placement: A study of time-lagged influence in online journalism. *Communication Research, 41*(4), 505–530.

Linden, C.-G. (2017). Decades of automation in the newsroom. *Digital Journalism, 5*(2), 123–140.

MacGregor, P. (2007). Tracking the online audience. *Journalism Studies, 8*(9), 280–298.

Mediana. (2017). *Mediana IBO*. Retrieved from http://www.mediana.si/medianini-aduti/mediana-ibo/

Mosco, V. (2014). *To the cloud: Big data in a turbulent world*. Boulder: Paradigm Publishers.

Napoli, P. M. (2003). *Audience economics: Media institutions and the audience marketplace*. New York: Columbia University Press.

Napoli, P. M. (2011). *Audience evolution: New technologies and the transformation of media audiences*. New York: Columbia University Press.

Napoli, P. M. (2014). On automation in media industries: Integrating algorithmic media production into media industries scholarship. *Media Industries Journal, 1*(1), 33–38.

Örnebring, H. (2010). Technology and journalism-as-labour. *Journalism, 11*(1), 57–74.

RTV SLO. (2014). *Letno poročilo 2013 [2013 annual report]*. Retrieved from http://www.rtvslo.si/strani/letno-porocilo-2013/4690

Slaček Brlek, S. (2014). Kvantifikacija občinstev kot ključni dejavnik odločanja v spletnih uredništvih. *Javnost-The Public, 21*(supplement), S93–S112.

Slovene Chamber of Advertising. *Rezultati merjenja obiskanoti spletnih strani* [Results of measurement of website visits]. Retrieved from http://www.mosssoz.si/si/rezultati_moss/obdobje/default.html

Splichal, S., & Dahlgren, P. (2016). Journalism between de-professionalisation and democratisation. *European Journal of Communication, 31*(1), 5–18.

Streeck, W. (2016). *How will capitalism end?* London/New York: Verso.

Tandoc, E. C., Jr. (2015). Why web analytics click. *Journalism Studies, 16*(6), 782–799.

Thompson, P. (1990). Crawling from the wreckage: The labour process and the politics of production. In D. Knights & H. Wilmott (Eds.), *Labour process theory* (pp. 95–124). Houndsmills/London: Macmillan.

Thurman, N. (2011). Making 'the daily me': Technology, economics and habit in the mainstream assimilation of personalized news. *Journalism, 12*(4), 395–415.

Thurman, N., & Schifferes, S. (2012). The future of personalization at news websites. *Journalism Studies, 13*(5/6), 775–790.
TSmedia. (2012). *Revidirano letno poročilo za leto 2011 [2011 revised annual report]*. Retrieved from http://www.ajpes.si/jolp/podjetje.asp?maticna=2169576000&leto=2011
TSmedia. (2013). *Revidirano letno poročilo za leto 2012 [2012 revised annual report]*. Retrieved from http://www.ajpes.si/jolp/podjetje.asp?maticna=2169576000&leto=2012
TSmedia. (2017). *Ciljano oglaševanje* [Targeted advertising]. Retrieved from http://www.tsmedia.si/ciljano-oglasevanje/
Turow, J. (1997). *Breaking up America: Advertisers and the new media world*. Chicago: University of Chicago Press.
Turow, J. (2006a). Cracking the consumer code: Advertising, anxiety and surveillance in the digital age. In K. D. Hagerty & R. V. Ericson (Eds.), *The new politics of surveillance and visibility* (pp. 279–307). Toronto: University of Toronto Press.
Turow, J. (2006b). *Niche envy: Marketing discrimination in the digital age*. Cambridge, MA/London: The MIT Press.
Turow, J. (2012). *The daily you: How the new advertising industry is defining your identity and your worth*. New Haven/London: Yale University Press.
Usher, N. (2013). Al Jazeera English online. *Digital Journalism, 1*(3), 335–351.
Vobič, I. (2011). Online multimedia news in print media: A lack of vision in Slovenia. *Journalism, 12*(8), 946–962.
Vobič, I. (2013). *Journalism and the web: Continuities and transformations at Slovenian newspapers*. Ljubljana: Založba FDV.
Vobič, I. (2014). Audience conceiving among journalists: Integrating social-organizational analysis and cultural analysis through ethnography. In G. Patriche, H. Bilandzic, J. Linaa Jensen, & J. Jurišić (Eds.), *Audience research methodologies: Between innovation and consolidation* (pp. 19–36). New York/London: Routledge.
Vobič, I., & Slaček Brlek, S. (2014). Manufacturing consent among newsworkers at Slovenian Public Radio. *Javnost-The Public, 21*(1), 19–36.
Vu, H. T. (2013). The Online audience as gatekeeper: The influence of reader metrics on news editorial selection. *Journalism, 15*(8), 1094–1110.
Welbers, K., van Atteveldt, W., Kleinnijenhuis, J., Ruigrok, N., & Schaper, J. (2016). News selection criteria in the digital age. *Journalism, 17*(8), 1037–1053.

Zamith, R. (2015). *Editorial judgement in an age of data*. Dissertation submitted to the Faculty of University of Minnesota. Retrieved from https://conservancy.umn.edu/handle/11299/175385

Zenith. (2017). *Top 30 global media owners 2017*. Retrieved from https://www.zenithusa.com/top-30-global-media-owners-2017/

Zuboff, S. (2015). Big other: Surveillance capitalism and the prospects of an information civilization. *Journal of Information Technology, 30*, 75–89.

Part IV

Contradictions in Democratic
Participation and Regulation

13

Media Use and the Extended Commodification of the Lifeworld

Göran Bolin

Introduction

The increased use of mobile personal media and web-based services (search engines, social networking sites, blog portals, etc.) has over the past couple of decades resulted in the development of new business models within the media and culture industries (Bolin 2011). Where older mass media models were based on selling media texts/content to audiences, or by selling 'eyeballs to advertisers', the new business models build on the extraction of economic value from web user activity, based in the aggregation of massive amounts of (big) data in an unprecedented scale, and in more socially intrusive ways compared to traditional survey methods and people meters (Bermejo 2009; Bolin 2012; van Dijck 2013).

One could say that there are basically two kinds of new industrial models for capturing the digital media user. Firstly, when users create profiles on, for example, Facebook, they are basically completing a questionnaire disclosing their personal data. In this way an 'audience commodity' is constructed based on self-reported sociological variables (age,

G. Bolin (✉)
Södertörn University, Stockholm, Sweden

gender, education, socio-economic status, etc.) very similar to the old survey technology. The second model builds on digital activity through the cookies that are installed on our computers and mobiles and through the tracking of user movement in digital space (Turow 2011; Andrejevic 2007). This 'data-base marketing' takes several forms such as 'stealth marketing', 'predictive behavioural targeting', etc., where telecom, advertising and media companies cooperate in order to capture 'the digital consumer' to the mutual economic benefit of all parties. This is also due to the increased integration and convergence between previously separate markets, where the telecom business and the media content producers today have become integrated, and where the Internet service providers based in the telecommunications business are key players, since it is through their cables and wi-fi networks that information travels (Bolin 2011, p. 119).

In the wake of this development arise the questions on how the media and culture industries generate economic value, what are the central components in this value-generating process, and what type of motor makes the production and consumption process tick. One part of this research is directed towards the organisational forms of the media and culture industries (e.g. Picard 2010; Wikström 2009). Others have identified changes *within* the media and culture industries, triggered by the changed relations between media producers and users. Peter Jakobsson (2012), for example, analyses the tension between the 'content industry' that are dependent on traditional copyrights, and the part that get their revenues from the appropriation of user-generated content. This 'openness industry' has no interest in strong immaterial rights since their business models build on the appropriation and use of the media users' creative efforts, to the contrary of the traditional mass media, who earned their revenues from the selling of content. This chapter is about this latter part of the media industries, where the media user is both the customer, utilising the services and the contents of the media industry, and the worker, providing the industry with their labour power.

If the appropriation of the media user's activity is obvious today, the discussion about the role of media use for media production was already initiated in the 1970s (Smythe 1977), and concepts such as 'watching as working' (Jhally and Livant 1986) were developed (for overview of debate, see Fuchs 2012). In the wake of digitisation and the interactive web this discussion on the role of user engagement has become revived. The more positively inclined emphasise participation, creativity and the non-hierarchical nature of the practices of media users (e.g. Bruns 2006; Jenkins 2006), how new, digital and algorithm-based media provide opportunities for 'distributed problem solving' and how 'the wisdom of crowds' build websites such as Wikipedia (e.g. Surowiecki 2004), or the industry benefits of 'crowdsourcing' (Brabham 2008). More critical researchers analyse the same phenomena in terms of increased and intensified surveillance (Andrejevic 2007; Vaidhyanathan 2011; Fuchs 2014), appropriation and 'free labour' (Terranova 2000; Hesmondhalgh 2010), 'playbour' (Kücklich 2005; cf. Hjorth 2017) or in terms of 'loser generated content' (Petersen 2008). Some have focussed co-produced journalism and computer game modulation with a focus on highly active media users (Deuze 2007; Banks and Humphreys 2008), others have directed their interest towards bloggers and social media influencers (Duffy 2017; Hearn and Schoenhoff 2016). Few have focussed on more 'ordinary' media users (i.e., not hackers or fans), and how they perceive of their role in these production-consumption processes focussed on media user behaviour that the media industries engage in (but see Kennedy et al. 2015 for an exception).

There are several studies on labour in the media industries, and how the professional creative workers regard their working conditions (e.g. Hesmondhalgh and Baker 2011; Mosco and McKercher 2009). There is also a wealth of theoretical reflections on 'labour in the digital age' (e.g. Fisher and Fuchs 2015). Empirical research on the ways in which ordinary users are drawn into production processes, and how they perceive of this, is more rare although it is mainly these broader layers of consumers that are the main source of 'labour' for the media and culture industries – especially the sector that build on openness. Yochai Benkler (2006) has made the important distinction between the kinds of production aimed at producing profit (the main goal for media industries), and the non-market motivated production by media users, which does not aim to produce surplus value. To understand the role of media users in these processes thus requires an approach that takes the users' own consideration into account. I have elsewhere (Bolin 2012) developed a theoretical understanding on why media users might negotiate the ambivalences brought on by the tension between being surveilled and the pleasures of media use, where users freely give away the rights to the fruits of their labour (that is, those things that are uploaded on social networking sites, where, for example, Facebook through their 'Terms of use' has secured the rights to dispose of this content in whichever way they find appropriate). This is one of the forms of what could be termed the labour dimension of media use. The other form concerns a more transient dimension of media user labour or activity, namely the construction of the 'traffic commodity', as search engine researcher Elizabeth Van Couvering (2008) terms it, that is, the information on search traffic and web behaviour that can be refined by the algorithms of search engines and social networking sites (and in portals of consumption such as Adlibris or Amazon). Now, one can distinguish between two types of traffic commodity, what I have elsewhere (Bolin 2011, p. 122) called the general traffic commodity and the specific traffic commodity. The *general traffic commodity* is what the telecom sector is interested in, that is, bits flowing through networks irrespective of the patterns of these bits. Swedish telecom provider Telia, for example, earns its revenues through subscriptions that allow users to use their networks for economic compensation. The *specific traffic commodity* is the refined version of these bits, where they are algorithmically processed in order to direct advertising or other kinds of messages to media users of certain behaviour profiles. This is the commodity at the basis for e.g. Google's enormous revenues (Bilić 2017), and it is this specific traffic commodity that is of concern in this chapter.

The difference between the audience commodity and the specific traffic commodity is that the former build on traditional sociological variables (sex, class, age, education, etc.) while the latter build on the digital persona constructed through the very activity and behaviour of the media user in the digital media landscape – both virtually through surfing the web, and in physical space/location with use of geo-social applications such as Foursquare on the smartphone (through its GPS functions), or through 'geo-tagging' on Facebook Places. The difference is between a social/psychological self and a 'data double', that is, the digital persona that is linked to the user's technological gadgets rather than him/her as an individual subject (Ruppert 2011). The surveillance of the data double can be perceived of as less intrusive and accordingly easier to live with, compared to if the person would be individually surveilled (through wiretapping the phone, for example). How users negotiate this is worth to explore further.

In order to add to the existing body of research into media work, this chapter wishes to contribute with empirical knowledge on various categories of 'ordinary' media users (as opposed to fans or highly specialised users). The aim of this paper is, then, to analyse how media users argue around their activities in online spaces in the context of the value creating processes of the media and culture industries. How do media users relate to their own media use, seen in relation to how the media industries take advantage of their activities? Where do media users draw a line for what they are willing to share (with others, with the industry) as individual persons (subjects) and as digital personas (user profiles, blog profiles, etc.)? And on what grounds do they draw this line? In short: how does it feel to be labouring in the symbolic factory of sign production and consumption?

The Model for Analysis

In Bolin (2012) is developed a theoretical model that aims to explain how and why media users contribute with their 'free labour' to the benefit of the media and culture industries. As theorized by Tiziana Terranova (2000), 'free labour' is the labour that is freely given by media users, but also 'free' for the industry in the sense that the labour is not remunerated. What remains unexplained by Terranova (and others) is why media users are giving away the fruits of their labour for free. The explanation given in Bolin (2012) is that the labour carried out by media users is rewarded in another field of cultural production than that in which the media industries act.

Media users could in fact be regarded as involved in two production-consumptions circuits (Table 13.1): in the first field (in the sense of Bourdieu), here tentatively labelled the field of prosumption for want of a better term, the user activities produce social difference (identities and cultural meaning) in a social and cultural economy. Through the postings

Table 13.1 Two fields of cultural production/consumption

Prosumption	Industrial production
Production of difference	Commodity production
Sign value	Exchange value
Social and cultural economy	Market economy
Non-profit motivation	Profit motivation

on social networking sites, and the interaction and communicative exchange performed there, the user receives rewards in terms of social prestige, recognition, sociality, identity and belonging. This labour, if one agrees to label it that way (and indeed, 'identity work' has been a common term in cultural studies analysis of media use since long), is non-profit motivated and its rewards are symbolic and result in sign value (cf. Baudrillard 1972/1981), circulated on the market for symbolic goods (Bourdieu 1993) within the framework of a social and cultural economy. It is a form of 'productive consumption' (Marx 1867/1976), or maybe more accurately 'consumptive production' (Baudrillard 1973/1975), as it is production as a result of consumption, that is, production as a consequence of media use.

This labour is then made the object of productive consumption as part of the activities of the media industries, the end product being economic profit. This means that the fruits of the labour of media users get appropriated by the media and culture industries, acting in another production-consumption field where activities are indeed profit-motivated and conducted within the framework of the commercial market economy. Media user labour is here used as raw material in the production process, and in that capacity the labour of media users is objectified and drawn into this new production-consumption circuit, productively consumed in the process and turned into economic value for the industry.

The premise that makes media user work more easily objectified and consumed in this new production-consumption circuit is the digitization process, and the fact that the active work of media users is increasingly materialized in textual form. If one considers the activities surrounded media consumption as being of three kinds, that is, subjective, social and textual (Fiske 1992), one can easily see that in the pre-digital world, the *subjective* and *social* productivity resulting in, for example, meaning and identity, was very hard for the media industries to objectify, turn into raw material and extracted economic value from. The *textual* productivity of, for example fans, could indeed occasionally be appropriated and taken advantage of by media industries (although the examples are sparse, but see Jenkins 1992), but the meaning making by the individual, or the social debates between media users on the quality of certain pop songs, were not accessible for the media and culture industries.

With digitization all this changes, as is illustrated in Table 13.2 below.

As is illustrated in Table 13.2, the textual productivity of media users – fan stories, reviews and features in photo-copied fanzines – was potentially accessible for media and culture industries already in the pre-digital world, although this was rather uncommon. In the digital world of interactive media and social networking sites, where fan stories, reviews on debates are published not in photocopied fanzines with small and alternative circulation, but on web-based blogs and social networking sites, the possibilities for the media and culture industries to access these multiply. And in addition, since the social productivity – the discussions with friends and colleagues at work on the latest pop song, yesterday's television drama or news story – is increasingly 'textualised' when conducted on social networking sites and in digital interactive media, it becomes accessible for the media and culture industry to appropriate and take advantage of in their production-consumption circuit. Thus one can claim that the parts of our lifeworlds that are exposed to appropriation have expanded.

Table 13.2 Different kinds of productivity in pre-digital and web 2.0 fields of consumption. Boxes indicate the degrees to which it is possible for media and culture industries to extract value

Pre-digital	Web 2.0
Subjective productivity	Subjective productivity
Social productivity	Social productivity
Textual productivity	Textual productivity

The analysis that will follow in the rest of the chapter draws on focus group and individual interviews with Swedish and German media users of different ages and backgrounds. I have based my analysis from two sets of data. Firstly, I draw from nine focus groups and eight individual interviews with Swedish media users, conducted between 2012 and 2015 (41 individuals in total). These interviews were made by me, and were fully taped and transcribed. Informants were chosen through snowballing. Secondly, I have used one focus group and nine individual interviews with German media users, conducted by MA students supervised by me in the autumn of 2016 (12 individuals in total). This data set was not planned for initially, but was generated in relation to a course I taught on audience labour in digital markets at Augsburg University. Also these interviews were fully taped and transcribed. The interviews were all semi-structured and focussed on questions of media use generally, more specifically social media use, questions of terms of use, privacy and relation between leisure use and vocational use. The ages of the interviewees varied between 16 and 66 years, with a bias towards the younger end of that spectrum. Interviewees were chosen to represent a wide range of occupations, including students, retired people, cultural occupations of professional and semi-professional kind, as well as a broad spectrum of blue- and white-collar non-managerial occupations (e.g. grocery store cashier, dentist, office worker, nurse, schoolteacher, etc.).

Media Use and the Labour Market

There are, as could be expected, vast differences among individual interviewees when it comes to the ways in which they use digital interactive media. Previous research has found that what is perceived of as most troubling with online sharing is related to privacy issues. But the worries most often concern social rather than institutional privacy (cf. Raynes-Goldie 2010). This means that people seem most worried over specific others sharing their photos or other uploaded material without their consent, while much fewer have concerns with the institutional privacy where social network media corporations are sharing their data. However, Kennedy (2016, p. 167) has pointed out that it is hard for interviewees to describe concerns about breeches of institutional privacy if one has no clue about what social networking companies are doing. In surveys, Swedish media users also reveal a sceptic attitude towards data mining, and roughly 60 per cent disagree with the statement that the benefits of companies registering internet habits outweigh the disadvantages (Leckner 2017), which indicates that – when prompted – people do find digital tracking problematic.

Contrary to privacy issues, that many informants have indeed thought about, there are as can be expected no informants that explicitly think of their general activities of communicating with friends and posting comments, photos and video clips on social networking sites in terms of labour, work, exploitation, etc. This aspect of media use has to be grasped through analysis. There are some informants who are conscious about what they post on open network sites in relation to their vocational or amateur cultural practices. This is especially so for those who work professionally or semi-professionally as cultural producers: photographers, filmmakers and musicians. As can be expected from a small qualitative study, approaches vary between interviewees. Where some are restrictive, others are more permissive:

> You wouldn't post... like, my job is to take photos, so I wouldn't post job photos without watermarks, as you never know where they could go. But it's like... if you post pictures of friends, yes... That's OK. Sure. But I wouldn't post something I have taken at work. (Emma, 21 years, university student and photographer)

Clearly, Emma distinguishes between her 'job', that is, what she earns money from, and her leisure activities – what she does 'with friends'. Others, however, have a more open approach to sharing:

> A lot of the music I have released on records, we have uploaded for free downloading. I think it is foolish to even try to fight that [i.e. the fact that others make money on his activities]. I am just happy that people want to take part of what I can offer. /.../ I think that the single individual's fight against... I don't think it's possible to get around that. People will make money on me irrespective of how I live my life, and I do not want to move into the woods and isolate myself. (Tage, 28 years, student and amateur musician)

The sharing attitude of Tage might reflect the fact that his musical activities are not professional, that is, are not profit motivated, whereas Emma's more restricted approach is related to the fact that she sees photographing as a job, that is, in order to make money of it. Tage is also displaying a resigned attitude in relation to the fact that media companies take advantage of his uploaded music, resembling the 'resigned' attitude described by Turow et al. (2015) in the US context.

Tage's approach is more similar to Monica's, who is a professional filmmaker on freelance basis. The way in which she funds her filmmaking is, however, different from Emma's, since she does not actually sell her films, but sells an idea, and then looks for ways to funding the actual film shooting. However, on her web-site she distinguishes between an open area where she posts things for everyone to see, but then she also has a password protected area on Vimeo, where she posts things that are 'work-in-progress' and/or that she wants comments and 'feed-back' on. In relation to open social networking sites such as Facebook, she is more restricted, however:

> Well, no, I never post anything that I think that I can sell, or… I know that many of my friends who are still photographers have posted their photos with watermarks. Its like a transparent text over the picture. But that felt kind of silly, so I have decided that what I post there, it is for everybody on Facebook. So, then I don't care so much about it. (Monica, 23 years, film photographer)

Most informants have very vague ideas about the legal frameworks and the terms of use that they have once signed. Prompted by the interview situation, they thus start to justify their relaxed attitude to ownership.

> *Marie*: It was a while when people said, like 'Facebook owns your pictures', as I remember. And then I kind of: 'Ok, but what does that mean really?' And then I remember that I tried to find out about that, but I don't think I found anything.
>
> *Interviewer*: Have you read on 'settings'?
>
> *Marie*: Eh, if you just go in and read under, like, 'settings', then there isn't so much you can find… and I think you have to dig deeper if you want to

find something about this... if they own the pictures or not. I don't know, I didn't find any answers, so I dropped it.

Tage: I dug a bit into that, and I think I came to the conclusion that it wasn't as bad as it sounded. And then, when I thought more about it, I thought that even if it had been that bad, I wouldn't have cared.

Interviewer: Because?

Tage: Because... I don't know. There's nothing on Facebook that I really would consider to be my intellectual property

(Marie, 23 years, nurse, Tage, 28 years, student and amateur musician)

This quote on the one hand point to the quite relaxed attitude to the tracking procedures by the social media platforms that they use. On the other hand it also reveals something about their attitude towards the textual production that they engage in. In the general public debate about social media, privacy and intrusive business models, one gets constantly reminded of what happens to media user data, and how the industry does feed on the images and postings that ordinary media users produce. In the interview situation there is a felt need to show concern and awareness about this fact in front of the interviewing media professor (Marie and Tage are, after all, also students). But in the end, as Tage expresses, the pictures, the music or the postings uploaded, are not considered to be part of a professional activity on part of the interviewees. Hence there is no need to claim 'intellectual property' to it, and they cannot imagine why Facebook would either.

For some of the interviewees, who have deeper technological insights into the organisation of social networking media, there is, however, a more specific kind of scepticism towards data extraction of user activity. A good example is Jonas, who works with ITC solutions for large corporations and public administration:

I do think about this a lot. These mobiles that we now have, they... What is happening today is a very good example of on this, like this company that was taken to the EU court by the German state because they did build in the predecessor of this operative system, and included an automatic GPS function that could download signals on where you and everybody else were. Talk about gigantic intrusion into your personal integrity! It is one thing if you as a customer make the choice, like… 'now I am activating this function', but I think it would have been really interesting to have been present on the meeting when they sat down and decided that, 'OK, now we are going to build in something that can automatically track all iPhones'. (Jonas, 50 years, ICT consultant)

The approach taken by Jonas is related to his specific role on the labour market in another way compared to Monica, Tage and Emma, since it is not related to him as a cultural producer, but rather in the capacity of him having insights into internet architecture and the tracking procedures that it allows for. Where Monica, Tage and Emma relate what they do to other users of the social web, Jonas is concerned about the web itself, and how it is organised as a tool for surveillance. He does not relate this to the business models of the media and culture industries, however, but rather to the way in which companies violate people's personal integrity. Thus also he misrecognises the basic economic models that the web is built on.

The Misrecognition of Social Productivity

As seen in the previous section, what media users worry about is their *textual* productivity. However, these worries are more about privacy concerns, just as is private information about bank account details, health information and telephone numbers, which, for example, are things that are of concern to the interviewees of the German focus group. It is very seldom that the *value* of one's productivity surfaces in the interviews, and when it does it is either framed negatively ('nothing I would consider my intellectual property'), or, in relation to one's profession (as photographer, or film maker).

The *social* productivity that is at the bottom of the specific traffic commodity remains misrecognised as a form of labour, and thus also as a source of value. This type of misrecognition of the sources of value generation in the media industries through the specific traffic commodity, however, reveals in many forms.

> *Eva*: Well, one can always leave, if one wants to. I know really many who has left.
>
> *Interviewer*: That has left Facebook?
>
> *Eva*: They think it is sort of unpleasant, and do not want to share their information. But I think that I am not a very interesting person. Because I am no criminal, [laughs] but... If someone is interested in looking at my pictures, so, 'be my guest, I sail a lot'. [laughs]
>
> (Eva, 42 years, activist, writer, artist)

Eva's approach is even more relaxed in relation to the social network provider. She knows of others who have opted out on privacy accounts, but her approach is more of 'I have nothing to hide'. In fact she takes great pride in exposing the different sides of herself – as a poet with her own web site, as an activist in the public sphere, and as a hobbyist building her own sailing boat and documenting the progress in pictures online, etc. When she says that 'I am not a very interesting person', she expresses clearly the discourse by the industry that seeks to convince users that 'you are not special' (cf. Deuze 2012, p. 143).

What interviewees very seldom, if ever, reflect on, is the activity of being present on social networking media as such. That is, the interviewees do not consider their activities in themselves of any worth *for others*, although they recognise the value the possibility of communicating with friends, or even anonymous others, *to themselves*. Theoretically, then, one could say that the interviewees recognise the value of social networking media within the cultural and social field of production in which they contribute with communicative activities, but they have a much harder time imagining how these activities contribute to the production and consumption circuit of the field of industrialised commercial media production. In that sense, the activities they are engaged in are misrecognised as labour appropriated by others, and only recognised as a labour of love that is freely given within the framework of a field of social and cultural production (cf. Duffy 2017). The extended commodification of the lifeworld that the business models of social networking media and other commercial actors on the interactive web thus never gets fully acknowledged.

The main reason for the misrecognition of media user productivity as labour is that it is only indirectly related to the field of industrialised production. The labour of media use is already rewarded in the form of social recognition, prestige, reputation and appreciation in the field of cultural 'prosumption' – that is, in the production-consumptions field that media users see themselves as actively productive in. Since this is a field driven by non-commercial logics the idea of having 'intellectual property' is nonsensical, since intellectual property only makes sense if you want to restrict access in order to be able to control the commodity. The field of prosumption works differently, since it is not centred on the commercial exchange value of the commodity, but on the statutory *sign value* that produces difference, status and social recognition (Baudrillard 1972/1981; Bolin 2011).

This also means that the activity of producing and distributing cultural artefacts on the social web is only to be considered as labour if seen in relation to the field of 'prosumption'. In the field of industrialised media production the reified form of this labour, alienated or decoupled from the labourer, is treated as raw material that can be tooled into other commodities: the general traffic commodity, the specific traffic commodity (including both the algorithmically and the sociologically produced specific traffic commodity).

Conclusions

I have in the above tried to analyse how media users relate to their own productivity on social networking media and the interactive web. More specifically, I have tried to analyse this as a form of labour that indirectly contributes to the valorisation process within the media and culture industries. There are, as can be expected, different approaches to these industries, and the media technologies through which they operate, depending on age, or on the more specific individual relation to the labour market, and especially in relation to one's own occupation. For those interviewees that are engaged in cultural production from which they earn a living, the approach is quite different, compared to if their cultural production is amateur, just to take the most obvious example.

Furthermore, I have shown that the ways in which media users think of their activities, and about value and propriety rights, is largely modelled on a very traditional understanding of media production and the business models that surrounds that production. This is the business model that is focused on the text as a material artefact and commodity that can be controlled and distributed for free or for money (which is also why social networking media corporations fiercely insists on not being media companies, since if they were, the content production and the distribution activities of the users, would stand out much more clearly as work). As a consequence, the media users largely misrecognise other commodity forms circulating within the frameworks of the media and communications industries, such as the specific traffic commodity, based in the extraction of value from social productivity of media users on the interactive web. The ideology that underpins the traditional media industries is firmly held on to among users, and thus the extended commodification of the lifeworlds of media users gets misrecognised as source of value.

The very fact that there are two valorisation processes going on simultaneously – one cultural and on economic – is seemingly too complex for individual media users to fully appreciate, and hence the social energy that is the resource algorithmically tooled into the traffic commodity at the basis for the social network business models is misrecognised as labour. The contradiction between the social networking media as *both* playground *and* factory (Scholz 2012) gets downplayed due to the very strong discourse on media production as text- or content-centred. While digital media has dramatically changed the ways in which economic value is produced, and extended its activities to the realm of the social, this extension is executed in a way that masks its role in the production-consumption circuit, and as capitalism expands, we can predict increased such expansions into the realm of the social, since these are but one of the few terrains not yet exploited by capital.

Acknowledgements I want to thank the students from my MA course at Augsburg University in the Autumn 2016 for conducting and transcribing the

German interviews: Janine Blessing, Marina Drakova, Lara Gauder, Constanze Küchler, Chloë Lamaire, Maria Leix, Ines Mayr, Julia Muhm, Daphne Noviant, Robert Pavcic, Katja Pfefferle. The research was funded by a grant from the Bank of Sweden Tercentenary Foundation, and through a visiting professorship at Augsburg University – a special thanks to Susanne Kinnebrock and Helena Bilandzic for the invitation. I also want to thank Fredrik Stiernstedt for comments on an earlier draft.

References

Andrejevic, M. (2007). *iSpy. Surveillance and power in the interactive era*. Lawrence: The University Press of Kansas.
Banks, J., & Humphreys, S. (2008). The labour of user co-creators: Emergent social networks markets. *Convergence, 14*(4), 401–418.
Baudrillard, J. (1972/1981). *For a critique of the political economy of the sign*. St. Louis: Telos.
Baudrillard, J. (1973/1975). *The mirror of production*. St. Louis: Telos.
Benkler, Y. (2006). *The wealth of networks. How social production transforms markets and freedom*. New Haven: Yale University Press.
Bermejo, F. (2009). Audience manufacture in historical perspective: From broadcasting to Google. *New Media & Society, 11*(1–2), 133–154.
Bilić, P. (2017). A critique of the economy of algorithms: Brief history of Google's technological rationality. *Westminster Advanced Studies* (5), 1–22.
Bolin, G. (2011). *Value and the media. Cultural production and consumption in digital markets*. Farnham: Ashgate.
Bolin, G. (2012). The labour of media use: The two active audiences. *Information, Communication & Society, 15*(6), 796–814.
Bourdieu, P. (1993). *The field of cultural production. Essays on art and literature*. Cambridge: Polity.
Brabham, D. C. (2008). Crowdsourcing as a model for problem solving. An introduction and cases. *Convergence, 14*(1), 75–90.
Bruns, A. (2006). Towards produsage: Futures for user-led content production. In F. Sudweeks, H. Hrachovec, & C. Ess (Eds.), *Proceedings: Cultural attitudes towards communication and technology 2006* (pp. 275–284). Perth: Murdoch University.
Deuze, M. (2007). *Media work*. Cambridge: Polity.
Deuze, M. (2012). *Media life*. Cambridge: Polity.

van Dijck, J. (2013). *The culture of connectivity. A critical history of social media.* Oxford: Oxford University Press.
Duffy, B. E. (2017). *(Not) getting paid to do what you love: Gender, social media, and aspirational work.* New Haven: Yale University Press.
Fisher, E., & Fuchs, C. (Eds.). (2015). *Reconsidering value and labour in the digital age.* Houndmills: Palgrave Macmillan.
Fiske, J. (1992). The cultural economy of fandom. In L. Lewis (Ed.), *The adoring audience: Fan culture and popular media* (pp. 30–49). London/New York: Routledge.
Fuchs, C. (2012). Dallas Smythe today – The audience commodity, the digital labour debate, Marxist political economy and critical theory. Prolegomena to a digital labour theory of value. *tripleC: Communication, Capitalism & Critique, 10*(2), 692–740.
Fuchs, C. (2014). *Digital labour and Karl Marx.* New York: Routledge.
Hearn, A., & Schoenhoff, S. (2016). From celebrity to influencer. Tracing the diffusion of celebrity value across the data stream. In P. D. Marshall & S. Redmond (Eds.), *A companion to celebrity* (pp. 194–211). Malden/Oxford: John Wiley & Sons.
Hesmondhalgh, D. (2010). User-generated content, free labour and the cultural industries. *Ephemera, 10*(3/4), 267–284.
Hesmondhalgh, D., & Baker, S. (2011). *Creative labour. Media work in three cultural industries.* London/New York: Routledge.
Hjorth, L. (2017). Ambient and soft play: Play, labour and the digital in everyday life. *European Journal of Cultural Studies.* Online First.
Jakobsson, P. (2012). *Öppenhetsindustrin.* Dissertation, Södertörn University, Stockholm.
Jenkins, H. (1992). *Textual poachers: Television fans and participatory culture.* New York/London: Routledge.
Jenkins, H. (2006). *Convergence culture: Where old and new media collide.* New York: New York University Press.
Jhally, S., & Livant, B. (1986). Watching as working: The valorization of audience consciousness. *Journal of Communication, 36*(3), 124–143.
Kennedy, H. (2016). *Post, mine, repeat. Social media data mining becomes ordinary.* Basingstoke: Palgrave Macmillan.
Kennedy, H., Elgesem, D., & Miguel, C. (2015). On fairness: User perspectives on social media data mining. *Convergence, 21*(4), 1–19.
Kücklich, J. (2005). Precarious playbour: Modders and the digital games industry. *Fibreculture Journal,* 5. http://five.fibreculturejournal.org/fcj-025-precarious-playbour-modders-and-the-digital-games-industry/

Leckner, S. (2017). *Sceptics of online privacy and supporters using online behavioral data. A study of changing attitudes towards sharing behavioral data in the Swedish population.* Paper presented to NordMedia 2017 conference, Tampere.

Marx, K. (1867/1976). *Capital. A critique of political economy* (Vol. 1). London: Penguin Books.

Mosco, V., & McKercher, C. (2009). *The labouring of communication: Will knowledge workers of the world unite?* Lanham: Lexington Books.

Petersen, S.M. (2008). Loser generated content: From participation to exploitation. *First Monday, 13*(3) http://firstmonday.org/htbin/cgiwrap/bin/ojs/index.php/fm/article/view/2141/1948

Picard, R. G. (2010). *Value creation and the future of news organizations: Why and how journalism must change to remain relevant in the twenty-first century.* Lisbon: Media XXI.

Raynes-Goldie, K. (2010). Aliases, creeping and wall cleaning: Understanding privacy in the age of Facebook. *First Monday* 15(1). http://firstmonday.org/ojs/index.php/fm/article/view/2775/2432

Ruppert, E. (2011). Population objects: Interpassive subjects. *Sociology, 45*(2), 218–233.

Scholz, T. (Ed.). (2012). *Digital labor. The internet as playground and factory.* New York/London: Routledge.

Smythe, D. (1977). Communications: Blindspot of western Marxism. *Canadian Journal of Political and Social Theory, 1*(3), 1–27.

Surowiecki, J. (2004). *The wisdom of crowds: Why the many are smarter than the few and how collective wisdom shapes business, economies, societies, and nations.* New York: Doubleday.

Terranova, T. (2000). Free labor. Producing culture for the digital economy. *Social Text, 18*(2), 33–58.

Turow, J. (2011). *The daily you. How the new advertising industry is defining your identity and your worth.* New Haven: Yale University Press.

Turow, J., Hennessy, M., & Draper, N. (2015). *The tradeoff fallacy. How marketers are misrepresenting American consumers and opening them up to exploitation.* Philadelphia: Annenberg School of Communication.

Vaidhyanathan, S. (2011). *The googlization of everything (and why we should worry).* Berkley/Los Angeles: California University Press.

Van Couvering, E. (2008). The history of the internet search engine: Navigational media and the traffic commodity. *Information Science and Knowledge Management, 14,* 177–206.

Wikström, P. (2009). *The music industry. Music in the cloud.* Cambridge: Polity.

14

Regulation, Technology, and Civic Agency: The Case of Facebook

Bjarki Valtýsson

In his work *The Hacker Ethic and the Spirit of the Information Age* (2001), Himanen juxtaposes Weber's Protestant work ethic with the hacker ethic, thereby creating a polarisation between two sets of values. On the one hand, money, work, optimality, flexibility, stability, determinacy, and result accountability. On the other hand, passion, freedom, social worth, openness, activity, caring, and creativity. Such polarisation has persisted in much of the literature describing the wealth of potentials brought about by digital communications and the internet. The first part of this chapter will account for these in terms of the apparently mutually exclusive concepts of *creativity* and *control*, both of which are inscribed in the technology of popular commercial social media services. While Himanen conceptualises these on the seemingly contradicting premises of the Protestant work ethic and the hacker ethic, Marcuse suggests a certain dialectic of technology. According to Marcuse, technology is both an instrument for control and domination and a mode of organising and changing social relationships. Further distinguishing between technology

B. Valtýsson (✉)
Department of Arts and Cultural Studies, University of Copenhagen, Copenhagen, Denmark

and what he terms 'technics', Marcuse emphasises this dialectic, as technics 'by itself can promote authoritarianism as well as liberty, scarcity as well as abundance, the extension as well as abolition of toil' (Marcuse 1998, p. 41).

In terms of technology, the present chapter focuses on Facebook, and apart from accounting for certain contradictions inherent in literature that mainly presents either elements of creativity or elements of control, this chapter mainly treats Facebook from the perspective of regulation and how citizens perceive their own use of Facebook in terms of space for civic agency. There are, of course, many ways of scrutinising the logics inherent in creativity and control in a service like Facebook, for instance by conducting an interface analysis or by focusing on Facebook's algorithmic logics, the role of content moderators, ownership structures, and business models. This chapter's approach seeks to capture certain complexities in Facebook's contractual agreements and how these relate to current EU regulatory frameworks. In addition, when accounting for motivational factors that relate to citizens' extensive use of Facebook, this chapter builds upon interviews with citizens that focus on their verbalisation of Facebook as a technology that allows for certain forms of civic agency. Including the voices of citizens and the contractual agreements they make with Facebook will further illuminate the dialectics between the hacker ethic and the Protestant work ethic, technics and technology, creativity and control.

Methodology

Facebook is chosen as the main platform of investigation because of its popularity and societal impact. The empirical bulk of this chapter consists of Facebook's data policy (as of 29 September 2016) and statement of rights and responsibilities (as of 30 January 2015) as well as EU regulation on audiovisual media services and telecommunications. The reason for choosing this particular aspect of EU regulations is that it specifically treats content and transmission and thus relates directly to user-generated content and its transmission channels. There are, of course, other important directives relative to social media, such as the EU's general data protection regulation and regulation on copyrights. However, to include these is beyond the scope of this chapter.

The analysis is inspired by Dahlgren's (2011) account of critical media politics. According to Dahlgren, a recurring theme in such analysis is tension between capitalist logics of media development and interests for public interest and democracy in a wider sense. Dahlgren ascribes specific roles to regulation when adjusting the balance between the two: 'The critical political economy of the media does not anticipate the elimination of commercial imperatives or market forces, but rather seeks to promote an understanding of where and how regulatory initiatives can establish optimal balances between private interest and the public good' (2011, pp. 234–235).

In order to account for the voices of citizens, I will refer to empirical data collected from June 2013–October 2015, composed of three focus groups (Bloor et al. 2001) and sixteen semi-structured qualitative interviews (Gaskell 2000; Cresswell 2009) with Danish citizens. These include a total of 36 respondents: twenty from the focus groups (8 male, 12 female; aged 22–67) and sixteen from the qualitative interviews (9 male, 7 female; aged 18–54). The data was thematically categorised using pre-established codes related to the research objective as well as codes that emerged from the data. The emerging themes are those of *regulation, data mining and digital labour, surveillance and privacy, collective emancipation,* and *individual emancipation.* Because there is no space in this chapter to explore this voluminous data in detail, I will mainly discuss these themes in general terms. I will, however, provide a few examples (anonymised and translated from Danish to English), providing only information on the gender and age of the respondents in question.

Creativity/Control

I began this chapter by noting Himanen's description of two sets of ethics because these ethics can conveniently be contained within discourses of creativity and control and because similar discourses have been persistently reproduced in much writing concerning the promise and potential of internet communication. Castells, for instance, refers to the 'interactive production of meaning' (2009, p. 132) generated by the creative audience, and Jenkins does the same by coining the term 'interactive audience' (2006). These empowering processes seem to turn citizens into 'produsers' (Bruns 2008), 'productive enthusiasts' (Gauntlett 2011) and 'interactive citizen-consumers' (Hartley 2005). In these instances, emphasis is placed on increased civic agency facilitated by digital technologies and communication. Gauntlett offers the following definition of 'creativity': 'Everyday creativity refers to a process which brings together at least one active human mind, and the material or digital world, in the activity of making something which is novel in that context, and is a process which evokes a feeling of joy' (2011, p. 76). In line with the hacker ethic, Gauntlett emphasises *novelty* and *joy* as important factors that in civic terms indicate activity and visible participation patterns. He furthermore discusses the wider cultural consequences of such engagement by suggesting a new form of polarisation between a *sit back and be told* culture and a *making and doing* culture. Creativity is at the heart of such dynamic cultural formations as '[t]his orientation rejects the passivity of the 'sit back' model, and seeks opportunities for creativity, social connections, and personal growth' (2011, p. 11). Lessig (2008) argues along similar lines with his oppositional pair RW (read/write) and RO (read/only) cultures, arguing mainly for the engaging role of RW in terms of education and online participation as a process in community building.

While these voices are certainly aware of critical dimensions of this creativity discourse, they hold onto views that focus on emancipatory and empowering aspects of online participatory cultures. Gauntlett, for instance, acknowledges that the profitable business side of web 2.0 services is largely facilitated by the creativity of their users. He furthermore maintains that this can be seen as exploitation 'from a macro point of view' (2011, p. 187) but not from the viewpoint of individual users: 'On the whole they never hoped or expected to be able to make any financial gain from sharing their work – for them, that's not the point, and in most cases it would be unrealistic to expect any' (2011, p. 187). In similar terms, Jenkins, Ford, and Green prefer to discuss audience labour not on the premises of exploitation but instead as *engaged labour*, since this term 'also recognizes that these communities are pursuing their own interests, connected to and informed by those decisions made by others within their social networks' (2013, p. 60).

Some of the literature concerning the hacker ethic emphasises individual and collective emancipation, with focus on the information commons of produsage (Bruns 2008), and by digital communication's facilitation of mass collaboration (Tapscott and Williams 2008; Shirky 2008), in which culture becomes more democratic, self-reflective, and participatory (Benkler 2006). A range of web 2.0 technologies are thus said to provide citizens with creative communicative tools and infrastructures through which everyone can make their voice and ideas known, for the better of democracy, culture, politics, and economics.

This is, however, an oversimplification of the complex relationships between processes of creativity and control. While acknowledging the culture of sharing, Freedman is attentive to commodification of user-generated content, in which the powerful drivers are precisely citizens' passion, joy, and creativity as well as the time, energy, and labour they put into generating content. Freedman thus highlights the dual nature of user-generated content: '[I]t is suggestive of a more participatory form of creativity and yet simultaneously very cost-effective as a means of generating free content that helps advertisers and marketers more precisely to identify and target desirable audiences' (2011, pp. 82–83). Fuchs is more direct in his account of the participatory web as ideology and maintains that platforms and services that are not built upon participatory economic models cannot be considered participatory in practice. He therefore advocates understanding these dynamics in terms of class, exploitation, and surplus value, with the audience constituting an internet prosumer commodity. This entails that the surplus value on Facebook, as a commercial social media, is partly created by citizens and partly by Facebook employees. While Facebook's employees get paid though, citizens, acting as users and content creators, are unpaid and thereby exploited. As a result, a 'product is not sold to the users, but, rather, the users are sold as a commodity to advertisers' (2013, p. 219). Fuchs is equally critical regarding the role of creativity since he maintains that the 'category of the produsage/prosumer commodity does not signify a democratization of the media toward a participatory or democratic system, but the total commodification of human creativity' (2010, p. 192).

Fuchs can therefore be firmly placed within discourse that analyses social media from the perspective of *control*, digital labour, exploitation, privacy, and surveillance.

Terranova uses the concept of *free labour* to signify that citizens are working not only because capital demands it of them but because they desire affective and cultural production: 'Free labor is the moment where this knowledgeable consumption of culture is translated into excess productive activities that are pleasurably embraced and at the same time often shamelessly exploited' (2013, p. 37). Terranova reaches, however, a conclusion that resembles Fuchs' vision of a communist internet, as she conceives of a liberation of free labour through the demand that profits be returned to living labour and that these platforms be deprivatised, i.e. 'that ownership of users' data should be returned to their rightful owners as the freedom to access and modify the protocols and diagrams that structure their participation' (p. 53).

The critical voices touched upon here emphasise elements of digital communications as well as creative and engaging participatory cultures in which focus is on data mining, exploitation of digital labour, surveillance capitalism (Mosco 2014), and communication without communicability. Dean, for instance, maintains that in much digital communication the exchange value of messages overtakes their use value, meaning that circulation alone is relevant: '[T]he message is simply part of a circulating data stream' (2008, p. 107). In order to explain the motivational factors behind such communicability that hinders, rather than facilitates, communication, Dean turns to the fantasy of participation: 'The paradox of the technological fetish is that the technology acting in our stead actually enables us to remain politically passive' (pp. 111–112).

Again, in contrast to the positive views concerning equal access to participation and creativity, this perspective is more prone to see such communication patterns in terms of Deleuze's (1995) account of the control society, which operates not by confining people but rather through continuous control and instant communication. A key characteristic of such a society is code, and it is deeply rooted in a mutation of capitalism that is directed towards metaproduction. The importance of these considerations has risen with the massive use of commercial social media. The complex relationships between social media as technology and citizens' use of social media as spaces for civic agency should not, however, be represented as a simple dichotomy of affirmative/creative and critical/control aspects. While theorists such as Bruns, Gauntlett, Castells, and Jenkins may lack a critical edge in much of their writing, their contribution is valuable in explaining the motivational factors for citizens who are dressed up as produsers, creative audiences, interactive audiences, and productive enthusiasts. Some of these views are also beneficial for further understanding the political, cultural, and economic potential of affective communication on commercial social media, their potential for dissemination, and their societal impact. At the same time, the critical theorists provide frameworks for further conceptualising the societal consequences of all this communication, for instance by pointing out that excessive online communication can indeed make citizens politically passive; that citizens are being economically exploited; and that the interface and algorithmic logics of commercial social media condition citizens' participative potentials to certain pre-programmed routes, which not only pushes them towards certain conditioned user patterns but also traces and capitalises them.

When scrutinising the dialectic between creativity and control, it is important to be aware of the context of use. Not all democratic communications and organisation on Facebook can be labelled 'slacktivism', even though much of it is. While Fuchs has a valid point that exploitation is inevitable when user-generated content is created and facilitated via commercial social media, citizens also seem capable of extracting and verbalising other forms of value while operating these services. Bolin (2012) addresses this in his account of the labour of media use, suggesting that audiences are involved in two production-consumption circuits, which account for individual meaning-making and cultural creativity as well as subordination to structural constraints. Bolin's two production-consumption circuits thus include elements of both creativity and control since, while 'the new information and communication technologies can provide more accessible tools for creativity on part of the media users, they also provide the media and culture industries with the means of surveillance and control' (p. 797).

In this vein, van Dijck's (2013) approach is also rewarding as she suggests that commercial social media platforms be perceived as both techno-cultural constructs and socioeconomic structures. As a result, when approaching a platform like Facebook, we must analyse technology, users, and content as well as the platform's ownership status, governance, and business model. This approach is useful because it takes into account not only how technology shapes user manoeuvrability but the wider contours of political economy—and significantly for the context of this chapter—*governance* and *regulation*.

Commercial social media such as Facebook are framed by explicit rules to regulate claims for privacy, property, community standards, etc. These are usually termed end-user license agreements, privacy policies, data policies, or terms of service. As van Dijck points out, these are contractual relationships into which users enter operating social media services. Because these contractual relationships are not law, they do not adhere to the same democratic and juridical processes as are, for instance, telecommunications directives negotiated at the EU level and later implemented by member states. Furthermore, these agreements constantly change, as do the interfaces and the functions of the algorithms of the services in question, and this does usually not entail users' prior consent.

It is nevertheless important to remember that there are regulatory frameworks for audiovisual media services and telecommunications that are continually amended to fit new societal and technological realities. Usually, technology moves faster, and because of this disconnect between regulatory and technological developments as well as current regulatory disparities between different geographical and cultural contexts, a global service such as Facebook brings with it a host of regulatory challenges that have real consequences for citizens' civic agency. This creates grey zones between current regulatory frameworks and the contractual relationships with which these social media bind their users.

The logics of algorithms play a large role in constituting such grey zones because, on commercial social media, these are essentially proprietary and thereby hidden. Like contractual agreements, such algorithms are constantly adapted to new business models and user patterns. This aspect of the logics of algorithms is an example of control, as is clear in Beer's account of the power of the algorithm: 'This is undoubtedly an expression of power, not of someone having power over someone else, but of the software making choices and connections in complex and unpredictable ways in order to shape the everyday experiences of the user' (2009, p. 997).

However, because algorithms react to citizens' stimuli on social media, Beer as well as van Dijck and Poell (2013) grant human agency key roles in their definitions of the power of the algorithm and the programmability of social media logic. Beer foresees reflexive citizens who 'may begin to actively shape the information so as to direct the way that the software reacts to them' (2009, p. 997), while van Dijck and Poell maintain that 'users retain significant agency in the process of steering programmability not only through their own contributions but also because they may resist coded instructions or defy protocols' (2013, p. 6). These contradictions between control and creativity are manifest in technology like Facebook. On the control side, Facebook conditions citizens' user manoeuvrability relative to certain forms for communication, which are tracked, stored, and sold to third parties. On the creativity side, empirical evidence demonstrates that while citizens are aware of Facebook as a technology of control, they still perceive their civic agency on Facebook as dynamic, providing spaces for creative, cultural, and political use. Before showing a few examples of such reflections by citizens, a few words will be dedicated to contractual agreements on Facebook and how these relate to EU regulation relevant to user generated content.

Facebook and Regulation

Contrary to popular assumptions, Facebook's data policy and statement of rights and responsibilities are not monstrous, incomprehensible documents. They are indeed quite explicit in stating that citizens acting as Facebook users accept that their data and their user manoeuvrability are *controlled* by Facebook Inc. Indeed, Facebook's statement of rights and responsibilities explicitly states that even though users own all content and information they post on Facebook, they still 'grant us a non-exclusive, transferable, sub-licensable, royalty-free, worldwide license to use any IP content that you post on or in connection with Facebook' (Terms of service n.d.). This is also the case concerning commercial content and advertisements: 'You give us permission to use your name, profile picture, content, and information in connection with commercial, sponsored, or related content (such as a brand you like) served or enhanced by us. This means, for example, that you permit a business or other entity to pay us to display your name and/or profile picture with your content or information, without any compensation to you' (Terms of service, n.d.). These are rather obvious examples of what the critical voices already touched upon term internet produsage/prosumer commodity, exploitation, free labour, and surveillance capitalism.

Facebook's data policy is not straightforward, for it discursively frames its policy in terms of creativity, passion, and citizen protection: 'We give you the power to share as part of our mission to make the world more open and connected' and 'We are passionate about creating engaging and customised experiences for people' (Data policy n.d.). Even though the policy is discursively framed on such terms, it reveals the extensiveness of collected information and the sharing of information with third-party partners and customers, relative to the things users do and information they provide: 'We collect the content and other information you provide when you use our Services, including when you sign up for an account, create or share, and message or communicate with others'. It also concerns things other users do and information they provide: 'We also collect content and information that other people provide when they use our Services, including information about you, such as when they share a photo of you, send a message to your, or upload, sync or import your contact information'. Facebook also collects information on networks, connections, payments, and devices. In addition, it collects information from websites and apps that use its services and from third-party partners.

The situation is further complicated by the fact that information collected by these integrated services is subject to Facebook's own terms and policies. As a result, when citizens engage in cross-mediated communication patterns, it becomes difficult for citizens to gain a comprehensible impression of how these terms and polices work in practice. Furthermore, if a citizen wishes to gain an overview of terms that concern their user-generated data, it is insufficient to just scrutinise Facebook's data policy and statement of rights and responsibilities, as Facebook also operates with specific payment terms, platform policies, advertising policies, self-serve ad terms, promotion guidelines, page terms, and community standards. Although these contractual agreements are clear concerning intellectual property rights and the overall framework for advertising, they are vague about exactly how finely filtered users' data is and how this more precisely affects the functions of Facebook's algorithms.

While there certainly is regulation, current law does not cover all the contours of commercial social media. This is primarily due to the converging characteristics of social media as technology as it makes use of various semiotic expressions and transmission formats that are treated separately by current EU regulation. Within the EU, audiovisual media services and telecommunication have been regulated through different directives, treating content and transmission/delivery systems within different regulatory frameworks. Commercial social media challenge these frameworks because the user-generated content that citizens create and distribute can in principle be framed in terms of social networks, venues for publishing, or the exchanging of TV streams and live casts. This kind of user-generated content mixes different semiotic expressions, thereby challenging notions of transmission and content as well as established frameworks for content jurisdiction, sender/user/audience, platforms, and public/private communication (Drucker and Gumpert 2010). Because these challenges have not been resolved, there is a lack of certainty regarding the alignment or otherwise of citizens' contractual agreement with Facebook and current EU regulatory frameworks on audiovisual media services and telecommunications.

This challenge is, however, not a new one. It was apparent already in the negotiations concerning EU's Audiovisual Media Service directive. Now, over ten years later, the proposal to amend the directive is once again grappling with these challenges, highlighting the rapid changes affecting the audiovisual media landscape on account of continued convergences between television and services distributed via the internet. Yet again, the proposal identifies the grey zone in which these converging processes situate citizens: 'However, TV broadcasting, video-on-demand and user-generated content are subject to different rules and varying levels of consumer protection' (COM (2016), 287 final, p. 2). This is really just a repetition of a similar discussion that took place a decade earlier, and although the proposal usefully identifies challenges, it falls short when it comes to proposing specific solutions. This is exemplified by its discussion of user-generated content, which maintains that the current AVMS directive 'does not apply to user-generated content offered on video-sharing platforms since the providers of video-sharing platforms services often do not have editorial responsibility for the content stored on those platforms' (p. 3). Instead, the proposal refers to the e-Commerce Directive, which covers information society services. However, the e-Commerce Directive does not require intermediaries to monitor the content they host, which again places citizens under uncertain terms when operating Facebook. The consequences of these shortcomings are quite grave for citizens as these proposals do not fill in the regulatory loopholes concerning user-generated content on commercial social media. The present chapter has, furthermore, only briefly touched upon this issue from the perspective of the EU and its member states; many commercial social media are not contained within the EU alone, meaning that it is necessary to develop frameworks that successfully operate on local, nation, and global scales.

Once again, this is not a recent dilemma. In 2006, the International Telecommunication Union published an account of the consequences of technological convergence, identifying similar challenges and potentials for conflict in regulation as different standards of content regulation are applied to telephony, sound, and TV broadcasting; print media, and internet. This is particularly challenging for areas that Dahlgren identified as within the realm of public interest and democracy in a broader sense: 'With convergence, polices may require change to achieve the common social objectives of promoting and protecting cultural traditions, public service, and protecting citizens from harmful material across all types of networks and delivery platforms' (ICT regulation toolkit 2006, p. 13). As a result, citizens are left in a regulatory grey zone, contributing to the perception of commercial social media as operating within a control framework.

Facebook and Civic Agency: Conclusion

I wish to conclude this chapter by briefly touching upon the data I collected amongst Danish citizens. I concluded my account of EU regulation and commercial social media by emphasising elements of control. One reason for this is the opaque manner in which Facebook's algorithms work, in how Facebook collects information based on user-generated content, and in how Facebook uses and sells this information to third parties. In terms of regulation, Facebook advocates a specific form of self-regulation, in which citizens are meant to work even harder to report offensive and criminal use. Seen from this perspective, it is hard not to think of Fuchs' point on internet prosumer commodity and Terranova's account of free labour. In similar vein, Beer as well as van Dijck and Poell are attentive to the algorithm's powerful role in shaping our everyday media practices and information circulation. Since Facebook's algorithm is propriety, we do not know its exact functions. This is a clear element of control.

I have also sought to account for the other side of the coin as well, the one which is celebrated using terms such as creativity, passion, joy, and empowerment. This is the side that Dahlgren ascribes to public interest and democracy and that Beer as well as van Dijck and Poell assign to human agency. This interplay between control and creativity is present in the data, as respondents articulate views that explain both the motivational factors behind their use of commercial social media and critical aspects related to uncertain regulation and governance of data mining, digital labour, surveillance, and privacy. Concerning the latter, many respondents shared stories in which the algorithm 'got it wrong'. Yet while commercial targeting is certainly an irritation, most citizens understand Facebook's business logics and emphasise that this is the price users have to pay since they do not pay for the service directly: 'Maybe they make too much money from me, but this doesn't make me angry because I appreciate the service they provide' (Female, 23a).

Citizens are less certain of their rights and contractual agreements: 'As a starting point, I can't trust it despite what it actually says' (Female, 33), also expressing curiosity as to 'why we give up so many of our rights' (Female, 23b). However, citizens are also unsure on this point, expressing doubts as to the extent and nature of information collection and their own rights: 'I think I've heard that Facebook acquires the rights over your pictures. I'm not sure if that's correct. So, I think a bit about that, but in reality, it doesn't change anything' (Female, 23a), and 'I'm doubtful about Facebook's rights over my pictures, how they can use them, and whether they can use them in other contexts' (Female, 33).

This uncertainty does not seem to bother citizens too much as they trust the law and the fact that it would be bad business for Facebook to violate its users' trust: 'There's almost too much conspiracy in it in terms of people blocking everything because Facebook is using your pictures for this or that purpose. I'm not so worried about that as it's hard for me to see what they'd be using my pictures for and why they'd abuse them. I don't know, perhaps I just trust the law blindly in terms of what they're allowed to do' (Female 23b). Such expressions of uncertain legal terms were accompanied by expressions of annoyance and discomfort when the algorithm 'got it right' as well as feelings of disempowerment and indifference: 'I think about this, but I'm not going to do anything about it. I just ignore it. It's not that I'm totally blind, but I won't fight it actively or get enraged about it' (Female, 23a). This lengthy excerpt expresses a similar lack of civic agency when confronted by the power of commercial social media companies: 'There are no states that offer citizens independent, free social platforms, where there's no surveillance, and it's too late to do that now. So, we can discuss this endlessly, but the point is that these companies are insanely powerful and can basically just govern. This talk about no gatekeepers anymore isn't true, as the gatekeeping is just more sophisticated and invisible than in the good old days' (Male, 54).

However, despite citizens' views on critical aspects of their use of Facebook, they also reflect more broadly on positive and negative aspects of internet communications: 'Generally, I don't trust the internet, but it's a bit silly, as it is both robber and police. It is both good and bad. And I think we can distinguish between the two' (Male, 51). In terms of collective and individual emancipation, citizens particularly mention Facebook's affordances in terms of organizing social and political events and reconnections to distant friends and people that offer inspiring proximity: 'One of the greatest values is to be inspired by friends but also people that you would normally never get in contact with, like Obama, Sarah Huffington and a lot of great people' (Female, 23b), directly mentioning as well that these positive dimension overrule the 'dodgy' parts of Facebook. Generally, citizens do therefore express views that have both elements of creativity and control, explaining the positive sides at the same time as adding critical remarks. Therefore, citizens feel that they are taking an informed decision by being on these platforms: 'Facebook and

Twitter are empty as users generate the content. This is the form which we accept as users. But I also get a lot from my use of these platforms. It is clear that they sell advertisements and these ads are there because of us and these profits do not come back to me. So, someone is making profits from me. If I were to perceive this from a sociological point of view, I find this an interesting consequence of capitalism' (Female, 40).

This kind of remark corresponds well with Bolin's two production-consumption circuits, which include dimensions of both creativity and control. The voices of citizens also confirm that a platform such as Facebook makes choices, frames creativity and connections in complex and unpredictable ways, at the same time as it provides citizens with cultural, political, and democratic tools and thereby provides them with a space of agency. However, while this kind of agency, driven by the passion, engagement, and joy associated with the hacker ethic, clearly is verbalised by citizens and reflected upon in contrast to Facebook's control and monetisation of their user-generated content, respondents are unsure about the regulatory aspects of this content production. This is hardly surprising, given that Facebook's contractual agreements and existing regulation leave users in a regulatory grey zone, a complex construction that needs to be tackled on a broad basis, including local, national, and global scales. It is thus not that citizens are uninformed and unclear in their perceptions of their commercial social media but instead that there is a lack of clarity within the regulatory frameworks that are meant to ensure citizens' rights. It is therefore obvious that regulatory initiatives have failed to provide the optimal balance between private interests and the public good, when seen from the regulatory perspectives concerning commercial social media such as Facebook.

References

Beer, D. (2009). Power through the algorithm? Participatory web cultures and the technological unconscious. *New Media & Society, 11*(6), 985–1002.
Benkler, Y. (2006). *The wealth of networks: How social production transforms markets and freedom*. New Haven/London: Yale University Press.

Bloor, M., Frankland, J., Thomas, M., & Robson, K. (2001). *Focus groups in social research*. London: Sage.

Bolin, G. (2012). The labour of media use. *Information, Communication & Society, 15*(6), 796–814.

Bruns, A. (2008). *Blogs, Wikipedia, second life, and beyond: From production to produsage*. New York: Peter Lang.

Castells, M. (2009). *Communication power*. Oxford: Oxford University Press.

COM. (2016). *287 final*. Proposal for a directive of the European Parliament and of the Council amending directive 2010/13/EU on the coordination of certain provisions laid down by law, regulation or administrative action in member states concerning the provisions of audiovisual media services in view of changing market realties. *European Commission*: Brussels.

Cresswell, J. W. (2009). *Research design: Qualitative, quantitative, and mixed methods approaches*. London: Sage.

Dahlgren, P. (2011). Mobilizing discourse theory for critical media politics: Obstacles and potentials. In L. Dahlberg & S. Phelan (Eds.), *Discourse theory and critical media politics* (pp. 222–249). London/New York: Palgrave Macmillan.

Data policy. (n.d.). *Facebook*. https://www.facebook.com/full_data_use_policy

Dean, J. (2008). Communicative capitalism: Circulation and the foreclosure of politics. In M. Boler (Ed.), *Digital media and democracy: Tactics in hard times* (pp. 101–122). Cambridge/London: The MIT Press.

Deleuze, G. (1995). *Negotiations, 1972–1990*. New York: Columbia University Press.

Drucker, S., & Gumpert, G. (2010). Introduction: Regulation convergence. In S. J. Drucker & G. Gumpert (Eds.), *Regulating convergence* (pp. 1–20). New York: Peter Lang.

Freedman, D. (2011). Web 2.0 and the death of the blockbuster economy. In J. Curran, N. Fenton, & D. Freedman (Eds.), *Misunderstanding the internet* (pp. 69–94). London/New York: Routledge.

Fuchs, C. (2010). Labour in informational capitalism and on the internet. *The Information Society, 26*(3), 179–196.

Fuchs, C. (2013). Class and exploitation on the internet. In T. Scholz (Ed.), *Digital labor: The internet as playground and factory* (pp. 211–224). New York/London: Routledge.

Gaskell, G. (2000). Individual and group interviewing. In M. W. Bauer & G. Gaskell (Eds.), *Qualitative researching with text, image and sound* (pp. 38–56). London: Sage.

Gauntlett, D. (2011). *Making is connecting: The social meaning of creativity: From DIY and knitting to YouTube and Web 2.0*. Cambridge: Polity Press.

Hartley, J. (2005). Creative industries. In J. Hartley (Ed.), *Creative industries* (pp. 1–40). Malden: Blackwell Publishing.

Himanen, P. (2001). *The hacker ethic and the spirit of the information age*. New York: Random House Trade Paperbacks.

ICT Regulation Toolkit. (2006). *Impact of convergence*. http://www.ictregulationtoolkit.org/6.4

Jenkins, H. (2006). *Fans, bloggers, and gamers: Exploring participatory culture*. New York/London: New York University Press.

Jenkins, H., Ford, S., & Green, J. (2013). *Spreadable media: Creating value and meaning in a networked culture*. New York/London: New York University Press.

Lessig, L. (2008). *Remix: Making art and commerce thrive in the hybrid economy*. New York: The Penguin Press.

Marcuse, H. (1998). Some social implications of modern technology. In D. Kellner (Ed.), *Technology, war and fascism: Collected papers of Herbert Marcuse* (pp. 41–65). London/New York: Routledge.

Mosco, V. (2014). *To the cloud: Big data in a turbulent world*. Boulder/London: Paradigm Publishers.

Shirky, C. (2008). *Here comes everybody: How change happens when people come together*. London: Penguin Press.

Tapscott, D., & Williams, A. D. (2008). *Wikinomics: How mass collaboration changes everything*. London: Atlantic Books.

Terms of Service. (n.d.). *Facebook*. https://www.facebook.com/legal/terms

Terranova, T. (2013). Free labor. In T. Scholz (Ed.), *Digital labor: The internet as playground and factory* (pp. 33–57). New York/London: Routledge.

Van Dijck, J. (2013). *The culture of connectivity: A critical history of social media*. Oxford: Oxford University Press.

Van Dijck, J., & Poell, T. (2013). Understanding social media logic. *Media and Communication, 1*(1), 2–14.

15

Spinning the Web: The Contradictions of Researching and Regulating Digital Work and Labour

Pamela Meil

The discourse surrounding the use of digital technologies and their impact on the world of employment and work is rife with contradictions: diverse uses of digital labor such as user-generated content, crowdsourcing or crowdwork, or cyber-physical systems are characterized as both divisive and uniting; liberating and constraining; mainly for the public good and mainly for private accumulation; commodifying and for the 'commons'. How can this be? The fact is that, depending on where you look and the example you select, it is certainly possible to identify both sides. In user-generated content, for example, forms of peer production or cooperative work abound and output such as Wikipedia or open source software are often cited to underscore the unifying, liberating and

---

Virtual work is very diverse and has many forms. This chapter leaves the exact designation of what virtual work is relatively open with one exception: forms of virtual labor exchange that are carried out locally such as for transport, accommodation, services, and so on, are excluded. All other forms, both paid and unpaid, are included, although the emphasis is largely on work on digital platforms.

P. Meil (✉)
Institute for Social Science Research (ISF Munich), Munich, Germany

'commons' aspects of digitalization. Here technology is often portrayed as a 'tool' and a means for peer production and collective use—free from capital constraints. Technology is thus neutral and liberating. In this view, digitalization engenders innovation, democratization, alternative forms of entry into professions, a shared economy with benefits to all, a shift to highly skilled and knowledge work, and social forms of production based on collaboration. The benefits of work in digital spaces are free access, promotion of creativity, increased autonomy, and entrepreneurial opportunities for employment. Conversely, it is also possible to identify aspects of user-generated content, crowdsourcing, and Industry 4.0 in which uses of technology are anything but free from capital constraints. From this perspective, digitalization brings a concentration of activities and an accompanying concentration of companies, worker displacement leading to skill polarization and job loss, deprofessionalization of a number of occupations, and a lack of protection for intellectual property particularly in the creative industries. Here the position is that traditional organizations and institutions are being bypassed thereby facilitating a deregulation of work, endangering intellectual property rights, and using virtual environments to exploit workers by profiting from unpaid labour.

It is questionable how fruitful it is to concentrate on a divisive discourse. However, this chapter picks up on a number of themes mentioned by both sides on the issue of digitalization by looking specifically at the effects on labour and employment in digitalization and focusing on three apparently contradictory relationships associated with the virtual or informational world: the compression of time and place vs. the global reach of virtual spaces; autonomy vs. control in virtual spaces; collaboration vs. competition in virtual work. Developments in the three contradictory relationships are examined through two topics that represent traditional areas of analysis for the sociology of work: institutional embeddedness and labour markets.

Time and Space

The general take on digitalization with regard to its effect on time and space is a, as Giddens expressed for the processes of globalization, 'lifting out of social relations from local contexts of interaction and their restructuring across infinite spans of time-space' (Giddens 1990, p. 21). In the digital world, there are theoretically no boundaries, which enables the restructuring of a global market in which emerging economies have an increasingly growing role, in which the boundaries between producer, user, consumer and distributor get blurred, in which labour moves freely across national boundaries to apply, bid, contribute, collaborate, or compete, and so on, for work. However, at the same time that there is an opening of economic and labour markets globally through digitalization, there is also an extreme compression of time and space. One consequence of the blurring of boundaries between production, distribution, and consumption is that, in terms of time, all three can theoretically be carried out simultaneously, thereby resulting in a dramatically changed landscape of production, exchange and consumption. Linear or sequential stages of production, exchange and consumption are transformed into more recursive, interactive and networked forms. Many of the terms used to depict the actors operating in digital spaces illustrates the blurring of boundaries between different stages of output as well as the means by which things get produced: prosumers, user innovators, peer production, produsers, co-creation, collective intelligence, citizen journalist. Furthermore, the process of value creation in these digital spaces takes place through a diverse mix of integrating actors: customers, business partners, regular employees, temporary employees, unpaid labour.

These processes have been referred to as 'digital shift' in which distribution, intermediaries and content are being rearticulated, thereby resulting in reconfigurations of value chains (Simon and Bogdanowicz 2012). Value chains are, in fact, a powerful conceptual tool for understanding changes occurring in digital spaces, particularly with regard to transformations in work and work processes. By asking how value chains are configured, it is possible to examine basic issues such as, who owns which part of the chain?; what is being outsourced by whom to whom and is the work that is carried out paid or unpaid?; what is the division of labour across the chain?; where is value being created and where is it being extracted or used (and by whom)? As Huws points out (2017), virtual work, particularly in the form of crowdwork, is basically a continuation and extension of outsourcing and offshoring processes that have been a part of company restructuring strategies for several decades. Outsourcing across value chains centres around the use of place as a strategic resource for company planning and rationalization (Sauer et al. 2017; Porter 1985). The topics that have been associated with it include governance between units across the chain, power relationships between various actors across the chain (Gereffi et al. 2005), the effects on conditions of work and employment (Flecker and Meil 2010), the quality of work (such as pay, job security, types of contract, regulatory problems and forms) and forms of control over workers.

The units of analysis and lessons learned from studies on outsourcing across value chains are valuable for understanding the developments and consequences of virtual work. Tracing the origins of a number of phenomena in digital worlds back to their predecessors in outsourcing strategies in analogue worlds, sheds light on their meaning for the organization of work, the role of institutions (or lack of them), and for the role of labour markets. In outsourcing simple tasks or functions, for example, the process generally involves standardizing and codifying processes in order for pieces of production or services to be broken up into individual tasks and moved abroad (mainly for cost reductions) (Huws 2006). A global division of labour utilizing cost saving benefits by tapping locations with low wage labour markets and often less regulated institutional contexts is the outcome (Meil et al. 2009).

The links with microtasking on crowdwork platforms are obvious (Huws 2017). Much of the research on crowdwork up to now has tended to concentrate on this type of low skill, low wage form of global/virtual crowdsourcing in which crowdworkers bid for jobs or tasks, which are designed to be carried out quickly and offer very low pay. The awarding process is heavily automated and hence there is little or no room for negotiating terms. This differentiates crowdwork from traditional forms of outsourcing in which companies are subcontracted to carry out work. In microtasking, as with traditional outsourcing of low value added tasks, global dispersion of work and the disembedding of institutions take place in the process of externalization and open global labour markets are created. The effects in both analogue and digital worlds are similar: a potential downward push on wages and enhanced competition between a larger pool of workers.

Another variation of traditional outsourcing also mirrors trends that can be found on crowdwork platforms, although those geared toward more highly skilled and less standardized work. In this variation of outsourcing, multinationals launch a call or invitation to submit designs or solutions for a particular task or product (such as designing an assembly hall or constructing an airplane or auto part). The multinational chooses the successful bid from among its subcontractors, based on price and solution, and this 'winner' then receives a contract for the work. Obviously the work involved in preparing the 'bid' is not compensated even for those who won the bid. For those who do not obtain the contract there is no payback or remuneration for the time and costs necessary to prepare the bid at all. Subcontractors complain bitterly about the tendency of large firms to launch vaguer and vaguer bids with fewer and fewer specifications, leaving them with the task of developing more and more complex solutions at higher and higher risks. Additionally they are increasingly responsible for integrating the solutions they develop at the customer's site. This is one of the contradictions in outsourcing: on the one hand, outsourcing leads to increased standardization and modularization of tasks and functions across longer and longer value chains. On the other, using alternative forms of control and governing processes, large, unspecific packages are outsourced in which the risk and costs of development are borne by the contractor. Here there are obvious parallels to bidding for jobs on creative work sites or entering into contests for designing a solution in a creative, technical or medical area. Examples of this kind of 'high-end' crowdwork are on platforms such as 99Designs, the German-based Jovoto, or the long-standing Innocentive.

These examples demonstrate the number of similarities evident in the processes and power imbalances between the outsourcing taking place in virtual environments and those found in earlier outsourcing practices. However, there are a number of differences as well. For one, the disembedding that takes place in virtual environments is very far reaching across a range of institutions and has crucial effects on work and employment (Drahokoupil and Fabo 2016). One very basic disembedding process involves the role of the company. Traditional outsourcing arrangements involve a company to company relationship. This is not the case in virtual environments in which there can theoretically be a direct relationship between a customer (company) and an individual. More common, however, is a characteristic 'triangular' relationship (Schörpf et al. 2017), involving customer, intermediary (platform) and producer (worker).

Usually the direct working relationship occurs between the platform and the worker/producer. Of course, platforms are a form of company. But platforms take on very diverse forms, target diverse workforces, and given their lack of physical locality, have a very unique position in terms of their responsibility (or lack of it), culpability, and accountability. Since companies in the traditional sense, as rationalized organizations with hierarchies and place-bound sites, basically play either no role or only an obfuscated one, traditional forms of regulating work such as through contracts or bargaining, traditional forms of resistance or negotiation and systems of worker protection are almost impossible to enforce.

It appears that in the globally dispersed, diffuse and disembedded world of virtual work, place loses meaning entirely. Yet, the contradiction is precisely that, although on the one hand the digital space is open and global, on the other it compresses time and space. One outcome of this process is that the potential for accumulation and concentrations of capital increases dramatically. In theory, the virtual world should present individuals, small businesses, new entrepreneurs and a variety of collaborative projects with the opportunity of having an open forum for their ideas, products, services, and so on. This side of digitalization does exist. However, digitalization and the 'information space' also give large corporations and powerful actors the forum to become increasingly dominant and to gain more and more control of digital space (Huws 2014). This is not only due to their dominant presence, but also to the fact that they can take over more pieces of the value chain—production, storage, and distribution—in the same space and in a very compressed time frame, making it possible to dominate in the production and distribution of commodities, both goods and services, in a variety of sectors.

In examining the relationship between outsourcing and virtual work, the role of platforms in mediating work, and the dominance of big players in the digital world reveals that despite disembedding and global labour markets, there is always 'real' work behind 'virtual' work. There is no such thing as purely virtual work unless perhaps if it is being performed by algorithms, which were nonetheless written, implemented and managed by real workers. The issue is really one of how the work is organized between the virtual spaces, or between real and virtual spaces, which institutions are involved and how labour markets are tapped.

Autonomy Versus Control

The conflictual space between autonomy and control is a long standing focus in the sociology of work and labour process theory. Taylorist forms of work organization demonstrated the lowest levels of workplace autonomy, since the time and effort designated for each task was pre-determined and technically controlled. Principles of Taylorist work organization were/are not limited to assembly lines in industrial production, but have also been transferred to contemporary service jobs such as in call centres (Holtgrewe et al. 2002). How much or little autonomy was evident in fordist or post-fordist forms of production are subjects of much debate in which institutional context and labour markets play significant roles (Jürgens et al. 1993; Peck and Tickell 1994). There is, however, agreement that the increasing share of knowledge intensive work in the production of goods and services has necessarily brought about different forms of control and potentially different and higher levels of autonomy (Edwards and Wajcman 2005). The argument is that in order to tap tacit knowledge, flexibility, innovation capacity and creativity of workers needed for knowledge intensive tasks, more autonomy in carrying out work is required. In the 90s, an entire management literature emerged on creating company cultures supposedly leading to organizational loyalty and a strong identification with the company (for example Drucker 1992), the reasoning being that you can grant more autonomy when workers have internalized company goals and ethics. Ways of binding highly skilled workers to the company is ongoing in management discussions, including the need to generate 'change competence' (Meyer 2014), develop soft skills, train team working abilities, and so on. Another related development is imparting an entrepreneurial ethos (Edwards and Wajcman 2005, p. 23) to employees. Increased autonomy does not mean that there are no controls on workers except for their identification to the employer or the task. The controls are simply less direct, or differ from bureaucratic forms found in the fordist era (Edwards 1979; Thompson et al. 2007). They often take the form of performance evaluation or monitoring, meeting deadlines or reaching targeted outcomes within time and resource constraints.

The extreme standardization of microtasks can, of course, be viewed as a type of Tayloristic division of labor and therefore subject to very direct forms of control. However, even with very standardized virtual work, the place of work, how long it takes, and to a certain extent, how work is performed, is left up to the crowdworker, making the form of direct control different from that in typical organizational settings. In discourses from the user or worker side, having autonomy in carrying out work is indeed mentioned as a central positive aspect of virtual work. Given that workers in virtual worlds can generally determine the place and the hours of work, they are free from the typical hierarchical and bureaucratic constraints of traditional work environments. They also have freedom in choosing which jobs to bid for. For bidding and contests in digital spaces that are geared toward a more highly skilled creative and technical workforce, there is also a high level of autonomy in when (the middle of the night), where, and, in contrast to microtasks, even what is produced. Having self-determination in carrying out work is a marketing tool for platforms and expressed as an internalized motivation for platform workers (Lehdonvirta and Mezier 2013). An online survey comparing creative and IT crowdworkers revealed that both groups mentioned 'fun' as their main motivation for engaging in crowdwork. Earning extra money and learning new skills also scored over 50 per cent. Earning a living was the least motivating factor to work on platforms (Lehdonvirta et al. 2014). This is corroborated by a newer survey on the extent of gigwork in five European nations which found that participation rates were much higher than expected, but that a very small percentage of respondents were using it as their main income source (Huws et al. 2016).

The employer's loss of traditional control is compensated in a number of ways: For instance, the saving of resources by not having to provide place of work and sanctions for inefficiency in the form of very low pay per hour or task. In many ways, the organization of work in digital environments appears to hark back to forms of pre-industrial piece-work—with the exception of a global labor market and technological controls that are no longer bound by place.

It would in any case be misleading to characterize crowdwork as largely autonomous. Several new forms of control are emerging for paid work on virtual platforms, occurring in a context of institutional disembeddedness and 'free' labor markets. Platforms, for instance, operating as the intermediaries, control the communication between customers and clients or companies and workers and they have a diffuse, often anonymous, relationship with both sides. Levels of uncertainty are rather high when dealing with anonymous workers on online platforms. To minimize these uncertainties, the platforms offer tools for supervision and control such as online surveillance of keystrokes or screenshots of work progress (Schörpf et al. 2017). While these forms of direct control are used for highly standardized micro-tasks, they are not effective for more complex tasks. For this work, the most important mechanism for controlling workers' behavior is ratings, reviews and statistics. There is a clear asymmetry in the communication channels between workers and customers: customers have extensive information on workers, but workers have little or no information about customers. On contest-based platforms, ratings are not so important, because customers simply assess the submitted work. Therefore in these forms of virtual work, control is based on output. Thus the bases for control for highly skilled creative and technical work are either performance monitoring in the form of ratings and reputation or alternatively, deadlines and evaluation of output.

The attractiveness of autonomy in the face of several means of practicing both direct and indirect control, and in light of institutional disembeddedness, where job protection, legal redress, and perhaps collective action for fair wages is precluded, raises the question of how sustainable virtual platform work is. Research on work-life balance raises the issue of whether autonomy in digital spaces is not simply an intensification of work which blurs the boundaries between work and private life so extensively that little private autonomy survives (Kreiss et al. 2011). In the end, the pull of autonomy appears to be grounded in a variety of circumstances: virtual platform work is only a supplementary form of income; creative work, in particular, has a long tradition of being carried out on a freelance basis; having autonomy regarding the place and time of carrying out work creates an open labor market, potentially benefitting workers in places with lower wage costs. Perhaps, therefore, there is no simple answer to this question.

Collaboration Versus Competition

Digital spaces have inherited a large burden in terms of high levels of expectation regarding collaboration. Rather than digitalization simply being a new way to organize work using a range of new technological tools, it has also been imparted with far reaching social and cultural meaning. In an environment in which answers or alternatives were being sought to a crisis arising from extreme forms of financialized capitalism, solutions were being offered in the form of shared values, social networking, and new forms of creating value and consuming goods and services. Some of the more well-known proponents of such positions were Rifkin (2014), who presaged a transition from an industrial production economy to a cultural production economy, and Benkler who saw the contemporary commons as 'a new paradigm for creating value and organizing a community of shared interests' (2006). Benkler saw the digital arena as a place where peer production allowed users to structure the rights to access as well as the use and control of resources, thus being an alternative to capitalized and private ownership (Benkler and Nissenbaum 2006, p. 403). Similar positions are found with the concept of the sharing economy and with the related concept of 'collaborative consumption', the latter being 'the creation of value out of surplus in combination with … communities of shared interests' (Botsman and Rogers 2010). These social network based transactional forms purportedly transform people from passive consumers to active creators and collaborators and simultaneously help create a less egocentric and more connected, social culture. These rather utopian visions, built upon the foundation of digitalization, are formulated as viable socio-economic models and not as simply countercultural fantasies. Even in less optimistic portrayals, collaboration as a principle and driving force is a very powerful one in the digital world.

Despite the role that collaboration certainly plays and the meaning that it has in the world of virtual work, a basic question remains of whether mainly societal use values are being created or mainly products (including commodities, services, creative effort) for profit? With regard to the sharing economy, for instance, Eckhardt and Bhardi (2015) argue that it has little to do with sharing, but is rather an economic exchange in which consumers are paying to access goods and services and that the value for all participants is essentially utilitarian and not social. Additionally unpaid labor in the form of collaboration is increasingly being used together with paid labor in value chains involving open access sites, platforms, and companies to produce economic outputs. Another most interesting development is the budding branch of management literature on how collaboration can be tapped in virtual communities in which the users are competing with one another in contests and bidding proposals (Ebner et al. 2010).

On virtual work platforms, offering a bid to carry out a task based on price, reputation and perhaps qualification, is a competitive activity, and one usually used on microtask sites, but also potentially on sites for highly skilled creative and technical labor. Another approach for obtaining work or carrying out a paid activity is the contest in which users submit a solution or design, often for a complex problem or innovation, and the winner or winners receive a (usually monetary) prize. Although clearly a competition, the contest is often described as a collaboration (Leimeister et al. 2015). In fact, collaborative processes are expressly desired in contest competitions, since 'research on open innovation shows that most innovations are the result of intensive collaboration processes in which many individuals contribute according to their specific strengths' (Blohm et al. 2010, p. 6). Thus fostering user collaboration enhances idea quality and is a 'viable design element for making idea competitions more effective' (ibid. p. 11). The role of platforms is to 'provide buyers with on-demand access to a specialized community of skilled suppliers who can be engaged on a project via a competition or contest. The buyer can choose from multiple competing inputs/deliverables and pay only for the one it finds most valuable. This outcome-driven selection also significantly reduces perceived risks for the buyer' (Kaganer et al. 2013). Basically contests on digital platforms are exploiting the inclination for people, particularly those operating in digital spaces, to collaborate and to make their unpaid labor available for solutions that ultimately belong to the company who launched the contest. Although there is an element of democratic experience in the idea generation and collaboration between contestants, business controls the entire process (Balkin 2012).

Another take on the collaborative approach is the term's more traditional use with regard to workers in projects or teams who have different jobs or tasks and work together to develop or produce a product or service. In company-based development processes which sometimes reach across regional or global value chains, cooperation and collaboration between workers towards the development of an end process or product is a well-established practice. In the digital world, this type of collaboration is also emerging, involving a new division of labor on crowdsourcing platforms, particularly geared to complex tasks. Platforms are offering new services by adopting the role of project manager or integrator for products or processes, making them online variants of engineering service suppliers. Named the 'governor' model of managing crowdwork in the management literature, the platforms overtake the task of monitoring and coordinating individual tasks with a small staffed workforce (human project managers) and a software enabled framework (Kaganer et al. 2013). The broken down parts of a project—conceptualization, requirement specification, architecture design, certification, and so on—are potentially launched as a series of online competitions or are simply put out for bids to the platform community. The offer for coordinating the collaboration is aimed at attracting more large enterprise clients since the platform becomes the singular interface and takes over a good share of the risk (which they generally pass on to their virtual workforce). Several characteristics of the digital form of coordinating collaboration display a divergence from its analog form, for instance, the very close relationship and in-depth knowledge that suppliers have of their customer's business. Another marked difference is the role of collaboration between project participants in these platform-based models, which looks less and less like collaboration and more like an explicit division of labor for increasingly standardized tasks.

Amorphous Labor Markets and Dis-embedded Institutions: A Challenge for Regulation

Labor Markets

Virtual environments have a major impact on how labor markets have functioned and been understood up to now. There have always been quite diverse types of labor markets: skill-based, segmented, low-cost, and so on, which have targeted different types of labor and involved different company ties. The unique 'unbounded' labor market found in digital spaces, however, makes existing categories for conceptualizing labor markets relatively obsolete. User-generated content in both paid and unpaid forms, collaborative work in competitive markets, an anonymous and replaceable workforce carrying out algorithm generated microtasks—all are difficult to place in the idea of labor markets as we have understood them up to now. Although markets for unskilled, replaceable labor on the one side, and high-skilled creative, freelance labor on the other, are not new, offering labor in the economy took place in a system of embedded institutions. This was one of the explanations for why labor markets looked and operated so differently depending on institutional context, as varieties of capitalism, comparative welfare state, and neo-institutionalist arguments claimed (Esping-Anderson 1990; Hall and Soskice 2001).

As with developments in the 90s to create company cultures and corporate identities, bargaining and negotiation on the parts of both labor and capital in industrialized post-war economies have been laying down pacts and principles to establish employment relationships which are the basis for institutionalized contract agreements. Since these pacts and principles center on a company-based form of organization, loyalties and ties in fordist and post-fordist relations have revolved around employers or firms, particularly in social welfare regimes (Smith 2010). Employee identities which are not so company-based, such as for creative workers including journalists, writers, designers, film and television personnel, and so on, tended to be linked to occupation as did their loyalty and professional orientation (Hesmondhalgh and Baker 2010). In this case regulation efforts were also connected to particular occupational initiatives or collectives such as authors' or journalists' or TV and film media unions.

Shifts in traditional employment relationships toward less regulated and open labour markets have been occurring for some time, again remindful of outsourcing and offshoring trends (Smith 2010). This has been leading to concomitant shifts in loyalty and commitment away from 'jobs' and their bureaucratic stability towards a more diffuse meaning of work based on content (Meil 2012), and possibly a more market-based orientation to work. The use of credentials, occupational identity, and professionalism has changed dramatically, if not disappearing entirely, in virtual labor markets. Thus with virtual work, the issue goes beyond closed or open labor markets, but rather what exactly or where exactly the labour market is. In this labour market context, how are qualifications determined, measured and defined? What role do institutions or regulation have for digital labor markets? And are careers now superfluous? Largely organized around the existence of internal labor markets, the construction of careers without them has to either occur in alternative ways or the idea of career has to be redefined or deemed irrelevant.

Finally, the absence of physical work places toward more amorphous places of working has consequences for social ties and social networks (Valenduc and Vendramin 2016). Although discourse on communities of cooperation and collaboration abound in digital spaces, virtual work and constantly changing working relationships on platforms makes collectivity of any type, whether to organize for better working conditions or to create communities of practice, a challenge.

(Dis)embedded Institutions

The most straightforward understanding of institutional embeddedness is the focus on the set of institutions and their relationship to one another that have developed historically in a particular regional or national framework. These institutions govern relationships between various actors in the society, such as capital and labor, in all areas of society—employment, education, finance, politics, law—and determine the rules and norms for negotiation, contract, participation, misbehavior, conflict, and so on. This is not simply an adaptive process: 'the creation and implementation of institutional arrangements are rife with conflict, contradiction, and ambiguity' (DiMaggio and Powell 1991, p. 28). Institutions are embedded because they have developed in an historical context within a set of particular social relations and therefore are different in different places and cannot simply be transferred from one place to another. Using a concrete example in the world of work, work contracts are shaped and constrained in their embeddedness in given institutional frameworks

(Tilly and Tilly 1998). The provisions in work contracts derive from market conditions, tradition, but also 'critically on degree of unionization, state enforcement' (ibid. p. 90) of rules and laws, protections for social exclusion, and so on.

The entire conception of embeddedness is anchored in the proposition that work is integrated in particular places, although these may be quite diverse, such as nations, regions, companies or value chains. Digital spaces present a real dilemma in this regard even though digital spaces are indeed places with a set of social relations (Thompson and Briken 2016). Additionally, the real work that is behind virtual work occurs in places with embedded institutional frameworks. Nonetheless, digital spaces do differ from existing places of work because the lines drawn between a variety of actors are indistinct, fluid, and contradictory and this makes identifying and defining social relations quite difficult. There are myriad examples for these blurring relationships in digital spaces: producers can also be consumers; workers can be sharers (co-creation or peer production); unpaid user-generator of content or freelance worker; employer or contractor of independent producers. Simultaneously the traditional locus of most worker-employer interaction—the company—becomes an internet platform or an anonymous client and loses its institutional grounding. Certainly it is possible to identify regular work relations in digital spaces which are governed by contracts, pay and have the same type of asymmetrical power relations that exist in traditional hierarchical organizations. However, precisely those work relations in which unpaid labor intersects with paid labor, in which motivations for participation involve desires for autonomy, collaboration, involvement in global networks, and the minimizing of time and space constraints, is where the determination of underlying social relations and institutional embeddedness becomes unfeasible. In many ways much of the non-contested interaction in digital spaces appears to have created its own habitus (Bourdieu 1984) in which shared typifications are internalized by actors sharing the space.

It would, however, be a misrepresentation to portray digital spaces as completely non-conflictual or uncontested. Although its institutional disembeddedness makes collective action, rule or law making difficult, there have been many actions both by individuals, groups, worker representatives and states to regulate work and employment (Milland 2016;

LaPlant and Silberman 2016; Prassl and Risak 2017; IG Metall 2016; Schulten et al. 2015; Wirsig and Compton 2017). These initiatives do tie into institutionalist orientations of establishing norms and rules in highly non-institutional environments.

Challenges to Regulation

As we have seen, virtual work has numerous implications for the regulation of work and employment. More broadly, the effects on labor markets, work contracts and the employment relationship also impact on social systems and the legal and institutional frameworks for governing work and employment at the societal level (Degryse 2016). Although labor force participation in digital platforms may still be used mainly as a supplement to other forms of employment and the wide variety in platforms and types of activities being offered on those platforms may still characterize virtual work, the potential for concentrations of capital and thus dominance in the determination of work looms. Is it legitimate to ask who controls the infrastructure in digital spaces or if there is an increasing concentration of ownership and how this might affect the ability to regulate it? How do new forms of indirect control and transparency affect the work process particularly in light of the intransparency of those who manage and control the work? Competition between workers in different regions is not a new phenomenon, but in the digital world they all belong to the same labor market. Furthermore, digital spaces take labor mix to a whole new dimension by using collaboration in competitive environments and unpaid labor for profit-based ventures. How should nations whose entire social systems and infrastructures are based on normal employment relationships (health benefits, pensions, unemployment compensation, taxation, and other obligatory payments) reorganize their models to adjust to the atypical employment relations in the digital world? Can regulations that protect workers and social systems be designed that don't destroy global access and marketplaces, autonomy and collaboration? Many of these questions and issues are being addressed by individuals, professional and occupational groups, professional organizations and guilds, regulatory institutions, unions and governments.

Finding answers requires analyses of the motivations, power relations, conflicting interests and mechanisms behind the developments and beyond the discourse.

References

Balkin, J. (2012, July 10). Mediating the social contradiction of the digital age. *Crooked Timber*. http://crookedtimber.org/2006/05/30/mediating-the-socialcontradiction-of-the-digital-age/

Benkler, Y. (2006). *The wealth of networks: How social production transforms markets and freedom*. New Haven/London: Yale University Press.

Benkler, Y., & Nissenbaum, H. (2006). Commons-based peer production and virtue. *The Journal of Political Philosophy, 14*(4), 394–419.

Blohm, I., Bretschneider, U., Leimeister, J. M., & Krcmar, H. (2010). Does collaboration among participants lead to better ideas in IT-based idea competitions? An empirical investigation. In R. H. Sprague (Ed.), *Proceedings of the 43rd Annual Hawaii International Conference on System Sciences* (HICSS) 2010, Kauai.

Botsman, R., & Rogers, R. (2010). *What's mine is yours: The rise of collaborative consumption*. New York: Harper Business.

Bourdieu, P. (1984). *Distinction: A social critique of the judgement of time*. Cambridge: Harvard University Press.

Degryse, C. (2016). *Digitalisation of the economy and its impact on labour markets* (ETUI working paper). Brussels: ETUI.

DiMaggio, P., & Powell, W. (1991). Introduction. In W. Powell & P. DiMaggio (Eds.), *The new institutionalism in organizational analysis* (pp. 1–38). Chicago/London: The University of Chicago Press.

Drahokoupil, J., & Fabo, B. (2016). *The platform economy and the disruption of the employment relationship*. ETUI policy brief, European economic, employment and social policy, no. 5/2016. Brussels: ETUI aisbl.

Drucker, P. (1992). *Management challenges of the 21st century*. New York: Harper Collins.

Ebner, W., Leimeister, J. M., & Krcmar, H. (2010). Community engineering for innovations: The ideas competition as a method to nurture a virtual community for innovations. *R&D Management, 39*(4, 2009), 342–356.

Eckhardt, G. M., & Bardhi, F. (2015, January 28). The sharing economy isn't about sharing at all. *Harvard Business Review*. https://hbr.org/2015/01/the-sharingeconomy-isnt-about-sharing-at-all

Edwards, R. (1979). *Contested terrain: The transformation of the workplace in the twentieth century.* New York: Basic Books.

Edwards, P., & Wajcman, J. (2005). *The politics of working life.* Oxford: Oxford University Press.

Esping-Anderson, G. (1990). *Three worlds of welfare capitalism.* Princeton: Princeton University Press.

Flecker, J., & Meil, P. (2010). Organisational restructuring and emerging service value chains—Implications for work and employment. *Work, Employment and Society, 24*(4), 680–698.

Gereffi, G., Humphrey, J., & Sturgeon, T. (2005). The governance of global value chains. *Review of International Political Economy, 12*(1), 78–104.

Giddens, A. (1990). *The consequences of modernity.* Cambridge: Polity Press.

Hall, P., & Soskice, D. (2001). *Varieties of capitalism: The institutional foundations of comparative advantage.* Oxford: Oxford University Press.

Hesmondhalgh, D., & Baker, S. (2010). A very complicated version of freedom: Conditions and experiences of creative labour in three cultural industries. *Poetics, 38*(1), 4–20.

Holtgrewe, U., Kerst, C., & Shire, K. (Eds.). (2002). *Re-organising service work in Europe: Call centres in Germany and Britain.* Aldershot: Ashgate.

Huws, U. (2006). The restructuring of global value chains and the creation of a cybertariat. In C. May (Ed.), *Global corporate power: (Re)integrating companies into the international political economy* (pp. 65–82). Boulder: Lynne Rienner Publishers.

Huws, U. (2014). *Labor in the global digital economy: The cybertariat comes of age.* New York: Monthly Review Press.

Huws, U. (2017). Where did online platforms come from? The virtualization of work organization and the new policy challenges it raises. In P. Meil & V. Kirov (Eds.), *The policy implications of virtual work* (pp. 29–48). Basingstoke: Palgrave Macmillan.

Huws, U., Spencer, N. H., & Joyce, S. (2016). *Crowd work in Europe: Preliminary results from a survey in the UK, Sweden, Germany, Austria and the Netherlands.* Brussels: European Foundation for Progressive Studies.

IG Metall. (2016). *Frankfurt paper on platform-based work—Proposals for platform operators, clients, policy makers, workers, and worker organizations.* Frankfurt.

Jürgens, U., Malsch, T., & Dohse, K. (1993). *Breaking from Taylorism: Changing forms of work in the automobile industry.* Cambridge: Cambridge University Press.

Kaganer, E., Carmel, E., Hirscheim, R., & Olsen, T. (2013). Managing the human cloud. *MIT Sloan Management Review, 54*(2), 23–32.

Kreiss, D., Finn, M., & Turner, F. (2011). The limits of peer production: Some reminders from Max Weber for the network society. *New Media & Society, 13*(2), 243–259.

LaPlante, R., & Silberman, M. S. (2016). *Building trust in crowd worker forums: Worker ownership, governance, and work outcomes, weaving relations of trust in crowd work: Transparency and reputation across platforms.* Proceedings of WebSci16. Workshop co-located with *WebSci'16*, May 22–25, Hannover. ACM.

Lehdonvirta, V., & Mezier, P. (2013). *Identity and self-organization in unstructured work* (Working paper, series 1, COST Action IS 1202). Hertfordshire: University of Hertfordshire.

Lehdonvirta, V., Barnard, H., & Graham, M. (2014). *Online labor markets*, presented at IPP2014, Crowdsourcing for politics and policy, Oxford.

Leimeister, J. M., Zogaj, S., & Durward, D. (2015). New forms of employment and IT—Crowdsourcing. In *4th Conference for the Regulating for Decent Work Network*, Genf.

Meil, P. (2012). Consent and content: Effects of value chain restructuring on work and conflict among highly skilled workforces. *Work Organisation, Labour and Globalisation, 6*(2), 8–24.

Meil, P., Tengblad, P., & Doherty, P. (2009). *Value chain restructuring and industrial relations: The role of workplace representation in changing conditions of employment and work.* Leuven: HIVA.

Meyer, B. (2014). *Agile: The good, the bad, and the ugly.* Cham, Switzerland: Springer.

Milland, K. (2016). *Crowd work: Shame, secrets and an imminent threat to employment. Global Labour Column* 238(June). University of the Witwatersrand, Johannesburg.

Peck, J., & Tickell, A. (1994). Searching for a new institutional fix: The after-Fordist crisis and the global-local disorder. In A. Amin (Ed.), *Post-Fordism: A reader*. Oxford: Blackwell Publishers Ltd.

Porter, M. E. (1985). *The competitive advantage: Creating and sustaining superior performance.* New York: Free Press.

Prassl, J., & Risak, M. (2017). The legal protection of crowdworkers: Four avenues for workers rights in the virtual realm. In P. Meil & V. Kirov (Eds.), *The policy implications of virtual work* (pp. 273–296). Basingstoke: Palgrave Macmillan.

Rifkin, J. (2014). *The internet of things, the collaborative commons, and the eclipse of capitalism.* Basingstoke: Palgrave Macmillan.

Sauer, D., Deiss, M., Döhl, V., Bieber, D., & Altmann, N. (2017 second edition, first published in 1992). Systemic rationalisation and inter-company divisions of labor. In N. Altmann, C. Koehler, and P. Meil (Eds.), *Technology and work in German industry* (pp. 46–62). London/New York: Routledge.

Schörpf, P., Flecker, J., & Schönauer, A. (2017). On call for one's online reputation—Control and time in creative crowdwork. In K. Briken, S. Chillas, M. Krzywdzinski, & A. Marks (Eds.), *The new digital workplace. How new technologies revolutionise work*. London: Palgrave Macmillan.

Schulten, T., Eldring, L., & Naumann, R. (2015). The role of extension for the strength and stability of collective bargaining in Europe. In G. Van Gyes & T. Schulten (Eds.), *Wage bargaining under the new European economic governance: Alternative strategies for inclusive growth* (pp. 361–400). Brussels: ETUI.

Simon, J. P., & Bogdanowicz, M. (2012). *The digital shift in the media and content industries: Policy brief.* European Commission, Joint Research Centre, Institute for Prospective Technological Studies. Luxembourg: Publications Office of the European Union.

Smith, C. (2010). Go with the flow: Labour power mobility and labour process theory. In P. Thompson & C. Smith (Eds.), *Working life—Renewing labour process analysis* (pp. 269–296). Basingstoke: Palgrave Macmillan.

Thompson, P., & Briken, K. (2016). Actually existing capitalism: Some digital delusions. In K. Briken, S. Chillas, M. Krzywdzinski, & A. Marks (Eds.), *The new digital workplace: How new technologies revolutionise work* (pp. 241–263). Basingstoke: Palgrave Macmillan.

Thompson, P., Jones, M., & Warhurst, C. (2007). From conception to consumption: Creativity and the missing managerial link. *Journal of Organizational Behavior, 28,* 625–640.

Tilly, C., & Tilly, C. (1998). *Work under capitalism.* Boulder: Westview Press.

Valenduc, G., & Vendramin, P. (2016). *Work in the digital economy: Sorting the old from the new* (ETUI working paper 2016.03). Brussels: ETUI aisbl.

Wirsig, K., & Compton, J. (2017). Workers, contradictions and digital commodity chains: Organizing with content creators in Canada. In P. Meil & V. Kirov (Eds.), *The policy implications of virtual work.* Cham, Switzerland: Palgrave Macmillan.

Index[1]

A

Adobe, 100, 101, 107
Advertising, 6, 10, 45, 47, 48, 50, 51, 57, 58, 61, 64, 66, 69, 71, 87, 101, 116, 214–217, 219–221, 223, 225–228, 236, 238, 262, 263
Affective economy, 6, 78, 80, 81, 199
Algorithm, 3, 5, 6, 13, 20, 32, 57–71, 77–90, 107, 165, 197, 211, 238, 260, 261, 263, 265, 266, 276, 283
Algorithmic capitalism, 58–63, 67, 71
Alphabet Inc., 57, 59, 64, 65, 69, 72n1, 72n6
Apps, 166
Application Programming Interface (API), 83
Apps, 9, 13, 15, 161, 163, 165, 169–172, 262
Assembly work, 30, 31
Audience, 9, 10, 51, 52, 64, 67, 100, 186, 211–216, 218, 221, 223–227, 235, 256, 257, 259, 263
Audience commodity, 213–216, 235, 238
Audience labour/work, 44, 242, 256
Audience metrics, 10, 211–218, 220–225, 227, 228
Audiovisual media services, 254, 260, 263
Automation, 5, 12, 19–25, 27, 29–33, 107, 206, 228
Automotive, 5, 22, 30, 31
Autonomist Marxism, 41

---

[1] Note: Page numbers followed by 'n' refer to notes.

Autonomy, 10, 11, 33, 43, 82, 83, 149–151, 155, 177, 205, 212, 213, 223, 224, 227, 272, 277–279, 285, 286

B

BIBB/BAuA Employee Survey, 22, 28
Blender, 100, 102–104, 112–116
Brands, 6, 45, 49, 78, 80, 84, 86, 87, 89, 199, 225, 262
Braverman, Harry, 2, 37, 40
Business models, 13, 68, 184, 199, 214, 215, 220, 228, 235, 236, 245–247, 249, 254, 260
Buzzard, Karen, 214

C

Capital, 2, 5, 6, 9, 12, 13, 15, 38–43, 45, 49, 50, 64, 131, 148, 155, 161, 167, 172, 199, 212, 213, 228, 249, 258, 272, 283, 284
Capital concentration, 276, 286
Capitalist surveillance, 213–216, 227
Civic agency, 11, 253–267
Class struggle, 40
Cohen, Nicole, 20, 212, 216
Collaboration, 4, 9, 11, 29, 175, 226, 227, 257, 272, 280–282, 284–286
Commodification, 10, 11, 48, 49, 58, 71, 72, 87, 196, 215, 235, 257
Commons, 9, 175, 178, 188, 257, 271, 272, 280
Commons-based peer production, 175
Computer graphics media, 100–103, 116

Contemporary literature, 9, 163
Contests, 116, 199, 275, 278, 281
Contractual agreement, 11, 15, 254, 260, 261, 263, 265, 267
Contradiction, 2–12, 14, 15, 19–22, 38, 52, 58, 59, 63, 70, 101, 104, 116, 117, 128, 155, 162, 172, 194, 197, 202–205, 249, 254, 261, 271–287
Control, 2–5, 9–11, 15, 23, 25, 31, 37, 40, 42, 43, 45, 48, 58, 60, 61, 67, 71, 78, 80, 83, 87, 89, 175–188, 194, 196, 198, 202, 203, 205, 212, 216, 248, 253–261, 264–267, 272, 274–281, 286
Crafts, 99
Craftsperson, 100, 104, 110–112, 115, 179
Creative industries, 7, 13, 121–135, 272
Creative labour, 7, 8, 121
Creativity, 7, 11, 15, 42, 43, 63, 64, 110, 130, 131, 135, 176, 237, 253–262, 265–267, 272, 277
Critical media politics, 255
Crowdwork, 2, 271, 273–275, 278, 282
Cultural politics, 6

D

Dashboards, 6, 9, 77, 162, 169
Data analytics, 81, 84, 89, 90
Datafication, 6, 12, 77, 194, 198, 202
Democratic rationalisation, 13–14, 61, 67, 70
Digital capitalism, 5, 19–22, 24, 28, 32, 33

Digital inclusion, 8, 141–156
Digitalisation, 5, 12, 99, 211, 272, 273, 276, 280
Digital labour, 3, 14, 58, 63, 175, 194, 197–199, 205, 255, 258, 265
Digital media, 44, 53, 62, 114–117, 197, 235, 238, 249
Digital practices, 7, 145, 146
Digital public relations (PR), 80
Digital shift, 273
Disadvantaged women, 8, 146–151, 155
Disembedded institutions, 279, 285
Division of labour, 125, 131, 143, 273, 274

E

Emancipation, 13, 15, 63, 150, 255, 257, 266
Engagement, 5, 6, 9, 78, 89, 127, 163, 198, 199, 201, 203–206, 237, 256, 267
Epistemology, 91n8, 107, 114–117
Everyday life, 15, 41, 63, 101, 122–124, 126, 128, 131, 132, 134, 167, 195
Exchange value, 5, 21, 23–26, 28, 52, 240, 248, 258
Experience, 4, 6, 9, 12, 26, 29, 30, 59, 61, 63, 66, 68–72, 82, 91n8, 106, 113, 121, 124–126, 129, 131–133, 135, 136n2, 142, 143, 145, 149, 151, 155, 162–164, 168, 169, 173, 194, 196, 198, 201, 202, 204, 205, 217, 261, 262, 281

F

Facebook, 5, 6, 10, 11, 37–53, 146, 215, 216, 220, 227, 228n2, 235, 238, 244, 245, 247, 253–267
Feenberg, Andrew, 4, 13, 61, 63, 67, 70, 71, 105
Feminist standpoint theory, 122, 124–127, 136n2, 136n4
Feminisation, 131–134
Foursquare, 200, 238
Free and open source software (f/oss), 9, 15, 175
Free labour, 102, 197–201, 215, 237, 239, 258, 262, 265

G

Game, 42, 46, 100, 101, 108, 193–196, 198, 201–205, 215, 237
Gamification, 9, 10, 193–206
Gender division of Labour, 125, 143
Gendered work, 122
Gender inequalities, 7, 128, 143, 146, 154
Gender perspective, 2, 143, 145, 146, 153–155
Gender roles, 123, 128, 129, 131, 134
GitHub, 183, 185–187
Global dispersion, 274
Google, 6, 10, 42–45, 57, 64, 65, 67–69, 72n1, 91n8, 215, 238
Governance, 80, 176, 178, 179, 183, 260, 265, 274
Grammars of action, 185

H

Hedonic logic, 204–206
Hierarchies, 9, 99, 125, 176, 177, 179, 180, 182, 188, 196, 276
Hochschild, Arlie Russel, 122, 128, 129
Home work, 125, 127, 133, 134

I

Ideology, 59, 62, 105, 128, 198, 249, 257
Immaterial labour, 48, 198
Industry 4.0, 5, 19–33, 272
Informational capitalism, 87
Internet use, 143, 145, 150, 154, 155

J

Job opportunities, 8, 141–156
Journalism, 212, 213, 218, 228, 237

K

Knowledge, forms of, 99, 102, 105, 106, 109, 114, 115
Knowledge work, 5, 26, 27, 59, 62, 63, 216, 272

L

Labour, 1–15, 19–33, 37–45, 48–50, 52, 57, 62–63, 65–68, 71, 79, 99, 100, 104, 105, 107–112, 117n1, 121–123, 125–134, 136n4, 143, 145, 151–155, 161, 167, 169, 172, 175–177, 179, 193–206, 212, 213, 216, 221–225, 228, 236–240, 243, 246–249, 256–259, 271–287
Labouring capacity, 22, 27, 28, 30–31, 33
Labour markets, 12, 14, 15, 20, 21, 24, 26–28, 33, 121, 122, 127, 141, 143–145, 151, 153, 154, 242–246, 248, 272–274, 276, 277, 283, 284
LC Index, 5, 22, 28–31
Lifelong learning programmes, 8
Linden, Carl-Gustav, 212, 228

M

Marcuse, Herbert, 6, 14, 58–61, 63, 67, 69, 71, 193, 196, 197, 204, 253, 254
Marx, Karl, 23, 38, 39, 41, 45, 61, 204, 240
Mechanical Engineering, 30
Medals, 9, 162–165, 169, 172, 173
Media industries, 11, 99, 101, 102, 107, 108, 110, 218, 236, 237, 239–241, 247, 249
Media practice, 52, 100, 102, 114–117, 265
Media production, 99–102, 108, 109, 114, 116, 117n1, 187, 236, 247–249
Media use, 10, 11, 44, 57, 235–249, 259

N

Napoli, Philip M., 212, 214
Native advertising, 224–227

Natural language processing (NLP), 64, 84, 85
Newswork/newsworker, 212, 213, 216, 225, 228

O

Online advertising, 220, 228n2
Online job search, 142, 143, 146–151
Online news, 9, 10, 82, 211–215, 217, 218, 220–223, 225, 227
Online reputation management, 80
Opinion mining, 84, 85
Organisation of labour, 111
Organisation of work, 29, 176, 177, 196, 274, 278
Örnebring, Henrik, 212, 213
Outsourcing, 63, 69, 273–276, 283

P

Participation, 10, 122, 149, 151, 155, 169, 178, 183, 184, 199, 205, 237, 256, 258, 278, 284–286
Peer production, 178, 184, 271–273, 280, 285
Peer-to-peer, 175
Pixar, 100, 101, 103, 110–112, 115, 116
Play, 8, 10, 12, 13, 25, 28, 31, 38, 41–43, 46, 78, 90, 134, 193–198, 200–202, 204, 206, 207, 212, 260, 276, 277, 280
Playbour, 10, 193–206, 237
Private sphere, 8, 38, 41, 43, 122, 123, 127, 132, 133
Production work, 5, 27, 28, 31, 32

Productive forces, 21–24, 27
Public sphere, 122, 127, 216, 247

Q

Qualification, 281, 284

R

Rationalisation, 58, 61, 63, 69, 213, 274
RedCritter, 202
Re-domestication, 123, 124, 131, 133–135
Reflective practice, 107, 114
Regulation, 10–12, 14, 68–70, 253–267, 282–287
Reification, 61
Robotics, 5, 19–22
Routine, 4, 5, 24–28, 30–33, 67, 134, 135, 206, 225

S

Sassi, Sinikka, 143, 145, 146, 150, 151, 155
Schön, Donald, 104–107, 109, 112–114, 117n1
Screens, 9, 88, 161–163, 169, 171, 172, 220
Search engine, 44, 58, 63–69, 84, 91n8, 185, 220, 235, 238
Search engine labour, 6, 58, 59, 63, 65, 67, 71
Second shift, 128, 129, 132
Sentiment analysis, 81, 84, 85
Smith, Dorothy E., 122, 124–126, 132, 136n2, 136n3

Smythe, Dallas W., 44, 53, 67, 236
Social coding, 185–187
Social death, 164, 173
Social inequalities, 1, 3, 8, 142–144, 155
Social media, 3, 6, 10, 11, 15, 43, 45, 47, 50–53, 78, 79, 81, 83, 86, 88, 171, 186, 197, 200, 211, 215, 237, 242, 245, 253, 254, 257–261, 263–267
Social media monitoring (SMM), 5–7, 77
Social stratification of the Internet use, 143, 145, 146, 151, 153–155
Software development, 103, 104, 107, 108, 113, 179, 181, 184, 186
Sponsored Stories, 45–49, 52
Streeck, Wolfgang, 214
Suchman, Lucy, 104, 106, 111, 112
Surveillance capitalism, 212, 258, 262

T

Task-based approach, 25
Technical artefact, 6, 59–62, 67, 71
Technical design, 6, 7, 67, 71
Technical rationality, 7, 99–117
Technics, 4, 14, 60, 61, 71, 254
Technological rationality, 59–63, 67, 71
Technology recession, 164, 165, 172, 173
Time, 5, 6, 11–13, 15, 25, 32, 33, 34n2, 37–53, 61, 63, 67, 68, 77, 79, 82, 88, 90, 99, 101, 107–111, 113, 116, 122, 126–129, 131–134, 136n1, 142, 149, 152, 164–171, 177, 182, 195, 196, 213, 215, 217, 220–226, 247, 257–259, 266, 267, 272–279, 283, 285
Turow, Joseph, 212, 215, 236, 244

U

Uber, 8, 9, 161–173
Unemployers, 142
User-generated content, 236, 254, 257, 259, 263–265, 267, 271, 272, 283
Use value, 5, 22–24, 27–29, 32, 258, 280
Utilitarian logic, 204, 206

V

Valorisation, 13, 14, 213, 248, 249
Value chains, 63, 212, 216, 273–276, 281, 282, 285
Version control, 181, 182, 185, 186
Virtual work, 11, 272–274, 276, 278–281, 284–286

W

Wajcman, Judy, 143, 145, 146, 150, 153, 155, 277
War, 9, 162–165, 167–169, 172, 173
Web 2.0, 43, 241, 256, 257
Web search, 6, 57–71
Women's work, 8, 121, 122, 124, 125, 127, 130, 132, 133, 136n3
Work-family conflict, 122, 127, 129

CPSIA information can be obtained
at www.ICGtesting.com
Printed in the USA
LVOW13*0859110518
576724LV00013B/269/P